U.S. Foreign Policy

FUTURE DIRECTIONS

Timely Reports to Keep
Journalists, Scholars and the Public
Abreast of Developing Issues, Events and Trends

Published by Congressional Quarterly Inc.
1414 22nd Street N.W.
Washington, D.C. 20037

About the Cover

The cover was designed by Richard Pottern, art director of Editorial Research Reports.

Editor, Hoyt Gimlin
Associate Editor, Sandra Stencel
Editorial Assistants, Patricia Ochs, Diane Huffman
Production Manager, I.D. Fuller
Assistant Production Manager, Maceo Mayo

Library of Congress Cataloging in Publication Data

Congressional Quarterly Inc.
    Editorial research reports on U.S. foreign policy.

    Bibliography: p.
    Includes index.
    1. United States — Foreign relations — 1977-I.
Title.
E872.C66   1979b   327.73   79-15637
ISBN 0-87187-187-4

Contents

Foreword

For some time after the Vietnam War, one of America's eminent pollsters tells us, "there was clearly a withdrawal of public attention" from foreign affairs. The Vietnam involvement had been so distasteful to a majority of Americans that they willingly shifted their attention back home — to Watergate, inflation, jobs, and a host of other concerns. Daniel Yankelovich, writing a year ago in the magazine *Public Opinion,* went on to observe that by then the pendulum had begun to swing back again, away from "the semi-isolationism of the early 1970s toward a new form of internationalism."

This "new internationalism" isn't easy to define precisely, for one characteristic seems to be ambivalence on the part of the American people toward how strong a role the United States should assume in world affairs. The public pulse-readings and the official record both indicate that caution is the keynote. In 1976, when a civil war in Angola began to show the potential of another Vietnam, Congress stepped in to thwart Henry Kissinger's larger aims in that African struggle.

While Americans seem to feel apprehensive about the potential consequences of U.S. military support abroad, such support continues with apparent popular backing wherever "another Vietnam" is not perceived. It can be argued, Marc Leepson writes in this book's Report on "America's Arms Sales," that this country's growing commitment to provide weapons to an expanding number of nations serves as a replacement for the commitment of U.S. armed forces abroad.

Nine other Reports in this book, written within the last year and a half, examine such other aspects of U.S. foreign policy as human rights, world trade, dollar problems abroad, nuclear proliferation, oil imports, China, Iran, Africa and the Middle East. Every Report, in addition to looking at the present situation and its background, also casts an eye forward in an attempt to discern likely or probable courses of action ahead.

Hoyt Gimlin
Editor

June 1979
Washington, D.C.

HUMAN RIGHTS POLICY

by

Richard C. Schroeder

**May 18
1 9 7 9**

HUMAN RIGHTS POLICY

MORE THAN halfway through the presidential term, Jimmy Carter's human rights program remains the center of controversy. Maligned by critics on both the right and left, and stoutly defended by the administration, the central question is whether the program is accomplishing the goals set out by Carter in his 1976 campaign, or whether it is counter-productive and harmful to American interests abroad.

Human rights supporters were buoyed by the release on April 26 of five leading Soviet dissidents, exchanged for two former Russian U.N. officials held in this country on espionage charges.[1] The White House viewed the exchange a clear-cut justification of the president's efforts over the past two years. Moreover, the Kremlin's ire over Carter's human rights efforts has subsided sufficiently for it to agree to a new strategic arms limitation treaty with the United States — despite oft-heard comments in Washington at the outset of Carter's program that human rights would scuttle détente. Soviet leader Leonid Brezhnev and Carter plan to sign the treaty in Vienna, June 15.

But success on one front was accompanied by failure on another. Only a few days before the Soviet exchange, a news dispatch from Buenos Aires noted that U.S. diplomatic efforts had succeeded in freeing only two of the thousands of political prisoners held by the Argentine government. "Almost everyone familiar with the humanitarian effort, including State Department officials, U.S. diplomats in the field, members of Congress and human rights groups, agrees that the two-year parole program — approved almost a year ago — has been a failure thus far."[2]

To administration officials, guerrilla terrorism and governmental counter-violence in such countries as Argentina, Uruguay or El Salvador provide a rationale for U.S. diplomatic intervention in defense of human rights. On May 4, a Salvadoran leftist group, the Popular Revolutionary Bloc, seized the French and Costa Rican embassies in San Salvador, demanding the release of political prisoners and an end to brutal suppression of peasant organizations in the countryside. Four

---

[1] Aleksandr Ginsburg, Valentin Moroz, Eduard Kuznetsov, Georgi Vins and Mark Dymshits.
[2] Charles Kraus, writing from Buenos Aires in *The Washington Post*, April 24, 1979.

days later, police fired on demonstrators supporting the embassy seizures and reportedly killed more than 20 persons.

An American businessman, the head of a large company doing business in El Salvador, told Editorial Research Reports that the administration was misguided in its belief that human rights was the motivating force behind the seizures. The embassy takeovers were carried out by "fanatical and obsessed radicals," he said. The "carrot-and-stick aid cutoff" techniques applied by "zealots of human rights" in Washington served only to intensify "mindless terrorism." The businessman said he had received a message advising him not to return to El Salvador, since he was on the "hit list" of the Popular Revolutionary Bloc. Another American, doing business in Chile, observed that "the time for the human rights policy has long since passed." The United States, he added, "may never recover the credibility it has lost."

Those assessments are not shared by the administration, and especially not by President Carter. Shortly after taking office, Carter declared:

> Our commitment to the concept of human rights is permanent, and I don't intend to be timid in my public statements and positions. I want them to be productive and not counterproductive. And also I want to assure that our nation and countries other than the Soviet Union are constantly aware that we want to pursue the freedom of individuals and their right to express themselves.[3]

Carter reaffirmed his commitment last December, in a speech marking the 30th anniversary of the Universal Declaration of Human Rights *(see p. 11)*. "As long as I am president," Carter said, "the government of the United States will continue, throughout the world, to enhance human rights. No force on earth can separate us from the commitment."[4]

In congressional testimony on May 2, Deputy Secretary of State Warren M. Christopher said: "... [T]here are many examples of tangible human rights progress. We do not claim credit for particular improvements. But we believe that we have contributed to an atmosphere that makes progress more likely to occur." In the past year, he said, "significant steps" were taken toward the transfer of power from the military to civilian democratic institutions in the Dominican Republic, Ghana, Nigeria, Peru, Brazil and Thailand. In Bangladesh, Sudan, Indonesia, Nepal and Paraguay, "substantial numbers" of political prisoners were released. Other prisoner releases occurred in Cuba, Guinea and South Korea.

---

[3] The statement was made in connection with the visit of Soviet dissident Vladimir Bukovsky at the White House, March 1, 1977.
[4] Quoted in the Department of State *Bulletin*, January 1979, p. 1.

In Eastern Europe and the Soviet Union [Christopher continued], human rights conditions remain a source of serious concern. But even there, we have seen some positive signs: prisoner releases in Poland and Yugoslavia; greater tolerance for dissent in Hungary and Poland; and significant increases in emigration from the Soviet Union. . . .

In my view, then, our policy clearly has been effective in improving human rights around the world. . . .[5]

Chorus of Critics; U.S. Business Opposition

Critics say the list of human rights failures is even longer than Christopher's list of successes. Countries where U.S. pressure has done little to stop massive and systematic brutality include Iran, both under the shah and under the Islamic provisional government that followed him; Uganda under Idi Amin and Equatorial Guinea under Macias Nguema; South Africa; Rhodesia; Cambodia under the Khmer Rouge; and such Western hemispheric nations as El Salvador, Nicaragua, Argentina, Uruguay and Chile. In some places, Carter's human rights efforts have produced an unexpected backlash. Argentina, Brazil, El Salvador, Guatemala and Uruguay all have rejected U.S. military assistance in protest of State Department monitoring of human rights in those countries.

Aside from the question of effectiveness, the tone and style of the administration's human rights effort is disturbing to some. A theologian suggests that it carries "overtones of moral arrogance" and speaks of the "extravagant claims" of some of its advocates.[6] On the political left, Professor Noam Chomsky writes that ". . . the human rights campaign is a device to be manipulated by propagandists to gain popular support for counter-revolutionary intervention."[7]

The U.S. business community sees the human rights push harming American trade and investment overseas. The new head of the Association of American Chambers of Commerce in Latin America, Alexander Perry, expressed this view last year to a congressional subcommittee, saying the world will not operate "according to an American design." Undue emphasis on "punitive, negative" measures, Perry said, runs the risk of provoking anti-American reactions and worsening the human rights situation.[8] In a letter sent to the president on May 2, the

---

[5] Warren M. Christopher, testimony before the International Organizations Subcommittee of the House Committee on Foreign Affairs, May 2, 1979.

[6] Elaine Pagels, "Human Rights: Legitimizing a Recent Concept," *The Annals* of the American Academy of Political and Social Science, March 1979, p. 58. Pagels is chairman of the department of religion at Barnard College.

[7] Noam Chomsky, *Human Rights and American Foreign Policy* (1978), p. 67.

[8] Testimony before the Western Hemisphere Affairs Subcommittee of the Senate Foreign Relations Subcommittee, Oct. 4, 1978. AACCLA is composed of American Chambers of Commerce in 15 hemispheric countries and is affiliated with the Chamber of Commerce of the United States. Perry, the head of a mining corporation in Argentina, was elected president of AACCLA at the group's annual meeting in Washington, May 4, 1979.

AACCLA said its membership adopted Perry's testimony as its own view.

In defense of the policy, administration officials insist that Carter's persistence has changed the climate of world opinion in

Derian

regard to human rights. America's ambassador to the United Nations, Andrew Young, told the General Assembly last Dec. 14: "For perhaps the first time in history we can truly say that there is a worldwide human rights movement and it is steadily gaining force." Patricia Derian, assistant secretary of state for human rights and humanitarian affairs, observes that human rights discussions now take place on the level of presidents and prime ministers. "It used to be," Derian said, "that this happened quietly in the hall or over a glass of brandy or between sets on a tennis court, because human rights things were not generally thought to be possible to discuss in diplomatic formal negotiations. That has changed. That happens now."[9]

Selective Application of Punitive Measures

Many observers comment on the arbitrary nature of actions taken against human rights violators. Efforts are concentrated where this country has some policy leverage — through aid programs, military alliances or trade relations. This leaves out such oppressive regimes as those in communist countries. Friendly countries of major importance to the United States — South Korea and the Philippines, for example — are sometimes wholly or partially exempted from pressures. "So the brunt of the Carter policy has fallen on those nations, notably in Latin America, that are still poor and friendly enough to qualify for U.S. aid, yet neither economically nor strategically important to this country," *The Wall Street Journal* observed last year.[10] A major new study of the state of human rights worldwide makes this observation:

> On the minus side, it must be admitted that the Carter administration's human-rights policy has been invoked selectively. It has been stated emphatically as applied to Western countries, such as South Africa, Chile, Brazil and Uruguay; in muffled tones where military allies or suppliers of oil are concerned, such as Iran or Saudi Arabia; and incoherently with regard to Communist regimes.
>
> On the subjects of continuing though diminishing human rights violations in mainland China, terrorism by Rhodesian and

[9] Department of State *Bulletin,* January 1979, p. 6.
[10] May 11, 1978.

SWAPO [South West Africa People's Organization] guerrillas . . . the administration has been wholly silent.[11]

That view is at least partly reinforced by recent congressional action on the administration's foreign aid request for fiscal year 1980. On May 1, the Senate Foreign Relations Committee recommended the elimination of bilateral economic aid to 10 countries, on human rights grounds for most of them. The countries affected are Panama, Pakistan, Ethiopia, Afghanistan, Haiti, Nicaragua, El Salvador, Guatemala, Paraguay and the Central African Republic. The committee also voted to end a U.S. ban on humanitarian aid to Uganda and to lift the trade embargo with that country in recognition of the ouster of Idi Amin.

The Soviet Union poses special problems for the president. Even before Carter took office, the Trade Act of 1974 denied trade concessions to the Soviets because of their restrictive policies on Jewish emigration. Last summer, the trials of dissidents Anatoly Scharansky and Aleksandr Ginzburg — in apparent contravention of the Helsinki Accords on Security and Cooperation in Europe *(see p. 18)* —presented a direct challenge to Carter's human rights policy. In protest, Carter canceled scheduled trips by American delegations to scientific and environmental conferences in Russia.

But he opposed any interruption in negotiations toward a new strategic arms limitation treaty (SALT), and he refused to call off a meeting Secretary of State Cyrus Vance had planned with Soviet Foreign Minister Andrei Gromyko in Geneva. Soviet suppression of dissent remains troublesome to Washington, but apparently there has been a liberalization of Jewish emigration. Jewish exits from the Soviet Union reached an all-time high of 4,418 in March and administration officials say the year-end total could be as high as 50,000.

Israel presents another kind of problem for the United States. The United States has — at some political cost to itself — consistently defended Israel in international forums against Arab and Soviet charges of suppression of civil and political rights of Palestinians in the West Bank and in Israel itself. But in February, the State Department's annual report on human rights[12] appeared to take a sharp turn away from traditional U.S. support. It stated that "instances of mistreatment" of Arab detainees appear to have occurred. Subsequently, copies of cables from the U.S. Consulate in Jerusalem surfaced in American newspapers.

---

[11] Kurt Glaser and Stefan T. Possony, *Victims of Politics: The State of Human Rights* (1979), p. xxii.

[12] *Report on Human Rights Practices in Countries Receiving U.S. Aid.* The report is required by 1976 amendments to the Foreign Assistance Act and is submitted yearly to the Senate Foreign Relations and the House Foreign Affairs Committees. The 1978 report detailed human rights conditions in 115 foreign countries.

The cables, drafted by consular official Alexandra U. Johnson, said that her consulate post had "assembled a body of firsthand testimony indicating that Israeli torture of Arab prisoners in the occupied territories may be a widespread and even common practice." The information, said the cables, "casts considerable doubt upon the fairness of the system of military courts in operation in the occupied territories. . . ." Israel reacted with outrage, and State Department officials were quick to point out that no evidence of "systematic" violations of human rights had been turned up.

Defining the Proper Scope of U.S. Concern

One built-in difficulty of the administration's human rights efforts is a lack of consensus on whose rights and what rights are properly the subject of American concern. This may stem, in part, from conflicts within the administration. So-called "hardline" rights activists, including Ambassador Young, Assistant Secretary of State Derian, and Derian's aide, Mark Schneider, have made it clear, for example, that Argentina's poor human rights record is a prime target for administration pressure. But that stand has been blunted by contrary signals sent out by Raul Castro, the U.S. ambassador to Argentina. Castro has recently been quoted as saying: "The issue of human rights absolutely does not interest me. I came to this country almost one year ago. . . . They received me with open arms, I ate good meals and good wine. . . . Our relations with Argentina are on the rise."[13]

The confusion goes deeper than the clash of political views within the State Department. There appears to be fundamental disagreement on the definition of human rights, and the scope of U.S. efforts to promote their observance. The fuzziness of the issue may contribute to popular disinterest. McGeorge Bundy has observed: "Americans are . . . a people ordinarily tolerant of special concerns, including those of presidents and foreign policy 'experts,' but deeply resistant to demanding political action in situations not clear and compelling."[14]

Traditionally, what Americans regard as "human rights" are those enumerated in the first ten amendments to the United States Constitution — the familiar Bill of Rights. These guarantee freedom of speech, press and religion, the right of petition, and protections against arbitrary acts of government. For many years, international discussions of human rights were built on that foundation. More than a decade ago, for example, two experts outlined the freedoms which, in their view, fell within the purview of the Inter-American Commission on Human

---

[13] Quoted in *Politics Today*, March-April 1979, p. 12.

[14] McGeorge Bundy, "The Americans and the World," *Daedalus*, winter 1978, p. 289.

Rights.[15] Most proceeded from the American Bill of Rights. There have been subsequent refinements, and new categories have been added, especially those having to do with human needs. In a speech to the American Bar Association last year, Warren M. Christopher outlined the administration's human rights priorities:

Christopher

> The right to be free from governmental violations of the integrity of the person.
>
> The right to fulfill one's vital needs such as food, shelter, health care, and education.
>
> Civil and political rights.[16]

In his recent congressional testimony, Christopher elaborated on the theme, saying:

> We attach fundamental importance to all three basic categories of internationally recognized human rights — that is, personal, economic and political rights. We are prepared to react to flagrant denials of any of these rights, but we have found in practice that we are most often called to respond to flagrant violations of personal rights such as widespread systematic torture or arbitrary executions.

The emphasis on "flagrant violations" lies at the heart of the confusion and controversy surrounding the Carter human rights program. Remarking that "only exceptional violations will produce significant response," one expert cites seven types of human rights crimes that are the object of international attention: genocide, official racism, large-scale official terrorism, totalitarian governance, deliberate refusal to satisfy basic human needs, ecocide (wanton ecological destruction) and war crimes.[17]

Complete as that list may appear, it omits some root causes of unrest in many countries: neglect and exploitation of the peasantry; wage and price policies that severely penalize industrial workers; and the status and rights of international migrants, ranging from Europe's oppressed "guest workers" and illegal Mexican immigrants in the United States, to the hundreds of thousands of Indochinese refugees piling up in temporary camps in that part of the world. A history professor has noted: "The

---

[15] These were: freedom of movement; due process of law; guarantees against arbitrary arrest and detention; equal protection of the law; the right of assembly and association; the right to peaceful petition; freedom of thought, speech, expression and the press; the right to protection of the courts; the right to a fair trial and the right to education. See Durward V. Sandifer and L. Ronald Scheman's *The Foundations of Freedom* (1966), pp. 43-95.

[16] Reprinted in the Department of State *Bulletin*, April 1978, p. 30.

[17] Richard Falk, "Responding to Severe Violations" in *Enhancing Global Human Rights*, by Jorge I. Dominguez, et al. (1979), p. 217.

Carter administration has shown more interest in international human rights than any since that of Woodrow Wilson; but it defines those rights chiefly as political. It avoids discussion of the right to a liveable environment, the right to be a wanted child, or other novel formulations of human rights."[18]

Foundations of Current Policy

MAURICE Cranston, a British scholar, warns that the notion of rights can be expanded so far that they lose their meaning. "An ideal is something one can aim at, but cannot by definition immediately realize. A right, on the contrary, is something that can and, from the moral point of view, must be respected here and now."[19] To insist that a human rights policy embrace the entire human condition is probably self-defeating.

Western concepts of human rights are rooted in Judaic, Christian and Islamic perceptions about the nature of man and his relationship to God. The notion that rights are universal, the "inalienable" possession of all men everywhere, is a secular development, however, the product of the Age of Enlightment. Among the major documents in the evolution of Western human rights theory were the English Bill of Rights (1689), Locke's *Civil Government* (1690), Montesquieu's *L'Espirit des Lois* (1748), the American Declaration of Independence (1776), the American Bill of Rights (1789-91), and the French Declaration of the Rights of Man and the Citizen (1789). It is noteworthy that slavery was abolished in the Western world between 1791 (Haiti) and 1888 (Brazil), some time after the doctrine of universal rights had made its appearance.

Receptive Post-War Climate for U.N. Action

While World War II had multiple and complex causes, it can be said to be the first major conflict in which human rights were a basic issue — the Nazi regime's inhuman treatment of Jews, especially, and many people in conquered lands. Even before U.S. entry into the war, President Roosevelt outlined the goals of American policy, in a speech Jan. 6, 1941, setting forth the "Four Freedoms": freedom of speech and expression, freedom of worship, freedom from want, and freedom from fear.

At the end of the war, the international community turned to

---

[18] Otis Graham, "The Problem that Will not Go Away: Illegal Immigration," *The Center Magazine* (published by the Center for the Study of Democratic Institutions), July-August 1977, p. 66. Graham is professor of American history at the University of California at Santa Barbara.

[19] Quoted by Niels C. Nielsen Jr. in *The Crisis of Human Rights: An American Christian Perspective* (1978), pp. 19-20. Nielsen is head of the department of religious studies at Rice University, Houston, Texas.

the task of creating an institutional mechanism for the defense of human rights. The U.N. Commission on Human Rights was established in 1946, with Eleanor Roosevelt as its first chairman. In 1948 the U.N. General Assembly adopted the Universal Declaration of Human Rights, listing a broad array of specific rights, such as life, liberty and security of person, freedom from slavery and arbitrary arrest, and freedom of opinion, to name but a few. The declaration was not binding on member states, but represented a first effort at achieving a worldwide consensus on the subject.

Four conventions — treaties — were drawn up in support of the aims of the declaration, covering genocide (1948), racial discrimination (1965), economic, social and cultural rights (1966), and civil and political rights (1966). The United States has ratified none of them, and the last three were not submitted to the Senate until last year, the second year of the Carter administration. In contrast, 83 countries adhere to the first treaty and 101 to the second.

Side by side with the U.N. human rights structure are regional institutions such as the European Convention on Human Rights, which is monitored by an investigatory European Human Rights Commission and enforced by a European Human Rights Court. In this hemisphere, the members of the Organization of American States signed an American Declaration of the Rights and Duties of Man in 1948 and an Inter-American Commission on Human Rights was created in 1959. Under the American Convention on Human Rights, which entered into force in July 1978, the commission's mandate will be strengthened. It will be joined by a new Inter-American Court of Human Rights, whose members are due to be named May 22 at special meeting of the OAS General Assembly in Washington.

U.S. Laws, Agencies Dealing With Rights

The U.S. record on human rights has been spotty. Fluctuating congressional interest or opposition, together with American involvement in overseas wars in Korea and Vietnam, have periodically deflected attention from the issue. American security interests, or at least the perception of such interests by different administrations, have also operated as a check on activism in the human rights arena.

Nonetheless, even before President Carter took office, human rights mandates were written into a number of laws governing American assistance programs overseas *(see table, p. 13)*. Among other things, existing statutes (with certain humanitarian exceptions) forbid economic assistance to countries that consistently violate human rights, and they require American directors of international financial institutions to oppose multi-lateral loans to such countries. Laws and executive branch regulations also prohibit or strictly control the extension of trade concessions and preferential financing for trade deals with human rights violators.

In the past two years, several proposed Export-Import Bank loans have been denied or delayed on human rights grounds, leading to protests from businesses penalized by these rulings. Also affected are technology transfers and the granting of most-favored-nation status and the extension of duty-free import privileges under the U.S. Generalized System of Preferences.[20]

To implement the series of laws and regulations, a new human rights bureaucracy has grown up, mainly within the State Department, but also in other departments, including Commerce and Defense. Within State, a new Bureau of Human Rights and Humanitarian Affairs was created in 1977, headed by Patricia Derian. While the application of sanctions against an offending country is a political decision, for which the president is ultimately responsible, the human rights bureaucracy monitors human rights situations overseas, carrying out a systematic collection and evaluation of data and providing decision makers with a constant flow of information and assessments.

U.S. diplomatic and consular missions abroad are primarily responsible for the collection of data. But the government, according to Warren M. Christopher in his congressional testimony, also relies on "the published reports of non-governmental human rights organizations, on reports of international organizations, on findings of congressional committees, on discussions with private U.S. citizens and on other information in the public domain." Critics have questioned whether unofficial sources can provide the degree of accuracy and impartiality needed, but administration officials insist that all such information is checked for reliability.

Work of Amnesty International and Others

The network of non-governmental organizations involved in monitoring human rights is extremely varied. It includes religious groups, such as the World Council of Churches, trade union organizations, political groups,[21] peace groups, organizations such as the YMCA and YWCA, women's groups, and special interest organizations such as Freedom House in New

---

[20] The most-favored-nation rule, under the General Agreement on Tariffs and Trade, is that non-tariff concessions offered to one country must be extended to all signatory nations. The U.S. Generalized System of Preferences provides duty-free entry into the United States for more than 2,700 products from nearly 140 eligible developing countries. See "Trade Talks and Protectionism," *E.R.R.*, 1979 Vol. I, pp. 21-40.

[21] See Donald M. Fraser and John P. Salzberg's, "International Political Parties as a Vehicle for Human Rights," *The Annals*, March 1979, p. 63.

Human Rights Legislation Before 1977

1973

PL 93-189 (Foreign Assistance Act). Declared the sense of Congress that the president should deny economic or military aid to foreign governments that imprisoned citizens for political purposes.

Directed the president to request Chile to protect human rights of all individuals.

1974

PL 93-559 (Foreign Assistance Act). Urged the president to reduce or terminate security assistance to any government which consistently violates internationally recognized human rights, including torture or cruel, inhuman or degrading treatment or punishment; prolonged detention without charges; or other flagrant denials of the right of life, liberty and the security of persons.

Prohibited all military aid to Chile; limited economic aid to $25 million.

1975

PL 94-161 (International Development and Food Assistance Act). Prohibited economic assistance to any country which consistently violates internationally recognized human rights unless the aid will directly benefit the needy.

1976

PL 94-339 (Security Assistance and Arms Export Control Act). Prohibited security assistance to governments that engage in a consistent pattern of gross violations of internationally recognized human rights.

Established within the State Department a coordinator for Human Rights and Humanitarian Affairs and required the secretary of state to report to Congress on human rights practices in each country proposed as an aid recipient.

Expressed the concern of Congress for the erosion of civil liberties in South Korea and requested the president to communicate this concern in forceful terms to the South Korean government.

Terminated military aid to Chile and limited economic aid to $27.5 million.

PL 94-441 (Foreign Aid Appropriations Act). Provided that no funds be used for military aid to Uruguay.

York, the Washington-based Council on Hemispheric Affairs, and the Washington Office for Latin America, a church-related human rights "watchdog."

Of all such organizations, the main ones are Amnesty International, the International Commission of Jurists and the International Committee of the Red Cross. Amnesty International was founded in 1961 in London to do something about "forgotten prisoners" detained in various countries because of dissenting political or religious views. Each year it publishes an encyclopedic report on human rights conditions in most countries of the world — including the United States.[22] For this work, the organization received the Nobel Prize for Peace in 1977.

The International Commission of Jurists was founded in West Berlin in 1952 and consists of not more than 40 distinguished judicial officials from all over the world who meet every three years. It issues annual reports and a biannual *Review,* and carries on a continuing program of public information on human rights issues. The International Committee of the Red Cross, founded in 1863 in Geneva, is a constituent element of the International Red Cross. It is composed of not more than 25 members, all of Swiss nationality, and has a specific prisoner-monitoring role assigned to it by the 1949 Geneva Convention on the Treatment of Prisoners of War.

Attacks on America's Human Rights Record

Andrew Young raised a political storm last year by remarking to the Paris Socialist newspaper *Le Matin* that American prisons hold "hundreds, perhaps even thousands, of people whom I would call political prisoners." His words were especially embarrassing to the White House since they appeared in print only hours before Secretary of State Cyrus R. Vance was due to meet Soviet Foreign Minister Andrei Gromyko on July 12 to protest Russia's treatment of its dissidents. Young received a strong rebuke from President Carter. Undaunted, Young returned to the theme of his speech to the U.N. General Assembly, in December. "There is no room for self-righteousness and self-congratulations in the field of human rights," he said. "Each of our nations has people of vision and people of fear, those who create and those who repress and torture."

Young's remarks point up the vulnerability of a nation that takes the lead in the international defense of human rights. The more forceful the effort, the greater the likelihood the country will be the target of propaganda to discredit its own human rights record. White House aides say the president is aware of the inherent risks, but is committed to the view, expressed in his first major foreign policy speech, that "no member of the United Nations can claim that mistreatment of its citizens is solely its own business. Equally, no member can avoid its responsibilities . . . to speak when torture or unwarranted deprivation of freedom occurs in any part of the world."

Amnesty International, in its 1978 report, said its main concerns in the United States were the use of the death penalty; the cruel, inhuman and degrading treatment of prisoners; and the fabrication of criminal charges against political activists. The

---

[22] *Amnesty International Report 1978* reports on 111 countries.

organization reported it had been monitoring two sets of well-publicized cases in North Carolina, one involving the so-called Charlotte Three on arson convictions and the other involving the Wilmington Ten on charges of firebombing a store during 1971 racial disturbances.[23]

In addition, Amnesty International has looked into cases of prosecution of individuals because of ethnic origin or political activity, and into specific complaints of mistreatment of jail inmates. Its volume of work in the United States has increased "due to the greater public attention given to American human rights issues as a result of President Carter's emphasis on human rights in relation to foreign policy." Observing that "it is difficult to identify prisoners of conscience in the United States," the organization is on balance much milder in its criticism of the American situation than of human rights conditions in other Western democracies.

Prospects for the Next Decade

NO TIME is ever really good for human rights," writes the editor of *Foreign Policy* magazine. "The 1980s are likely to see an intensification of trends that could lead governments increasingly to violate human rights . . . the 1980s may be a gloomy decade. . . ."[24] This dour assessment is based on an analysis of such factors as rising unrest generated by excessive population growth, food shortages, urban crowding, resource scarcities, and stricter controls on the "safety valve" of international migration. In addition, the author cites "technological progress that steadily enhances the ability of the state to spy upon and bring repressive force against targeted individuals and groups. . . ." The observation suggests that George Orwell's vision of 1984 may indeed be fast approaching.

As justification for repressive measures, governments commonly point to the need to control and eliminate the plague of terrorism. Indeed, the most glaring abuses of human rights are often found in countries facing serious opposition from organized guerrilla groups. For such governments, repression of opposition becomes a holy crusade waged in the name of the greater good of the nation, or even its survival as a nation. Argentina, for example, frequently justifies the clandestine kidnapping of thousands of political opponents on these grounds. In a news

---

[23] The three Charlotte defendants were Earl Grant, Charles Parker and T. J Reddy; the 10 Wilmington defendants were the Rev. Benjamin F. Chavis, Reginald Epps, Jerry Jacobs, James McKoy, Wayne Moore, Marvin Patrick, Connie Tindall, Ann Shepard Turner, Willie Earl Vereen, and William Wright.

[24] Richard H. Ullman, "Human Rights — Toward International Action," in Dominguez, *op. cit.*, pp. 1, 4.

conference in Los Angeles in September 1978, Argentine Finance Minister José Alfredo Martinez de Hoz explained his government's position: "Wars are never fought with white gloves. We have used against the terrorists the same drastic methods that they have employed."[25]

Terrorism is usually defined as violence directed against unarmed non-combatants in pursuit of a political or military objective. Aircraft hijacking, the massacre of members of the Israeli Olympic team in Munich in 1972, and the kidnapping of foreign diplomats all qualify under this definition. Unconventional or guerrilla warfare waged against military personnel or targets, on the other hand, is generally regarded as a legitimate tactic, although the dividing line is often indistinct.

Official terrorism is often the response of governments driven to the wall by violent opposition. Arbitrary arrests, beatings, kidnappings and torture are not the exclusive hallmarks of military dictatorships. The Indian government, for example, arrested thousands of "prisoners of conscience" during the 1975-1977 emergency under provisions of the Maintenance of Internal Security Act. Amnesty International has frequently complained about "inhuman treatment" and even "torture" used by Britain against prisoners in Northern Ireland.

Uruguay, once one of the premier democracies of the Western Hemisphere, has been under *de facto* military rule since 1973, when the armed forces took over control of the government and dissolved the elected parliament. Uruguay's troubles began in the 1960s, with the appearance of the Tupamaros, an urban guerrilla group that kidnapped prominent businessmen and diplomats, staged bank robberies and detonated bombs in public buildings. The military's response was to arrest thousands of suspected "subversives," torturing and killing many prisoners as a matter of course. According to the State Department's 1978 report on human rights, official Uruguayan figures indicated that at least 5,700 persons had been detained since 1972 on such charges as "undermining the morale of the armed forces," and "disrespect to military authorities."

Current Trouble Spots on Four Continents

Since the end of World War II, Southeast Asia has been a primary locus of guerrilla warfare and terrorist activity. Most attention has been focused on Indochina, but civilian populations have been ravaged by guerrillas and government forces alike in the Philippines and Indonesia. A second major area of terrorism is the Middle East, where Palestinian guerrillas have long waged a campaign against Israel and have, in turn, been

---

[25] Quoted in a statement by Amnesty International, reprinted in the *Congressional Record,* March 26, 1979, p. S 3373.

periodically devastated by Israeli military and paramilitary forces.[26]

In Africa, the central and southern parts of the continent, along with the Horn of Africa, have seen increased savagery and terrorism in recent years. The victims of the bloody regime of Idi Amin in Uganda may number as high as 100,000, according to some estimates, and the crimes ascribed to Amin range from skull-smashing to forced cannibalism. A close competitor of Amin is President Macias Nguema of Equatorial Guinea in West Africa whose victims may number in the tens of thousands.

The struggle for black majority rule in Rhodesia, South Africa and South West Africa (Namibia) has likewise claimed thousands of lives and, particularly in South Africa, resulted in widespread rioting and mass arrests. In the Horn of Africa, the revolutionary government of Ethiopia has mounted a sweeping campaign against "counter-revolutionaries," calling its action "justifiable terror," a category which, in the view of two experts, is "unknown in legal philosophy or social science."[27]

In Europe, Italy has come to the fore as a center of terrorist violence. Assassinations, bombings and kidnappings, mostly carried out by the so-called "Red Brigades," occur with monotonous frequency. The most notable outrage was the kidnapping and murder of former Italian Premier Aldo Moro last year. In this hemisphere, violence seems endemic to a majority of the Latin American republics. Amnesty International reported in 1978 that "throughout the region there continues to be a high level of political violence: abductions, disappearances, torture and extra-legal executions or assassinations."

> The incidence of these violations [the report continues] ranges from an estimated 15,000 dead or disappeared in Argentina since 1976 to an estimated 1,500 disappeared in Chile since 1973, and more limited numbers in rural parts of Mexico.

> Guatemala was the first Latin American country where, in recent times, political killings of this type have occurred on a large scale (an estimated 20,000 victims since 1966). In the past year, in both El Salvador and Nicaragua, there have been numerous disappearances and assassinations.

No country — not even the United States is immune to the virus of terrorism. A decade ago, H. Rap Brown, the black militant, remarked that "violence is as American as cherry pie."[28] Underscoring that observation, the past decade has witnessed urban riots, skyjackings of domestic airliners, and bombings of public buildings.

---

[26] See "International Terrorism," *E.R.R.*, 1977 Vol. II, pp. 909-932.

[27] Glaser and Possony, *op. cit.*, p. xvi.

[28] See "Violence in American Life," *E.R.R.*, 1968 Vol. I, pp. 405-424.

Carter administration officials profess to be encouraged by two developments in the international human rights scene. The first is the increasing effectiveness of human rights machinery in this hemisphere. The Inter-American Commission on Human Rights has recently begun to show some muscle for the first time since its creation in 1959. During 1978, the commission issued three hard-hitting reports, condemning human rights violations in Nicaragua, Paraguay and Uruguay, and it began an intensive investigation of the human rights situation in Argentina and Haiti.

Some Advances Abroad; Helsinki Accords

Last July, the American Convention on Human Rights entered into force, when Grenada, the newest and smallest member of the Organization of American States, ratified its provisions. The treaty gives broader powers to the Human Rights Commission and sets up an Inter-American Court of Human Rights. The seven members of the court, to be selected at a special meeting of the OAS General Assembly in Washington on May 22, will hear complaints on violations by OAS member governments and it can order payment of indemnification to victims. One serious limitation is that jurisdiction extends only to the OAS member states that have ratified the treaty. More than half the members have not yet done so, and among them are the big countries of the hemisphere: Argentina, Brazil, Mexico — and the United States. The treaty has been submitted to the Senate for approval, but it is far down the list of Senate priorities and unlikely to be acted on in the near future.[29]

The second encouraging international development is the world attention now being focused on the Final Act of the Conference on Security and Cooperation in Europe, the so-called Helsinki Agreement, signed in 1975 by the leaders of the United States, the Soviet Union, Canada and 32 European nations at the Finnish capital. The agreement recognizes the collective rights of peoples to self-determination and equal status in the international community. Under its terms, signatory states agree to respect human rights and fundamental freedoms, including freedom of thought, conscience, religion and belief, and to participate in periodic reviews of their human rights performance.[30]

Although the agreement is not legally binding as a treaty would be, it has served to spotlight the human rights records of the Soviet Union and its eastern European allies. Surprisingly, citizen groups have sprung up in several of the East Bloc countries, demanding compliance with the terms of the agreement.

[29] See Richard C. Schroeder, "In Defense of Human Rights," *Americas* magazine, October 1978, pp. 28-29.
[30] See Karl E. Birnbaum, "Human Rights and East-West Relations," *Foreign Affairs*, July 1977, pp. 783-799.

The most significant is the Helsinki Watch Committee, formed in Russia in May 1976 by Professor Yuri Orlov and 10 other Soviet activists, which has become the rallying point for dissidents in the Soviet Union. In the three years since its founding, many of the original members of the Helsinki Committee have been arrested and sentenced to prison terms, but the group continues to speak out, now under the leadership of Nobel Peace Prize-winner Andrei Sakharov.[31]

Campaign for Human Rights After Carter

No one doubts the sincerity and determination of President Carter to press human rights issues, even in the face of bitter domestic and international criticism. And even opponents of Carter's policies acknowledge that some forward movement has taken place. The nagging question is: what happens when Carter leaves the White House? With a human rights bureaucracy now in place at the State Department, and an Interagency Group on Human Rights and Foreign Assistance coordinating policy among several executive departments, it is likely that future administrations will continue at least a nominal effort in the direction initiated by Carter. But there are several constraints. One is that "the easy steps" have been taken.[32]

A second constraint is the influence that can be brought to bear by opponents of the human rights policy — particularly in the business community and in Congress — when the going gets rough. President Carter is apparently willing to sacrifice a certain amount of American export potential in order to enforce his human rights policies in such countries as Argentina or the Soviet Union. A future president may decide that U.S. prosperity is more important than the condition of Soviet dissidents.

A third element is that, without Carter's leadership, the constituency for a strong human rights program may evaporate. The campaign, from the beginning, "was seriously flawed as a unifying theme," wrote the managing editor of *Foreign Affairs* magazine.[33] Its appeal to the political left was that it seemed a way to "get tough" with such dictatorial governments as those of Chile or South Korea. The political right viewed it as a hardline policy toward the Soviet Union. If the human rights program depends on whose ox is being gored, it is not likely to have a long life-span. The hope of human rights advocates is that the crusade, once begun, will gather its own momentum and continue even after its originators have disappeared from the national and international political scene.

---

[31] See two recent articles by Rep. Dante B. Fascell, D-Fla.: "The Helsinki Accord: A Case Study," *The Annals* of the American Academy of Political and Social Science, March 1979, pp. 69-76, and "Did Human Rights Survive Belgrade?" *Foreign Policy*, summer 1978, pp. 104-118.

[32] See David Hawk's "Human Rights at Half-Time," *The New Republic*, April 7, 1979, p. 23.

[33] James Chace, "Is a Foreign Policy Consensus Possible?" *Foreign Affairs*, fall 1978, p. 8.

Selected Bibliography

Books

Chomsky, Noam, *Human Rights and American Foreign Policy,* Spokesman Books, 1978.

Dominguez, Jorge I., et al., *Enhancing Global Human Rights,* McGraw-Hill (for the Council on Foreign Relations), 1979.

Glaser, Kurt and Stefan T. Possony, *Victims of Politics: The State of Human Rights,* Columbia University Press, 1979.

Jiryis, Sabri, *The Arabs in Israel,* Monthly Review Press, 1976.

Nielsen, Niels C., *The Crisis of Human Rights: An American Christian Perspective,* Thomas Nelson Inc., 1978.

Sandifer, Durward V. and L. Ronald Scheman, *The Foundations of Freedom: The Inter-Relationship Between Democracy and Human Rights,* Frederick A. Praeger, 1966.

Veenhooven, Willem A. (ed.), *Case Studies on Human Rights and Fundamental Freedoms: A World Survey* (5 Vols.), Martinus Mijhoff, The Hague (for the Foundation for the Study of Plural Societies), 1975.

Articles

Birnbaum, Karl E., "Human Rights and East-West Relations," *Foreign Affairs,* July 1977.

Bundy, McGeorge, "The Americans and the World," *Daedalus,* winter 1978.

Chace, James, "Is a Foreign Policy Consensus Possible?" *Foreign Affairs,* fall 1978.

Fascell, Dante B., "The Helsinki Accord: A Case Study," *The Annals of the American Academy of Political and Social Science,* March 1979.

Hawk, David, "Human Rights at Half-Time," *The New Republic,* April 7, 1979, pp. 21-23.

Pagels, Elaine, "Human Rights: Legitimizing a Recent Concept," *The Annals,* March 1979, pp. 57-62.

Shulman, Marshall D., "On Learning to Live with Authoritarian Regimes," *Foreign Affairs,* January 1977.

Reports and Studies

Amnesty International Report 1978, Amnesty International Publications, 1979.

Warren, Christopher M., "Testimony Before the International Organizations Subcommittee of the House Committee on Foreign Affairs," May 2, 1979.

Editorial Research Reports: "Political Prisoners," 1976 Vol. II, p. 721; "International Terrorism," 1977 Vol. II, p. 909.

Freedom House *Comparative Survey of Freedom,* January 1979.

Inter-American Commission on Human Rights, "Report on the Situation of Human Rights in Nicaragua," November, 1978; "Report on the Situation of Human Rights in Uruguay," April 1978; "Report on the Situation of Human Rights in Paraguay," January 1978

U.S. Department of State, *Report on Human Rights Practices in Countries Receiving U.S. Aid,* submitted to the Senate Foreign Relations Committee and the House Foreign Affairs Committee, Feb. 8, 1979.

AMERICA'S ARMS SALES

by

Marc Leepson

May 4
1979

AMERICA'S ARMS SALES

G OVERNMENT-TO-GOVERNMENT transfers of conventional weapons — not nuclear arms — have been an integral part of American foreign policy since World War II. Recent events in the Middle East seem to indicate that at least for the immediate future U.S. arms shipments abroad will continue to play an important role in the relationship between this country and its allies. Arms supplied by the United States, the largest seller of arms in the world, were important factors in the Egyptian-Israeli peace treaty signed March 26, the rise and fall of the Shah of Iran and the simmering war between North and South Yemen.

The political machinations in the Middle East are being played out against the backdrop of the worldwide competition between the United States and the Soviet Union — the second leading seller of arms — to gain influence and win friends around the world. Neither the United States nor the Soviet Union sells nuclear weapons, and the two countries are now completing talks leading to a new agreement for limiting the deployment of offensive nuclear weapons *(see box, p. 26)*.

President Carter came to office two years ago promising to cut down U.S. arms sales. During the 1976 presidential campaign he constantly criticized the extent of arms sales under the Nixon and Ford administrations. "We cannot be both the world's leading champion of peace and the world's leading supplier of weapons of war," Carter said numerous times during the campaign. Soon after taking office, Carter ordered a review of U.S. military sales practices. He then outlined his new arms sales policy on May 19, 1977, announcing that "the United States will henceforth view arms transfers as an exceptional foreign policy implement. . . ." Warning of the "threat to world peace embodied in this spiraling arms traffic," Carter said he would "place the burden of persuasion . . . on those who favor a particular arms sale rather than on those who oppose it."

On Feb. 1, 1978, Carter imposed an 8 percent cut in the $8.6 billion ceiling on arms sales to countries other than the 14 NATO allies,[1] Japan, Australia and New Zealand during that fiscal year. The following Nov. 29, he announced a further 8 percent reduction during the 1979 fiscal year.

---

[1] The member countries of the North Atlantic Treaty Organization, in addition to the United States, are: Belgium, Britain, Canada, Denmark, France, West Germany, Greece, Iceland, Italy, Luxembourg, the Netherlands, Norway, Portugal and Turkey.

Carter's policy has provoked criticism on two counts: (1) that it is selective, and (2) that overall U.S. arms shipments have increased each year since he has been president. The Department of Defense's Security Assistance Administration reported recently that worldwide arms transfers by the United States totaled $15.2 billion in fiscal year 1978, 16 percent more than in 1977. "Transfers" — or shipments — include not only arms purchased abroad directly from the U.S. government or from private American dealers and manufacturers, but also arms provided to foreign governments as U.S. aid. However, in general usage, "sales" are often synonymous with "transfers." [2]

Congress enacted legislation three years ago expanding its authority to review and reject foreign arms sales proposed by the executive branch. Congress acted after President Ford vetoed an earlier version of the bill, to put a $9 billion ceiling on sales of weapons abroad and allow Congress to reject certain commercial sales. The bill that became law, the Arms Export Control Act of 1976, required advance reporting for all military sales over $25 million and sales of defense equipment worth more than $7 million. Congress has not rejected any proposed sales since the law was passed, but both the Ford and Carter administrations have been forced to modify some earlier arms sales in the face of congressional opposition. The law allows the president to bypass the congressional review process if he determines a sale is required by U.S. national security.

President's Plans for Arming North Yemen

President Carter invoked the bypass provision for the first time on March 9, 1979, when he announced that the United States would sell some $450 million worth of jets, tanks and other arms to North Yemen without waiting for congressional review. The arms shipments came in the wake of increased fighting between North Yemen and its Marxist neighbor, South Yemen. In February, troops from South Yemen, supported by Soviet-supplied tanks and planes, invaded North Yemen at four places. By late March, the fighting had died down, but U.S. officials announced that this country would still deliver the arms to North Yemen.

In the past fiscal year (1978), according to State Department information, the United States provided no military equipment to North Yemen and $763,000 worth of military aid in the form of military education and training programs. There had been no plans to sell it arms in the current year until Carter made his recent decision. Now North Yemen will become the third-biggest recipient of American weapons (after Israel and Saudi

---

[2] A further complexity in terminology is the Department of Defense's reference to arms "orders," which are items contracted for but not yet delivered. For information on the various elements of the arms program, see the middle section of this report.

U.S. Military Sales Orders from Abroad*

Fiscal year	Amount (in thousands)	Fiscal year	Amount (in thousands)
1955-1968	$10,547,482	1974	10,740,639
1969	1,183,723	1975	13,938,200
1970	1,155,817	1976	13,233,157
1971	1,388,955	1977	11,341,906
1972	3,065,867	1978	13,534,389
1973	4,480,390	1979	13,962,161**
		1980	14,000,000**

*Excluding Commercial Sales
**Estimated

Source: Department of Defense

Arabia), according to the calculations of Rep. Les Aspin, D-Wis., a member of the House Armed Services Committee and an outspoken critic of high U.S. arms spending.

Drawing a parallel to U.S. arms support of South Vietnam in the 1960s and 1970s, Aspin wrote recently: "Yemen is an unwise spot on which to stake our prestige. It is yet another case where the United States . . . will be unable to exert much control over events with sophisticated military gear. And yet the sale of such equipment sucks us into the whirlpool and puts American prestige on the line. Selling such vast quantities of advanced weapons is almost certainly not the best way of dealing with the sort of tribal conflicts that have beset Yemen for years." [3]

There were other members of Congress who joined in criticizing the presidential action. Rep. Gerry E. Studds, D-Mass.,

---

[3] Rep. Les Aspin, "Report on Yemen and U.S. Arms Sales," issued by his office March 19, 1979, p. 6.

Containing Nuclear Proliferation

Neither the United States nor the Soviet Union sells nuclear weapons to other countries. Nonetheless, the two superpowers share a concern about the spread of such weapons, and about the costliness of an arms race between the two.

In 1972, the two countries signed two strategic arms limitation pacts. One was a treaty limiting the missile defenses of both countries and the other was technically an executive agreement placing a numerical freeze on U.S. and Soviet missile launchers for five years at existing levels.

Although both agreements are sometimes referred to as SALT I, the tendency now is to speak of SALT I in terms of the second agreement — on offensive weaponry. The other is usually called the ABM (anti-ballistic missile) treaty.

SALT I envisioned SALT II, a new agreement extending and expanding the original one. That a SALT II agreement will be signed in the coming weeks is a foregone conclusion in Washington. There is every expectation that the new agreement, in treaty form, will be presented to the Senate for ratification in the late spring or early summer.

maintained at a House Foreign Affairs subcommittee hearing on March 12 that congressional aquiescence about Carter's arms sales policy reflected ignorance rather than support. Members of Congress are now beginning to realize the scope of the administration's arms sales program, he said, and skepticism is developing among some liberals. Rep. Lee H. Hamilton, D-Ind., one of Congress's leading critics of U.S. arms sales, said that these sales since the early 1970s "have represented a disproportionate part of our total foreign policy effort, to the detriment of our economic development, political and diplomatic efforts."[4] Hamilton, chairman of the Foreign Affairs Subcommittee on Europe and the Middle East, protested that the president's waiver of the congressional review was unwarranted since the weapons could not possibly have an immediate effect on the border war.

Congressional criticism was reflected in two provisions the Foreign Affairs Committee has put in the foreign military assistance bill for the next fiscal year, beginning Oct. 1. The bill, as approved by the committee March 24, offers an alternative to the presidential waiver provided in the 1976 law. The president could instead create a stockpile of arms for delivery to specific "friendly" countries in case of emergency. Another provision of

[4] Speech at the National Defense University, Washington, D.C., April 19, 1977.

the bill would require that any future waiver of congressional review on grounds of national security be justified to Congress in detail, explaining the U.S. interests that are endangered by the emergency.[5]

State Department officials have defended the emergency sales to North Yemen. William R. Crawford Jr., the acting deputy assistant secretary of state, told Hamilton's subcommittee March 12 that congressional review of the North Yemen sale had been waived because "we felt speed to be of the essence" — to bolster North Yemen's defenses and to signal U.S. resolve to other nations, especially Saudi Arabia. The Saudis were reported to have been shaken by Washington's lack of support of the Shah of Iran preceding his downfall.[6]

In the past decade, Saudi Arabia has embarked on a rapid military modernization program. In 1974-76, the desert kingdom bought almost $6 billion worth of arms from the United States. In fiscal year 1978, its purchases amounted to $4.1 billion, more than those of any other country. Sixty supersonic F-15 fighters were sold to Saudia Arabia last year over some objections in Congress. Saudi officials denied that they felt threatened by Iran during its big arms buildup, but outside observers saw that as one reason behind their spending spree. Until Iraq recently assumed a more pro-Western stance, it also was perceived in Saudi Arabia as a potential threat.

Peace Treaty Aid to Both Egypt and Israel

One of the ironies in the Egyptian-Israeli peace treaty is that the United States agreed to provide massive aid — much of it in the form of arms — to both nations. A week before the treaty-signing ceremonies on the White House lawn, March 26, 1979, the Carter administration pledged $1.5 billion worth of planes, tanks and anti-aircraft weapons to Egypt and about $3 billion worth of armaments to Israel. Some $2.2 billion of the Israeli total will be in the form of long-term loans to enable Israel to purchase an array of arms from the United States. The Egyptian aid also will be in the form of grants and long-term loans. All of the arms shipments are subject to approval by Congress, which is expected to be forthcoming.

The United States has been supplying arms to Egypt only for the last three years. The new commitments represent the opening of what Bernard Weinraub of *The New York Times* on March 29 called a "far-reaching defense relationship" between the United States and Egypt. The United States has provided some $4.2 billion in foreign aid to Egypt since 1973, including

---

[5] See *Congressional Quarterly Weekly Report*, March 31, 1979. p. 612.

[6] For background, see "Iran Between East and West," *E.R.R.*, 1979 Vol. I, pp. 65-84, and "Saudi Arabia's Backstage Diplomacy," *E.R.R.*, 1978 Vol. I, pp. 21-40.

some $1 billion in the form of arms and security assistance in fiscal year 1979, according to Department of Defense statistics.

Israel has been a main beneficiary of U.S. arms sales in recent years. Israel has agreed to buy, in this fiscal year alone, some $1.8 billion worth of arms from the United States. Since 1973, this country has provided $11.4 billion in arms and security assistance support to Israel. Some concerns have been voiced in Congress about public opposition to the $4.5 billion outlay but overall reaction from Congress seems to be favorable. Observers say Congress will approve the arms shipments to both Egypt and Israel. "We will find that the price for peace represents the best investment this country has ever had," said Frank Church, D-Idaho, chairman of the Senate Foreign Relations Committee. That price "will fall well below the price we have paid over and over again for wars in the Middle East during the last 30 years."

Aftermath of Large Sales to the Shah of Iran

With the massive new shipments of U.S. arms, Egypt will need American technology and manpower to keep the weaponry operable — just as Iran did. The now-deposed shah had been by far the largest recipient of American-made arms. Iran agreed to buy some $20.7 billion worth of U.S. arms between 1955 and 1978, according to the Defense Security Assistance Agency.[7] The bulk of the U.S. arms sales to the shah — some $19 billion — were sold after President Nixon visited Iran in 1972. Nixon decided to "sell Iran virtually any conventional weapons it wanted," according to a Senate Foreign Assistance Subcommittee staff report issued Aug. 1, 1976.

Iran's annual arms purchase from the United States quadrupled in 1973, as the following table shows:

Fiscal Year	Amount	Fiscal Year	Amount
1971	$ 363,884,000	1975	$2,447,140,000
1972	472,611,000	1976	1,794,487,000
1973	2,171,355,000	1977	5,713,769,000
1974	4,325,357,000	1978	2,586,890,000

According to a study completed by the International Institute for Strategic Studies in London,[8] Iran's defense expenditures for 1975-76 amounted to $10.4 billion, about a third of the nation's gross national product. Britain, whose GNP was five times larger than Iran's, spent less for defense.

Why did the shah pour so much money into arms? "The more

---

[7] U.S. Department of Defense, Security Assistance Agency, "Foreign Military Sales and Military Assistance Facts," December 1978, p. 1.

[8] "The Military Balance, 1975-76."

powerful we get, the more responsible we feel," the shah told author Anthony Sampson in a 1975 interview. "We don't want the land of others; we don't need the wealth of others, we have enough. . . . The strength that we have now in the Persian Gulf is ten times, twenty times, more than the British ever had." [9]

Along with the massive arms shipments to Iran came American military and technical personnel to instruct the Iranians on how to use and maintain the weapons and equipment. The number of American citizens in Iran working with the military sales program climbed from 15,000 in 1972 to a peak of 24,000 in 1976. Of the 45,000 Americans living in Iran when the shah fell in January 1979, observers believed that about 10,000 were working with the military. Nearly all Americans left Iran in the chaotic days following the shah's downfall.

The shah's fall had immediate consequences on American arms sales policy. For one thing, there was concern that advanced American arms, including a large number of F-14 jet fighters equipped with Phoenix air-to-air missiles, would fall into the hands of the Soviet Union, giving the Russians valuable information about some of

F-14 Fighter

the most sophisticated American weapons. The F-14s' Phoenix missiles, which cost about $250,000 each, are capable of engaging moving targets at distances of up to 200 miles.

In addition, there are indications that the new Iranian government wants to sell the F-14s back to the United States. Adm. Ahmad Madani, Iran's defense minister, said March 27 that disorganization in the new government and military has prevented the Iranian armed forces from using the complicated equipment. Madani told *The Washington Post* that the government also wants to sell back 600 of 900 helicopters the shah purchased from the United States. Informal discussions between U.S. embassy officials and representatives of the new revolutionary government dominated by the Ayatollah Khomeini were held in Tehran to work out details on returning the arms and equipment. Also discussed was the possibility of sending a small number of American advisers to Iran to show the Iranians how to use the highly computerized American-produced military supply system the shah had purchased.

The new Iranian government has cancelled the bulk of some $12 billion worth of U.S. arms ordered by the shah but not yet

---

[9] Anthony Sampson, *The Arms Bazaar: From Lebanon to Lockheed* (1977), p. 256.

delivered, including seven highly advanced flying radar command posts called AWACS (Airborne Warning and Control System). Also included in the cancelled orders were four destroyers, three submarines, 160 F-16 fighter jets with Phoenix missiles, 16 F-4 Phantom fighters and 14,000 missiles of various kinds.

The cancellations, among other things, have com-

E-3A Aircraft With AWACS

plicated Department of Defense spending plans for the immediate future. The Pentagon was forced to ask Congress for substantial revisions in a supplemental defense appropriations bill to provide for the purchase of weapons ordered by the shah but cancelled. In order to absorb this cost, the Pentagon dropped 42 items totaling more than $700 million that it had initially sought.

Pentagon officials have said that some of the cancelled arms could be sent to Egypt and Israel. Observers say that the cancellations will not harm the U.S. arms makers significantly because of a worldwide demand for American-made arms. The new sales to Egypt, Israel and Yemen also will fill some of the void. "The beauty of this is that Iran is a drop in the bucket," an unidentified aerospace industry analyst was quoted as saying in *The Washington Post*, March 25. "The military and commercial cycles of the [arms] companies are clicking on all cylinders." Moreover, many of the arms ordered by the shah have yet to be built. AWACS, for instance, were not scheduled for production by Boeing until the 1980s.

Arms Policy Since 1940

A MERICA began its role as a big international arms supplier about a year before it entered World War II and while it was still trying to maintain the facade of a neutrality policy. Franklin D. Roosevelt, fresh from his third presidential election in 1940, searched for a way to aid beleaguered Britain without being thwarted by the isolationist spirit in Congress. As explained to a cluster of newsmen gathered around his Oval Office desk that Dec. 17 and in a radio speech to the nation 12 days later, he proposed that the United States lend, lease, sell or transfer billions of dollars worth of war supplies (including food, machinery and services) to nations whose defense was vital to this country.

As reluctantly approved by Congress on March 11, 1941, the Lend-Lease Act provided that a country should receive aid on such terms as "the president deems satisfactory" and that repayment was to be "in kind or property, or in any other direct or indirect benefit which the president deems satisfactory." Lend-lease, originally intended for Britain primarily but also China, was extended later that year to include Russia. Upon America's entry in the war after Pearl Harbor, wartime aid went to every ally. When terminated by President Truman on Aug. 21, 1945, total lend-lease aid had exceeded $50.6 billion. So it was that the United States had assumed the role of "the great arsenal of democracy," which Roosevelt spoke of in his radio talk to the nation announcing the lend-lease program.

Cold War Aid Under the Truman Doctrine

In the post-war years, the United States continued to distribute arms, but the object no longer was to help allied countries fight Germany and Japan. The Cold War had begun and the foe was the Soviet Union and international communism. The fear of communist domination was dramatically sounded in Winston Churchill's famous "iron curtain" speech at tiny Westminster College in Fulton, Mo., March 5, 1946. He warned that an "iron curtain [had] descended across the [European] continent" and threatened all of Europe. A civil war in Greece between government and communist forces, coupled with the withdrawal of British assistance, prompted President Truman to set forth a policy that essentially was an extension of the idea behind lend-lease. The Truman Doctrine, spelled out to Congress in March 1947, committed the United States to give economic and military aid to free nations anywhere in their resistance of aggression or subversion, whether external or internal.

The first step in implementing the Truman Doctrine was securing congressional approval for $400 million in aid to Greece and Turkey. About 59 percent of the aid to Greece and nearly all of the aid to Turkey was in the form of military equipment. The loan of American civilian and military advisers also was part of the deal. The establishment of the North Atlantic Treaty Organization and passage of the Mutual Defense Assistance Act in 1949, the Mutual Security Acts of 1951 and 1954, the formation of the Southeast Asia Treaty Organization in 1954 and the Foreign Assistance Act of 1961 all tended to increase U.S. military aid throughout the world, through both grants and sales.[10]

During the first years after World War II, the United States and Britain gave away most of their obsolete military equipment

---

[10] For background, see chapters on "Foreign Policy" and "National Security" in Congressional Quarterly's *Congress and the Nation, 1945-1964*, Vol. I (1965).

Arms Control Agency

The U.S. Arms Control and Disarmament Agency, established by Congress in 1961, advises the president, the National Security Council and the secretary of state on the implications of specific arms sales abroad. The  agency evaluates the likely reactions of nations that neighbor the recipient of U.S. arms, the possibility of international conflict in a region where American weapons are sold, and the impact that a sale would have on arms control negotiations.

Today the arms-control negotiations attracting the most attention are on strategic arms involving nuclear weapons. These are SALT II negotiations between the United States and Russia *(see box, p. 230)*. However, other talks have been conducted for years by the two countries and their allies on troop and arms reductions in central Europe.

Representatives of 19 nations have been meeting regularly in Vienna since November 1973 to discuss what is formally known as a Mutual and Balanced Force Reduction. The NATO nations want the outcome of reductions to put their strength in central Europe roughly on par with that of the Warsaw Pact (communist) nations. The communist nations want, instead, equal percentage reductions on each side, permitting them to retain superior strength.

to friendly nations. But by the mid-1950s, it became evident that many recipient countries were economically capable of purchasing arms. At about the same time, the Soviet Union entered the world arms trade in a significant way. Communist-bloc countries, seeking to increase their influence, felt compelled to compete with the West in the world arms market.

JFK-McNamara Emphasis on Arms Sales

When President Kennedy took office in 1961, the goals of the foreign military sales program changed.[11] Secretary of Defense Robert S. McNamara realized that continued overseas deployment of U.S. troops and equipment would lead to a balance-of-payments deficit. He therefore tried to persuade America's allies to begin purchasing U.S. weapons in substantial quantities. By 1966, most of the Western European nations had completed their economic recovery and the United States reduced the military aid programs in Europe, as well as in Japan, Canada and Australia. Arms sales began to take the place of grants.

---

[11] See "World Arms Sales," *E.R.R.*, 1976 Vol. I, pp. 323-342.

Outright grants since then have been confined mostly to nations like Taiwan, South Korea, Greece and Turkey, so-called "front-line" countries bordering on communist countries or areas of influence. The United States also continues to make grants to nations where large American military bases are located, such as in the Philippines and Spain. By fiscal year 1967, military sales figures topped those for grants for the first time. Since then, the trend has been toward a "declining use of military assistance and an increasing reliance on arms sales." [12]

Mechanics of Exporting American Weapons

Foreign countries in the market for U.S. weapons today can buy from the Department of Defense or directly from licensed commercial sources. The department oversees the mechanics of the sales and notifies the foreign affairs committees in the House and Senate, but the State Department — sometimes the president — ultimately decides if a proposed sale is consistent with U.S. foreign policy and may proceed. If credit is necessary for the purchase of arms, it is arranged by the U.S. government or obtained through private sources with a government guarantee.

Before a foreign country is allowed to purchase U.S. military equipment, the nation must agree (1) not to transfer the equipment to a third country without U.S. consent, (2) to use the supplies only for the purposes stated, and (3) to maintain security over the material. According to the Department of Defense, no decision to sell equipment is made until three factors are weighed: the requirements of U.S. forces, military needs of the recipient nations, and the "anticipated contribution to peace and stability" a sale would make.

The transfer of weaponry and security assistance from the United States to foreign countries comes about through commercial sales or through one or another of four government-run programs. In commercial sales, private American arms suppliers negotiate with and sell weaponry directly to foreign governments. According to Department of Defense records, commercial exports by U.S. private companies totaled $1.48 billion in fiscal year 1978. The other four categories of arms transfers are on a direct government-to-government basis.

The largest volume of U.S. arms transfers by far — some $13.5 billion in 1978 — comes under the *Foreign Military Sales* program. Under FMS, the Department of Defense buys military equipment from U.S. suppliers or takes equipment from military stocks and sells it to foreign governments. Department services, training and management advice also fall under the

---

[12] U.S. House Committee on International Relations, Subcommittee on Europe and the Middle East, "United States Arms Transfer and Security Assistance Programs," March 21, 1978, p. 4.

Leading Purchasers of U.S. Arms

(Fiscal Year 1978)

Country	Purchases	Country	Purchases
Saudi Arabia	$4,136,000,000	Japan	$338,000,000
Iran	2,586,000,000	Australia	337,000,000
Israel	1,749,000,000	Spain	191,000,000
Egypt	937,000,000	Sudan	187,000,000
Britain	485,000,000	Turkey	171,000,000
Germany	430,000,000	Greece	121,000,000
South Korea	390,000,000	Indonesia	112,000,000
Taiwan	346,000,000	Thailand	111,000,000

Source: Department of Defense

same program. The president is authorized to finance procurement of defense articles and services or to guarantee financing for friendly foreign countries or international organizations. The fiscal year 1979 financing program is due to cost just under $2 billion. Financing will be provided to 26 countries;[13] Israel will receive about $1 billion, or more than half, of that total.

Military Assistance Program provides loans or outright grants to foreign countries for defense items and services, including technical assistance, repair, supply operations, and administrative support. The program, born during the early stages of the Cold War to strengthen non-communist countries, has been scaled down greatly in recent years. It is used today mainly to provide military assistance to countries in which the United States has received permission to operate military bases. In fiscal year 1979, the MAP program will cost some $210.4 million and apply to only five countries — the Philippines, Jordan, Greece, Portugal and Spain. Some $144.6 million has been requested for fiscal year 1980.

International Military Education and Training (IMET) offers military training and education primarily in the United States to foreign military and civilian personnel. Some 456,000 foreign personnel have been trained under the program; this year's trainees represent 38 countries.[14] Their training will cost the U.S. government $28.8 million.

Security Supporting Assistance provides assistance to friendly countries or organizations to promote or support economic or

---

[13] Bolivia, Cameroon, Colombia, Dominican Republic, Ecuador, Greece, Haiti, Honduras, Indonesia, Israel, Jordan, Kenya, Korea, Lebanon, Liberia, Malaysia, Morocco, Panama, Philippines, Peru, Spain, Sudan, Thailand, Tunisia, Turkey and Zaire.

[14] Afghanistan, Austria, Bangladesh, Bolivia, Chad, Colombia, Dominican Republic, Ecuador, Egypt, Finland, Ghana, Haiti, Honduras, India, Indonesia, Jordan, Kenya, Korea, Lebanon, Liberia, Malaysia, Mali, Mexico, Morocco, Nepal, Pakistan, Panama, Peru, Philippines, Portugal, Senegal, Spain, Sudan, Thailand, Tunisia, Upper Volta, Yemen and Zaire.

political stability. The Marshall Plan, under which this country gave Western Europe billions of dollars in economic aid after World War II, is the forerunner of the SSA program. In fiscal 1979, the program is slated to cost just under $2 billion. Egypt, Israel, Jordan and Syria will receive about 90 percent of that aid. The other nations scheduled to receive SSA funds this year are Botswana, Cyprus, Spain and Turkey. In addition, organizations supported by the program currently include the Sinai Support Mission, other projects in the Middle East, and support for U.N. forces in Cyprus.

Trends in the Arms Trade

PRESIDENT CARTER has stressed that his program to reduce the flow of American arms abroad is only a first step toward the worldwide reduction of arms sales. He has said on numerous occasions that the United States cannot go very far toward reducing its shipments unless other selling nations also cut back. "We continue to believe that all nations have an interest in restraining transfers of conventional weaponry which threaten the stability of various regions of the world and divert recipient resources from other worthy objectives without necessarily enhancing national security," Carter said last Nov. 29. "We are making a maximum effort to achieve multilateral cooperation on the arms restraint issue."

The major arms sellers in the world are the United States and the Soviet Union, followed by France and Britain, according to the U.S. Arms Control and Disarmament Agency *(see table, p. 38)*. The United States has asked each nation to cut back its sales program. French President Valery Giscard d'Estaing has endorsed Carter's reduction proposal but France has put no ceiling on arms sales, apparently for economic reasons. "Without arms sales abroad," said Professor Alfred Grosser of the School of Political Science in Paris, "there is no question that more thousands of [French] people would be unemployed. What is more, the sales are needed to help finance the complex process of producing weapons for France's own army." [15]

For many years France and Britain have vied for third place among the world's arms dealers. Their principal markets are in the Middle East, Latin America and former African colonies. Among the major buyers of British and French arms are South Africa, India, Brazil, Peru and Taiwan. The best-selling French products are supersonic jet fighters, tanks, helicopters and anti-

---

[15] Quoted in *The Washington Star,* Dec. 14, 1978.

ship missiles. France sold more than $4 billion worth of sophis-
ticated aircraft last year alone. Britain's arms industry also has
become important to the national economy. The British sell
frigates, submarines, patrol boats and tanks, among other weapons. Both France and Britain currently are negotiating with
China on the sale of anti-tank missiles, helicopters and vertical
takeoff and landing aircraft.

Talks With Russians on Restricting Sales

Russia's status as a major arms supplier arises mainly from its
relationship with Warsaw Pact nations,[16] North Korea and Vietnam. It also has become the principal supplier of many Third
World nations, offering low prices and liberal credit. The Central Intelligence Agency reported recently[17] that in 1974-77, the
Soviet Union sold and delivered to less-developed countries
more fighter and bomber aircraft, tanks, anti-aircraft guns and
artillery pieces than did the United States. The Soviets also sold
ships with a greater total value. The United States topped the
Soviets in the number of trainer and transport aircraft, helicopters, armored personnel carriers and self-propelled artillery
pieces.

---

*"I have absolutely kept my promise [to
reduce arms sales.] I have met my standard
very accurately, even exceeded those reductions, and I am very proud of that
achievement."*

President Carter, March 30, 1979

The Carter administration began to enlist Soviet cooperation
in restricting worldwide arms sales two years ago. American and
Russian negotiators have met four times since March 1977 in
talks aimed at finding common ground on reducing conventional
arms transfers. The latest round of talks took place in Mexico
City in December 1978. No substantive agreements came out of
the first three negotiating sessions, primarily because the United
States wanted to concentrate on arms sales in Latin America
and Africa, two areas where the Russians have been sending
increasing amounts of weaponry. The Soviet Union instead
wanted to discuss arms sales in Iran, China and South Korea.

Observers saw some possibility that the Mexico City talks

---

[16] Bulgaria, Czechoslovakia, East Germany, Hungary, Poland, Romania and Russia.
[17] CIA study, "Arms Flows to LDCs: U.S.-Soviet Comparisons, 1947-77," November 1978.

Arming Switzerland and Luxembourg

Most Americans are aware that this country sells arms worth billions of dollars annually to countries like Israel, Egypt and Saudi Arabia. But far less publicity is given to the dozens of other countries, from Afghanistan to Zaire, that receive smaller shipments of American-made arms. Two seemingly unlikely recipients are Switzerland and Luxembourg.

Switzerland is well known as Europe's neutral nation. Switzerland has maintained the principle of neutrality since 1815, and has avoided involvement in Europe's wars since then. Nevertheless, 650,000 Swiss citizens spend a few weeks of the year in military training and even keep arms in their homes for instant duty. Switzerland currently is modernizing its armed forces and has ordered $173.5 million worth of arms and equipment from the United States this year.

Luxembourg, with a 630-man army defending the nation of 360,000, is a NATO member and close ally of the United States. A large part of this year's military budget will go toward buying about $15 million worth of arms from U.S. commercial suppliers.

would result in compromises by both powers and provide some basis for agreement. But a dispute within the U.S. delegation — primarily between presidential assistant Zbigniew Brzezinski and the chief U.S. negotiator, Leslie H. Gelb, director of the State Department's Bureau of Politico-Military Affairs — caused last minute changes in the American bargaining position and provoked anger and distrust from the Russians.

Continuation of Record U.S. Arms Exports

It is difficult to imagine that the United States will not continue to export great amounts of arms in the next few years. The U.S. commitment just to Israel and Egypt will amount to about $1 billion a year for at least the next four or five years. Total U.S. arms sales reached record levels in fiscal year 1978 and Department of Defense officials estimate that sales in 1979 and 1980 will be slightly higher. A study by the Library of Congress found that President Carter's policy has "yet to demonstrate a significantly reduced role for arms transfers as an instrument of U.S. foreign policy" and concluded that "U.S. arms transfers continue to occur on a rather routine basis." [18]

Carter vigorously defends his program. "I have absolutely kept my promise" to reduce arms sales, Carter told a group of newspaper editorial writers at the White House on March 30, 1979. "The promise I made was outside of our NATO commitments, where we have defense alliances, that we would cut down . . . whether or not other nations did the same, our total defense

---

[18] Library of Congress, Congressional Research Service, "Implications of President Carter's Conventional Arms Transfer Policy," Sept. 22, 1977.

Arms Transfers of Major Suppliers, 1967-1976

(in billions of current dollars)

Country	Amount	Country	Amount
United States	$38.3	West Germany	$ 2.0
Soviet Union	22.1	Czechoslovakia	1.4
France	3.8	Canada	1.3
Britain	2.8	Poland	1.1
China	2.2	All others	4.2
	World Total	$79.2	

Source: U.S. Arms Control and Disarmament Agency

sales at least 8 percent per year. Last year we cut back in excess of 8 percent. . . . And this year we will do the same. . . . I have met my standard very accurately, even exceeded those reductions, and I am very proud of that achievement."

Post-Vietnam Thinking; Economic Factors

The American failure to contain communism in Vietnam, Cambodia and Laos has changed the focus of U.S. foreign policy in a way that affects how this country sells arms abroad. "One lesson we must surely learn from Vietnam is that new commitments to our national honor and prestige must be carefully weighed," former Secretary of State Henry A. Kissinger said several years ago. "We must weigh carefully — as we failed to do in the early sixties — the long-term consequences of new engagements. We must not overextend ourselves, promising what is not either in our interest or within our capability." [19]

The United States has not committed troops into battle since the last American combat soldiers were withdrawn from Vietnam in March 1973. It can be argued that the growing commitment of U.S. arms around the world since then has served as a replacement for the commitment of U.S. armed forces. Neither course is entirely satisfactory and neither constitutes the entire commitment the United States makes to an ally. But most Americans would no doubt prefer to risk the loss of American arms rather than the loss of American lives in furthering this country's national interest.

One other important reason why U.S. arms sales are likely to remain high is the impact of the arms industry on the American economy. A U.S. Department of Labor study[20] estimated that

---

[19] Quoted in *The Defense Monitor*, September 1975, p. 2. For background, see "American Global Strategy," *E.R.R.*, 1976 Vol. I, pp. 85-104, and "Foreign Policy After Kissinger," *E.R.R.*, 1977 Vol. I, pp. 1-20.

[20] "Foreign Defense Sales and Grants, Fiscal Years 1973-75, Labor and Material Requirements," July 1977.

every $1 billion worth of U.S. arms delivered overseas provides some 52,000 American jobs. A study prepared by the Department of the Treasury found that a cut of 40 percent in orders for U.S. arms sales abroad would result in the displacement of 132,000 U.S. workers.[21]

"Weapons of war are generally technology-intensive," former Rep. Dale Milford, D-Texas, said in a House speech in 1977, "requiring a solid base of research and development. . . . It is not a coincidence . . . that the R&D base nurtured both the world's best commercial aircraft and finest military fighter planes. . . . Such a development has resulted in a very favorable balance of trade for the United States and the attendant benefits of increased employment and high standard of living."

Hawk Missile

The impact of the U.S. arms industry on the American economy; the nation's resolve not to commit troops overseas unless U.S. national interest is directly threatened; the impasse in U.S.-Soviet arms sales reduction talks — all of these factors are contributing to growing U.S. arms sales, and there is little indication that the flow of American arms abroad will lessen in the immediate future.

---

[21] The study was cited by the U.S. House Committee on Inernational Relations, Subcommittee on International Security and Scientific Affairs, "Conventional Arms Transfer Policy: Background Information," Feb. 1, 1978, p. 77.

Selected Bibliography

Books

Chan, Anne H., et al., *Controlling Future Arms Trade*, McGraw-Hill, 1977.
Farley, Philip J., et al., *Arms Across the Sea*, Brookings Institution, 1978.
Sampson, Anthony, *The Arms Bazaar: From Lebanon to Lockheed*, Viking, 1977.
U.S. Defense Policy: Weapons, Strategy and Commitments, Congressional Quarterly, 1978.

Articles

Aviation Week & Space Technology, selected issues.
Ball, Nicole and Milton Leitenberg, "The Foreign Arms Sales of the Carter Administration," *Bulletin of the Atomic Scientists*, February 1979.
Gervasi, Tom, "Eagles, Doves and Hawks: Arming the World in Order to Arm Ourselves," *Harper's*, May 1978.
Rothschild, Emma, "Carter and Arms: No Sale," *New York Review of Books*, Sept. 15, 1977.
Smith, Carlton, "Making the Sale for America," *Politics Today*, March-April 1978.

Reports and Studies

Advanced International Studies Institute, "President Carter's Arms Transfer Policy: A Critical Assessment," Jan. 23, 1978.
Arms Control and Disarmament Agency, "World Military Expenditures and Arms Transfers, 1967-1976," July 1978.
Arms Control Association, "Arms Control Today," newsletter, selected issues.
Central Intelligence Agency, National Foreign Assessment Center, "Arms Flows to LDCs: U.S.-Soviet Comparisons, 1974-77," November 1978.
Department of Defense, Security Assistance Agency, "Foreign Military Sales and Military Assistance Facts," December 1978.
Editorial Research Reports: "World Arms Sales," 1976 Vol. I, p. 325; "International Arms Sales," 1970 Vol. II, p. 647.
Library of Congress, Congressional Research Service, "Implications of President Carter's Conventional Arms Transfer Policy," Sept. 22, 1977.
House Committee on International Relations, Subcommittee on Europe and the Middle East, "United States Arms Transfer and Security Assistance Programs," March 21, 1978.
House Committee on International Relations, Subcommittee on International Security and Scientific Affairs, "Conventional Arms Transfer Policy: Background Information," Feb. 1, 1978.
——"Review of the President's Conventional Arms Transfer Policy," Feb. 1, 1978.
Senate Committee on Foreign Relations, "Prospects for Multilateral Arms Export Restraint," April 1979.

I RAN BETWEEN EAST AND WEST

by

D. Park Teter

**Jan. 26
1 9 7 9**

IRAN BETWEEN EAST AND WEST

THE REVOLUTION unfolding in Iran is revealing to the world powerful historical forces that not only contend for the destiny of Iran but challenge Western assumptions about the Middle East and the Third World. Iran's deepening crisis has baffled Western observers focusing on surface political developments rather than on the underlying transformation of a whole culture. Iranians themselves, torn by ambivalence, were groping for coherence in this latest episode in the ancient conflict between East and West.

When Shah Mohammed Reza Pahlavi, whom the United States had championed as a guardian of stability in the turbulent Middle East, left on Jan. 16 for an indefinite "vacation"[1] that was almost universally regarded as the end of his 37-year reign, the population took to the streets in delirious expressions of joy. But the state had no authority, the economy was in shambles and rival forces prepared for a showdown.

Mass demonstrations and crippling strikes overwhelmed the shah's regime and could bring down its appointed successor, but could not establish the foundations of a new order. A new prime minister promised sweeping reforms to end corruption and repression, religious leaders called for establishment of an Islamic republic that would reverse Westernizing trends, and the shah's Western-trained army waited nervously while the populace dominated the streets and fraternized with conscript soldiers. The rest of the world watched anxiously to see what Iranians would now make of their country.

For the West the stakes were high. Iran has been the world's second largest exporter of oil, after Saudi Arabia, and is strategically located between the Soviet Union and the Persian Gulf region, the source of more than half of the oil imports of the industrial free world.[2] The United States attached so much

---

[1] The shah, accompanied by his wife, the Empress Farah, and a large entourage, went to Egypt where, reportedly at U.S. insistence, he was greeted by President Anwar Sadat. On Jan. 22 the royal party flew to Morocco for what was officially described as a stay of two or three days. The Iranian ambassador in Washington, Ardeshir Zahedi, said that day in a *New York Times* interview that the shah had put off his plans to come to the United States and would find some other country in which to spend the rest of his "vacation." A subsequent *Times* dispatch from Cairo said the shah had accepted an invitation from Sadat to take up residence in Egypt.

[2] According to estimates derived from the Central Intelligence Agency's *International Energy Statistical Review*, Persian Gulf states were the principal sources of crude oil and refined products imported in 1977 by the United States (34.1%), Western Europe (61.7%), Japan (72.1%) and Canada (42.4%). Also *see box, p. 83.*

43

importance to Iran that it gave the shah wholehearted support, selling him vast quantities of the most advanced weapons, encouraging his ambitions for regional dominance, and overlooking a reputation for violation of human rights considered among the worst in the world *(see box, p. 55).*

The United States became so closely identified with the shah that the hatred for his regime spilled over into virulent anti-American sentiments. By the time the shah departed, all but 12,000 of the 41,000 Americans living in Iran, drawn there primarily by the economic boom that followed the quadrupling of oil export prices in 1973-74, had been driven away by the hostility expressed in demonstrations, in threats and in occasional acts of terrorism. In the United States, a public debate sought to determine how Iran had been "lost," and the lessons eventually drawn from the continuing drama in Iran were likely to influence U.S. policies toward the Third World in the years ahead.

Conflicting Forces Within Iranian Society

Among the rival groups competing for power in the wake of the shah's departure, the United States placed its hopes in a new government formed by Shahpour Bakhtiar, who had been appointed prime minister by the shah and confirmed by Parliament hours before the shah left the country. Bakhtiar, 62, was a minor figure in the National Front government of Mohammed Mossadegh, the popular political leader who in 1953 had forced the shah to flee the country briefly — until a CIA-backed *coup d'état* quickly ousted Mossadegh.

When the Front re-emerged last year after a long period of suppression, Bakhtiar ranked second in its leadership after Karim Sanjabi, 74. But the Front expelled Bakhtiar for accepting the shah's mandate to form a new government. During their

years of political impotence, the Front's aging leadership lost any command of a mass following but it remained the umbrella organization for secular opposition to the shah's government. Members of Bakhtiar's cabinet are generally described as little-known technocrats.

Bakhtiar's acceptance of his appointment at a time when other opposition leaders were spurning such overtures from the shah led observers to conclude —AP Photo he hoped to reduce chances that the army

Shahpour Bakhtiar might try to reimpose order with a massive show of force and thus cause a bloodbath or civil war. Bakhtiar, who had been imprisoned for opposition to the shah, promised to dissolve SAVAK, the shah's hated secret police, release political prisoners, guarantee freedom of expression and association, dismiss unneeded foreign workers, abandon Iran's efforts to be "policeman" of the Persian Gulf, cut off oil exports to South Africa and Israel,[3] and cooperate with the country's Moslem leaders.

But the chief religious leader, Ayatollah Ruhollah Khomeini, 77, from his exile in France[4] denounced the Bakhtiar government and called for demonstrations and strikes to bring it down. On Jan. 13 Komeini announced the formation of a Provisional Islamic Revolutionary Council as the first step toward establishing an Islamic republic. Khomeini earlier had described his goals in an interview published in *The Middle East,* a London-based magazine, in December:

—AP Photo

Ayatollah Khomeini

> The purpose of a future Islamic republic — and it is the will of the Iranian people — will be to eliminate Western influence in our country. By the same token, our purpose is to break the hold of Western domination, in all its forms, in Iran. This Western influence is found in all walks of Iranian life. Since the entire Iranian nation has risen up against this state of affairs, nobody can now expect this movement to be stopped.

Moslem Leadership in Anti-Shah Protests

In January 1978, a government-inspired article in the Tehran newspaper *Etelaat* accused Khomeini of conspiring with communists against the regime and impugned his character. When the article touched off a protest in Qum, a city dominated by Iran's Shi'a clergy, army troops fired into the crowd. The resulting deaths launched a cycle of escalating violence in which Shi'ite mourning ceremonies, at traditional 40-day intervals, produced yet more deaths to be mourned.[5]

---

[3] While most Western observers see anti-Zionism as an aspect of the Islamic revival in Iran, Sadegh Ghotbzadeh, a spokesman for religious leader Ayatollah Ruhollah Khomeini, told news reporters on Jan. 12 that if it had not been for Israel's close identification with the repressive side of the shah's rule, particularly assistance to the secret police, "we would most probably have continued to supply them oil, especially in light of Arab hostility or indifference to our movement."

[4] When Khomeini originally went into exile following Moslem-led anti-shah protests in 1963, he went to Iraq, but in 1978 the Iraqi government, concerned with maintaining good relations with Iran, expelled Khomeini and he went to France in October 1978, living in Neauphle-le-Chateau near Paris. Khomeini said on several occasions he planned to return to Iran, most recently naming Jan. 26 as the date of return, despite the displeasure of the Bakhtiar regime.

[5] While most U.S. press reports estimated deaths in the year before the shah's departure at more than 1,500, the Journalists' Syndicate in Iran and the Iranian Doctors Association estimated that at least 10,000 had been killed.

Twelve cities were placed under martial law early in September after hundreds were killed when troops fired into a crowd of demonstrators in Tehran. And the shah installed a military government on Nov. 5 after rioters, protesting killings on the campus of the University of Tehran, went on a rampage of destruction in the city's center. The most spectacular demonstrations occurred on Dec. 10 and 11, holy days of mourning for Shi'a Moslems. While the army withdrew to the northern sector of the city, crowds that may have reached one million marched through the streets in protest against the regime.

The size of the demonstration removed any lingering doubts that the opposition to the shah was a mass movement. Even more indicative of the universality of opposition was the fact that large demonstrations repeatedly took place in provincial cities and towns across the country. Strikes, which had been virtually unknown in Iran for years, increasingly crippled the economy. Workers and civil servants did not respond to large wage concessions and defied orders to return to work in their determination to force the shah from power.

The oil industry, which normally produced six million barrels of oil a day, was gradually shut down, denying the government $20 million per day in revenues, depriving the population of all but a trickle of gasoline and heating and cooking fuels, and paralyzing the already-staggering economy. Even the hardships imposed on the population did not abate the public clamor against the government.

46

The 168,000-member Moslem clergy[6] provided much of the initial impetus for the demonstrations. Mosques provided meeting places and a network of communication for demonstrations and strikes, and Khomeini served as a national symbol behind which Iranians could rally. To some extent, reliance on religious leadership was necessitated by the shah's success in stamping out, even at the local level, all other independent forms of voluntary association. In part, the role played by religious leaders reflected a revival of interest in Islam in the face of frenetic "Westernization" and the many frustrations of rapid technological change. But virtually all classes and shades of opinion, including the most Westernized, were well represented in the opposition to the shah.

Criticism That U.S. Intelligence Had Failed

Historical movements of such magnitude take time to grow. And yet the uprising in Iran obviously came as a surprise to the U.S. government. *The New York Times* said that as late as last August the Central Intelligence Agency reportedly had circulated an evaluation of the Iranian situation stating: "The shah, who firmly holds the reins of power, will preside over a peaceful and prosperous Iran for the next 10 or 15 years."[7] And on Oct. 5 a State Department official testifying before a congressional committee compared the protests in Iran to Shays' Rebellion in 18th century Massachusetts.[8]

As the scale of the opposition to the shah became obvious, there was a scramble to explain the lapse in U.S. intelligence, especially since a former director of the CIA, Richard Helms, was ambassador to Iran from 1973 to 1977. It was widely reported that U.S. diplomats and intelligence agents were prohibited from establishing substantial contacts with the opposition lest this offend the shah. "We maintain some contacts — very informal, very low key — but it's just not worthwhile going beyond that," an American diplomat in Tehran was quoted as saying last July. "The strength of the opposition and its future are both limited."[9]

[6] While Shi'a Islam does not have a priesthood with a sacramental function, its clergy is a more distinct body than the relatively informal organization of Sunni Islam. Mullahs — the religious leaders — are expected to have satisfied formal religious educational requirements and they wear distinctive dress and beards. Higher authorities among the Shi'a generally reach their influence through consensus of their peers, and interpreters of the Koran and the law are expected to have advanced religious education.

[7] *The New York Times*, Dec. 21, 1978. According to the *Times*, a CIA official contended that such an estimate existed only in draft form and was withdrawn after the State Department's Bureau of Intelligence raised objections.

[8] Testimony by Under Secretary of State Lucy Wilson Benson before the House Committee on International Relations. Shays' Rebellion refers to an uprising in 1786-87 by a group of Massachusetts farmers aggrieved by high taxes and mortage foreclosures. Led by Daniel Shays, the farmers marched on Boston to take control of the state government by force but disbanded when troops were called out.

[9] *The New York Times*, July 9, 1978. The *Times* added that the U.S. Embassy's "only contact with the Moslem leaders who have led the anti-shah demonstrations is carried out by a second secretary who makes infrequent visits to their stronghold in Qum, which is 90 miles from Tehran."

Professor James A. Bill, a University of Texas specialist on Iranian politics, recently wrote that "few American officials have had the linguistic fluency, intellectual curiosity, personal fortitude or occupational time to pierce the crust of Iranian society." He accused U.S. ambassadors and their deputies of being "more concerned with confirming Washington's stereotype of Iran than encouraging their diplomats to develop a true understanding of Iranian society."[10]

"Iran under the great leadership of the shah is an island of stability in one of the more troubled areas of the world. This is a great tribute to you, Your Majesty, and to your leadership, and to the respect, admiration and love which your people give to you."

—President Carter, New Year's Toast, Tehran, Dec. 31, 1977

The shah conducted an extensive public relations campaign in the United States to promote an image of his regime as not only benevolent but invulnerable. In particular, he convinced many Americans in and out of government that there was no viable alternative to his rule — a situation which he had done everything in his power to create. His purchases of an arsenal of America's most advanced weapons also created an aura of invincibility that may have impressed his suppliers even as it intimidated his subjects. But probably nothing was as persuasive as the remarkable fact that, in a region as turbulent as the Middle East, his regime had survived for 37 years.

The means by which it survived, it is now clear, were such that revolutionary passions continued to accumulate beneath the surface until, when they finally burst into the streets, they were overwhelming. The forces that finally captured headlines in 1978 had long been observed by persons with intimate knowledge of Iranian culture. As long ago as 1962, Princeton Professor T. Cuyler Young had concluded an analysis of historical trends in Iran with the warning: "Amidst such tension and turmoil, much of it seething beneath the surface, some sudden coup or lightning accident could alter the scene overnight. The present pattern cannot persist without explosion or significant change."[11]

Ironically, it may have been the very importance which the United States attached to Iran that led to the failure to see what

---

[10] James A. Bill, "Iran and the Crisis of '78," *Foreign Affairs,* winter 1978-79, p. 339.

[11] T. Cuyler Young, "Iran in Continuing Crisis," *Foreign Affairs,* 1962, Vol. 40, p. 275.

was happening there. Because of Iran's oil and its position between Russia and the Persian Gulf, the country was viewed primarily in terms of its role in global power struggles. Attention was focused on its relations with other states rather than on its internal affairs, and therefore on its government rather than its people. But the experience in Iran is not really an isolated phenomenon. Behind the facades of repressive governments, similar conflicts between tradition and modernization are building throughout the Third World.

A Clash of Civilizations

THE SPECTACLE of conservative Moslem religious leaders rallying mass support against a government committed to "modernization" has surprised and unsettled most Western observers. But British historian Bernard Lewis, writing in 1964, had observed: "This much is obvious. Of all the great movements that have shaken the Middle East during the last century and a half, the Islamic movements alone are authentically Middle Eastern in inspiration."

> Liberalism and fascism, patriotism and nationalism, communism and socialism [he continued], are all European in origin, however much adapted and transformed by Middle Eastern disciples. The religious orders alone spring from the native soil, and express the passions of the submerged masses of the population. Though they have all, so far, been defeated, they have not yet spoken their last word.[12]

In the current upheaval in Iran, Islamic protest is most visible in violent attacks on Western institutions such as banks and movie theaters, and in the resumption by women of the chador, the Iranian version of the veil. But the power of Islam derives from its appeal to deeper satisfactions.

The dominant message of Islam is the exaltation of God to an utterly transcendent majesty. While accepting Jesus as a prophet and revering the prophets of the Old Testament, Islamic thought and feeling stress the distance between the human and the divine more emphatically than Jewish and Christian beliefs. The Moslem concept of God is not humanized by the Judeo-Christian belief that man was made in God's image, let alone by the central Christian faith that God actually took on human flesh.

From this sense of the absoluteness of God, joined to the constant invocation of God as "the merciful, the compas-

---

[12] Bernard Lewis, *The Middle East and the West* (1964), p. 114.

sionate," Moslems gain a feeling of ultimate security and meaning no matter how chaotic or cruel temporal affairs may seem. Since nothing in the universe can happen except as a distinct act of God's will, the Moslem path to peace and virtue lies in Islam, which means surrender to that divine will.[13]

While such a faith lends itself to the fatalism that has so handicapped Middle Easterners in their pursuit of Western standards of living, it also lends itself to a sense of great righteousness in the face of those who have not yet bowed to God's final revelation in the Koran. The early history of Islam seemed to confirm God's pleasure with those who accepted the message He sent through Mohammed in the seventh century; the first generations of Moslems swept all before them, from Central Asia to Spain, and established a civilization far more advanced than existed in Christian Europe.

Unlike the Jews, whose biblical history was full of God's punishments for the transgressions of his chosen people, or the Christians, who began as a persecuted sect in a world dominated by the Roman Empire, the Moslems in their formative historical years experienced worldly power as a confirmation of their faith. The modern domination of Islamic peoples by the infidel West has, therefore, posed psychological problems for the faithful which have not yet been resolved.

Distinctiveness of Iran's Shi'ite Moslems

However, in the Shi'a branch of Islam, to which more than 90 percent of all Iranians adhere, the Moslem's sense of historical confirmation is somewhat qualified by an initial experience of defeat. The Shi'a trace the legitimate succession to Mohammed through a series of imams, the descendants of Mohammed's cousin and son-in-law Ali. When Ali's son Hussein led a small group of rebels in a political revolt, they were massacred by the forces of the ruling Caliph at Karbala in Iraq in 680. The political failure, however, launched Shi'ism as a religious movement, and the martyrdom of Hussein became a powerful symbol as the Shi'a sect emerged as a champion of the discontented masses against the established political order. Acceptance of the political order meant conformity to the Sunni, or orthodox, branch of Islam.

Indeed, when up to one million Iranians marched in protest against the established political order in Tehran on Dec. 10 and 11, the occasion was the annual Shi'a commemoration of the defeat at Karbala. While the version of Shi'ism that became established as the official religion of Iran in time assumed

---

[13] Derived from the word "salam," which means primarily peace but in a secondary sense "surrender," its full connotation is "the perfect peace that comes when one's life is surrendered to God" — *The Religions of Man* (1958), p. 193, by Huston Smith.

attitudes of orthodoxy not unlike Sunni Islam, in its origins it still contains the seeds of revolution.

In centuries of struggle against the majority Sunni Moslems, the Shi'a developed a capacity for survival in spite of political domination. They also developed a singular survival mechanism, the doctrine of *taqiya* or "dissimulation," which encouragd Shi'ites to adopt outward conformity to the dogmas of those in power while inwardly strengthening the fervor of their true beliefs. This defense enabled the Shi'a to preserve their deepest beliefs not only against the surrounding Sunni, but also against the later domination of the West, whether embodied in imperialist politics or the values of "modernization." Indeed, "dissimulation" evolved from a religious doctrine to a behavioral pattern that baffles foreigners and serves Iranians as a defense against their own rulers or others in authority. But it inhibits real communication between the powerful and the weak.

Even Shi'ism itself can be used as a mask for other objectives, a banner behind which diverse political groups can rally. It is a particularly convenient banner in Iran, where Shi'ism has long served as an expression of nationalism. Shi'ism was established as the official state religion in the 16th century by the Safavid dynasty as a means of unifying the country against Sunni neighbors. Even today, religion plays an important role in unify a country of immense ethnic diversity. Of Iran's 35 million people, less than two-thirds speak Persian *(Farsi)* as their native language, while more than 90 percent profess Shi'ism.[14]

While Iranians in time of crisis may fall back on the traditional values of Islam, there is also a deep counter-tradition to official religion. Much-loved Iranian mystics, poets and storytellers have challenged all dogmatism in religion, not only with vision but with humor, and humor remains to this day a popular Iranian defense against the clergy as well as the state. Playful, skeptical and even cynical attitudes toward established religion are not uncommon among Iranians, who on the whole have been much readier than Arab Moslems to adopt Western lifestyles.

Influence of Western Culture; Shah's Rise

Although contacts with the West date from the 16th and 17th centuries, when the Safavid kings received European ambassadors seeking allies against Ottoman Turkey, and continued through the rival imperialisms of Britain and Russia in the 18th and 19th centuries, it was not until the current century that

[14] Iranians who speak *Farsi* as their native language, 63 percent; ethnic groups speaking related languages (including Bakhtiaris, Lurs, Baluchis), 13; Turkic (Azerbaijani, Turcoman, Qashqai), 18; Kurdish 3; Arabic and other Semitic, 3; other, 1. Religious groupings: Shi'a Moslem, 93 percent; Sunni Moslem, 5; other (Christian, Zoroastrian, Bahai, Jewish), 2 — Central Intelligence Agency, National Intelligence Survey, *Basic Intelligence Fact Book*, July 1974, p. 163.

Western values became a disruptive force within Iranian society. They found their earliest political expression in the Constitutional movement of the first decade of the 20th century, but did not become a full-fledged movement for "modernization" until an army officer named Reza Khan staged a successful coup in 1921 and subsequently proclaimed himself shah.

In an impatient style resembling the revolution Kemal Ataturk was leading in neighboring Turkey, Reza Shah reorganized the military and the civilian bureaucracy, promoted Western forms of education, and pursued such social changes as the abolition, by decree, of the veil for women. He also adopted "Pahlavi" (the term for Iran's pre-Moslem Persian dialect) as the family name of his dynasty, and sought in other ways to encourage Iranian identification with traditions antedating the Moslem Arab conquest.

Perhaps the dominant motive for adopting Western-style reforms was to provide Iran with the strength to throw off Western imperialism, especially the pervasive interference of the Russians and the British. It was this same need which led Reza Shah to flirt with Nazi Germany, as the long sought "Third Force" that might help Iran escape its two ancient enemies. But because of his German sympathies, in August 1941 the British and the Russians invaded Iran and deposed Reza Shah, placing his 21-year-old son, Mohammed Reza Pahlavi, on the throne.

Beginning his career under the tutelage of his father's enemies, the present shah's initial experience of kingship was one of profound insecurity. Subsequent experiences reinforced that sense of insecurity, especially the 1953 crisis when the shah fled Iran to escape the burgeoning power of Prime Minister Mohammed Mossadegh and was quickly restored by an army coup aided by the CIA. The shah's resulting passion for security helps to explain why he was to place heavy reliance on a pervasive and brutal security police and to build up military forces of 400,000 men, equipped with the most modern weapons, rewarded with high pay and privileges, and kept exclusively under his command.

The maintenance of public order has always been a high priority for Iranian governments trying to survive in a country whose diverse and restive ethnic groups have for centuries engaged in rebellions, civil wars and connivance with foreign enemies. It was precisely the Iranian record of anarchy that the shah sought to counter by celebrating, in lavish ceremonies at Persepolis in 1971, "2,500 years of monarchy" since the founding of the Persian Empire.

But while the shah struggled to suppress old sources of disorder, he created new ones. He embarked on a technological and social revolution that inevitably created deep conflicts in Iran. Especially after he proclaimed a "White Revolution" in 1963, the shah's government pushed forward with programs of land reform, education, social services, and emancipation of women.[15] While there is both scholarly and partisan debate about the effectiveness of these reforms, there is no question that everyday lives and personal relations among Iranians were rapidly, and profoundly, changed.

The pace of change reached dizzying speed with the forced industrialization, mass consumption and inflation that followed the heavy inflow of oil money after 1973. The rush of new opportunities was exhilarating, but also deeply disquieting. Geographic, economic and social mobility robbed existence of its familiarity, leaving in the wake of trusted patterns of behavior not only a free-for-all scramble for the new wealth but a confusion of values and a longing for restored security. Most disquieting of all, perhaps, as Iranians embrace a "modernization" inspired by Western science, was the undermining of the feeling of ultimate security that had been provided by Islam.

Ambivalence Toward New Social Values

The conflict between tradition and modernization is being waged not only between different groups in Iran, but also, at least unconsciously, within the hearts of individuals of every religious and political persuasion. In his study of *Modern Islam: The Search for Cultural Identity,* G. E. von Grunebaum observed that for Westerners, "The stability of our mental and social universe hinges, as it were, on its rapid change." In contrast, he added:

> In his dreams of the future the reform-minded Middle Easterner sees himself not merely in a technologically and politically improved "Westernized" society, but in a society of the same binding absoluteness as the one in which his ancestors grew up; he envisages himself as secure in a stable network of dependencies and protectively limited, that is government-shouldered, responsibilities.
>
> The new truth, more effective than the old but just as final, is not to throw him on the road to everlasting transformation but to shield him from being abandoned to the whims of the foreigner, the tortures of self-criticism, the unpredictable risks of an expanding universe.[16]

The attempt to assimilate the fruits of Western "progress" without the passion for change that produces it explains much of the conflict now erupting in Iran. But the problem lies neither in Iran's traditions nor in its Westernization. It lies rather in the

---

[15] See "Resurgent Iran," *E.R.R.*, 1974 Vol. I, pp. 303-322.

[16] G. E. von Grunebaum, *Modern Islam: The Search for Cultural Identity* (1962).

absence of a real dialogue between the two. Cuyler Young observed:

> ...[T]here has been no real creative interaction of Western and Islamic thought at the deeper levels of faith and philosophy. This is primarily caused by the lack of understanding between the intellectual and spiritual leaders in the old Iranian tradition, and the dynamic group, mostly of the younger generation, which is determined upon carrying through an Iranian cultural revolution consonant with Western science and technique. This schism must be healed before Iran can have a fighting chance in solving its problems.[17]

Questions in Post-Shah Iran

W HOEVER GOVERNS Iran after the current upheaval will be confronted by four main tasks at the same time: re-establishing order, appeasing popular hatred of corruption and repression, restoring the shattered economy, and resolving conflicting attitudes toward social change. The relative urgency of these four demands will play a major role in determining which groups achieve dominance. None of the competing forces in Iranian society can alone deal with all of these problems.

Maintaining the authority of the state is the primary task of the army and the police, which combine a virtual monopoly on weapons with professional instincts that abhor public disorder. If any new government is seriously challenged by violent protest, it will need army support to survive. And the longer anarchic conditions exist, the more willing ordinary Iranians will be to accept a restoration of order by force.

However, the present leadership of the army has been tainted by its close association with the shah, and the troops, which fraternized with demonstrators in the last days before the shah's departure, might not obey orders to put down civil disturbance, especially if religious leaders appeal to their Moslem loyalties.

The religious leaders are free of identification with the old regime, and the ascetic lifestyle of Khomeini in particular stands in symbolic contrast to the opulence and corruption of the shah's court. At present, the clergy has the greatest command over the kind of mass protests and strikes that brought down the government. If fresh leadership were to emerge from the army and to pursue policies that won the blessing of the clergy, it might establish a government able to control more Westernized dissidents.

---

[17] T. Cuyler Young, ed., *Near Eastern Culture and Society* (1951), p. 146.

Human Rights in Iran

"I think I speak accurately for the American people in saying that United States' commitment to the enhancement of human rights on a worldwide basis is a sound policy." President Carter made that statement Dec. 14 in an ABC television interview in response to an observation by Barbara Walters that "some highly placed Iranians close to the shah have said that your insistence on human rights was a factor weakening his position." Walters also noted that former Secretary of State Henry Kissinger had said that Carter's human rights policy is "a weapon aimed primarily at allies and tends to undermine their domestic structure."

Noting that the shah was unable to pacify a "groundswell of criticism, passionate rejection and bitterness" by offering "hearty and decisive promises of reform," the *Swiss Review of World Affairs* said recently the situation in Iran seemed "a precise illustration" of an observation by Alexis de Tocqueville: "Experience shows that the most dangerous moment for a bad government is usually that point at which it begins to reform itself."

Martin Ennals, head of Amnesty International, the human rights organization, called the shah's claims of reform "gross hypocrisy." Amnesty International reported Dec. 11: "Political prisoners in Iran continue to be tortured and suffer cruel treatment at the hands of the police and SAVAK agents despite frequent assurances by the shah that the practices had been halted."

The army and the clergy, however, share a different kind of limitation. Neither has the education, experience and skills required to run a modern bureaucracy and economy. A government dominated by the military and supported by the clergy would need at least some cooperation from those in the middle class and the technocracy, including large numbers educated in the United States and Europe. These groups are poorly equipped either to raise up or to put down mass protests, but their influence will reassert itself whenever a new regime settles down to the business of restoring the economy and public services. Then their demands for a more open society than the army might like, and a freer lifestyle than the clergy might like, will be felt.

In spite of bitter resentment of the shah's political repression, the modern middle class shared his goals of social modernization. That was a big reason why they could compromise their political aspirations and work for his government. It would be much more difficult for them to share the goals of a theocratic state that sought to stamp out Western influences. And once the negative power of the clergy has completed the task of purging the old political order, popular anti-clerical traditions may well resurface if the fun of Western movies, fashions and courtship are threatened by puritanical regulation.

Iranian women, in particular, are not likely for long to accept a reversal of the trend toward liberation. Even though many have recently returned to wearing the chador, either from fear of insults from reassertive religious conservatives or to express solidarity against the shah, the taste of freedom and hope for greater freedom from anti-feminine traditions will not be soon forgotten or quietly abandoned. Great numbers of Iranian women have become educated, and some have achieved prominent positions in public life. And in private life the influence of educated women as wives and mothers will be felt by the men dominating the government and by the younger generation.

Frustration of Western-Educated Iranians

Whatever combination of political forces consolidates power in the wake of the current upheaval, the conflict between Middle Eastern and Western civilizations will continue in Iran.

Iranians educated in the West have been the vanguard of "modernization" in Iran. In 1965 there were about 15,000 Iranians studying in the United States alone, and that number today is between 40,000 and 60,000. Even after allowances are made for the sizable minority who remain in the West, the number now in Iran who were educated in the United States or Europe is a significant part of the population. In the competition for positions of influence in government, business and education, their educational credentials have usually been favored over Iranian degrees.

As bureaucrats, managers, and above all as teachers, they have passed on to large numbers of Iranians who have never been abroad not only the skills and ideas learned in Western classrooms, but also attitudes, values and habits learned from living in a more open society. Such a simple thing as a teacher encouraging questioning behavior from students or a manager asking advice from a subordinate challenges authoritarian traditions in the classroom and the office, and also in the wider arenas of politics and religion.

The political frustration of Iranians returning to Iran from the West has been extreme. The freedom of expression they had learned to take for granted in the West was severely limited, and criticism of the regime was liable to be cruelly punished. In place of that freedom, the Western-educated were often offered high positions and high salaries. Many of them participated in the technical and administrative decisions of the shah's campaign to turn Iran into a modern industrial state. But the fundamental questions of the form of government and the overall directions it would pursue were not theirs to ask, let alone answer.

They were not allowed to form organizations of their own or to develop any independent popularity or influence. Because they had no real alternative, except perhaps to live in a foreign land, those with public ambitions usually let themselves be co-opted by the regime. This compromise, however, often left the most talented deeply embittered, outwardly conforming to the regime's demands while inwardly nurturing hatred of the shah.

Inner Conflicts in Individuals and Society

The shah was also a convenient symbol for other frustrations. Because he went out of his way to take credit for every kind of achievement in Iran, he was inevitably blamed — privately — for every kind of failure. Even inner conflicts unrelated to politics could be unconsciously projected onto a leader who claimed a divine mission for his nation.

Iranians returning from Western education experienced many inner conflicts. For example, the return to the traditional family usually provided a warmth and security sorely missed while living in Western cultures, but traditional family expectations and ties were now also felt as restrictive of personal freedom. The broadening experience of living and studying abroad also fostered impatience with the views and habits of Iranians with narrower horizons, especially the older generation, the poor and the clergy.

The personal freedom Iranians found in the United States and Europe, freedom not only from a repressive state but also from confining religious traditions and suffocating family demands, was profoundly attractive. It will not easily yield to efforts to return to simpler traditions. But freedom is not the only thing Iranians experienced in the West.

In the recent novel *Identity Card,* F. M. Esfandiary described the anguish of an Iranian who lost his sense of identity while living in the West and tried to regain it in Iran. The book concludes with the protagonist's suicide. An author who was a literary standard-bearer of young Iranians, Sadiq Hedayat, in real life killed himself in Paris. Mohammed Mehdevi, describing his experiences of American culture named his book for what he failed to find there: *Something Human.*

Most Iranians also failed to find something else — something divine. The triumphs of Western science and technology, like the triumphs of Western imperialism in earlier generations, undermined their confidence in the civilization of Islam. But science, unlike Islam, offered no answers to ultimate questions about the meaning of life, questions of great urgency to men and women uprooted, whether by foreign travel or by modernization at home, from the culture of their childhood.

U.S. Arms Sales to Iran

(military sales agreements in thousands of dollars)

Fiscal Year	Amount	Fiscal Year	Amount
1955-68 (total)	$ 505,412	1974	4,325,357
1969	235,821	1975	2,447,140
1970	134,929	1976	1,794,487
1971	363,884	1977	5,713,769
1972	472,611	1978	2,586,890
1973	2,171,355	1955-78 (total)	$20,751,656

Source: Department of Defense Security Assistance Agency

Roger M. Savory, professor of Islamic studies at the University of Toronto, has observed: "By 1976 many Iranian intellectuals realized that Western technology had not produced human happiness. The psychic disorders prevalent in the West, the direct result of the psyche's being deprived of its basic relationship with the non-rational, or spiritual, had given Iranian thinkers pause. Both Marxists and so-called Massachusetts-trained technocrats were now seen by some as alien to Iranian society."[18]

Alienation from the West was intensified by another experience of Iranians. They saw the United States violate the values it taught by selling billions of dollars of arms to a regime that repressed their human rights. The fact that the United States did so from fear of communism and dependence on oil only deepened Iranians' doubts about the spiritual foundations of Western civilization.

Political, Cultural Repercussions Abroad

Henry Kissinger, who was Secretary of State when the Nixon administration greatly increased arms sales to Iran, warned in a *Time* magazine interview appearing shortly before the shah's departure: "The more that the United States looks out of control of events, the more it appears as if our friends are going down without effective support or even effective American understanding of what is occurring, the more this process will accelerate."[19]

While acknowledging that "there existed objective reasons for discontent" and that the clergy probably were not "triggered" by the Soviet Union, Kissinger said that the coordination of anti-shah strikes, whether or not they were actually organized by Soviet-trained dissidents, was "certainly the result of Soviet support of radical movements on a global basis, which has also now reached Iran."

[18] Roger M. Savory, "Social Development in Iran during the Pahlavi Era," in *Iran Under the Pahlavis* (1978), p. 126; George Lenczowski, ed.

[19] *Time*, Jan. 15, 1979, p. 29.

Iranian Oil

(as a percentage of each nation's crude oil imports)

	Sept. 1973	Aug. 1978
United States	5.9%	9.1%
Japan	31.9	16.4
United Kingdom	16.5	16.8
West Germany	10.8	21.1
France	7.8	12.9
Italy	11.0	12.7

Source: Central Intelligence Agency

In the same issue the Kissinger interview appeared, *Time* reported: "There is no convincing evidence that the Russians have been subversively operating to get rid of the shah in Iran. . . ." The fact there are 40 million Moslems in Russia might well make the Kremlin hesitate to encourage a revolution led by Iran's Moslem clergy. But even if the Russians did seek to win adherents in Iran, they would be burdened by a great handicap. Iranians have a 200-year history of fear of Russian expansion, and Russia is the only big power that has annexed Iranian territory.[20] In the 19th and early 20th centuries, Moscow's intervention in internal Iranian politics provoked a popular hatred of Russia that remains to this day.

The U.S. government had believed that the shah's well-armed and repressive regime was among the least "fragile" social and political structures in the Third World. Events have now proved that belief profoundly mistaken. And yet American diplomats, intelligence officials, and policy-makers clung to that belief long after there was dramatic evidence to the contrary. Until the motives for such rejection of evidence are understood, the United States is in danger of repeating in other Third World countries the mistakes it made in Iran. Where will they lead?

In his effort to explain the psychological appeal of totalitarianism revealed in the rise of Nazism in Germany, Erich Fromm first examined the breakup of traditional society in Europe at the end of the Middle Ages. He observed in *Escape From Freedom:* "Freedom *from* [Fromm's emphasis] the traditional bonds of medieval society, though giving the individual a new feeling of independence, at the same time made him feel alone and isolated, filled him with doubt and anxiety, and drove him into new submission and into a compulsive and irrational activity." A similar breaking of traditional bonds is taking place throughout the Third World, but both the speed of change and the number of people involved dwarf the experience of Europe at the end of the Middle Ages.

---

[20] In the early 19th century Russia annexed Georgia and the provinces now forming the Soviet republics of Armenia and Azerbaijan.

Selected Bibliography

Books

Amouzegar, Jahangir, *Iran: Economic Profile,* Middle East Institute, Washington, D.C., 1977.

Baraheni, Reza, *The Crowned Cannibals: Writings on Repression in Iran,* Vintage Books, 1977.

Bill, James, *Politics of Iran: Groups, Classes and Modernization,* Merrill Co., 1972.

G. E. von Grunebaum, *Modern Islam: The Search for Cultural Identity,* University of California Press, 1962.

Lenczowski, George, ed., *Iran Under the Pahlavis,* Hoover Institution Press, Stanford University, 1978.

Lewis, Bernard, *Middle East and the West,* Indiana University Press, 1964.

Ramazani, Rouhollah K., *Iran's Foreign Policy, 1941-1973,* University Press of Virginia, 1975.

Zonis, Marvin, *Political Elite in Iran,* Princeton University Press, 1971.

Articles

Bill, James, "Iran and the Crisis of '78," *Foreign Affairs,* winter 1978-79.

Gage, Nicholas, "Iran: Making of a Revolution," *The New York Times Magazine,* Dec. 17, 1978.

"Iran's Long Record of Censorship: Is it About to Crack?" *IPI Report* (publication of the International Press Institute), December 1978.

"Iran's Upheaval Derails a Dynamic Economy," *Business Week,* Nov. 27, 1978.

Klein, Ira, "The 70-year Roots of Iran's Turmoil," *The Washington Post,* Dec. 24, 1978.

Kraft, Joseph, "Letter from Iran," *New Yorker,* Dec. 18, 1978.

Lewis, Bernard, "Return of Islam," *Commentary,* January 1976.

Rovere, Richard, "Affair of State," *New Yorker,* Jan. 22, 1977.

Teter, D. Park, "Future Shock in Iran," *The Washington Post,* Dec. 10, 1978.

Young, T. Culyer, "Iran in Continuing Crisis," *Foreign Affairs,* 1962 Vol. 40.

Reports and Studies

Editorial Research Reports: "Resurgent Iran," 1974 Vol. I, pp. 303-322; "Middle East Transition," 1978 Vol. II, pp. 881-904; "Oil Imports," 1978 Vol. II, pp. 621-640.

International Commission of Jurists, "Human Rights and the Legal System in Iran," March 1976.

Tahtineh, Dale R., *Arms in the Persian Gulf,* American Enterprise Institute, 1974.

U.S. Department of Defense, Security Assistance Agency, "Foreign Military Sales and Military Assistance Facts," December 1978.

U.S. House of Representatives, "Hearings Before the Committee on International Relations: U.S. Arms Sales Policy and Recent Sales to Europe and the Middle East," Oct. 5, 1978.

TRADE TALKS AND PROTECTIONISM

by

Richard C. Schroeder

**Jan. 12
1979**

Editor's Note: The Geneva trade negotiations ended April 12 with most of the participating nations initialling an agreement that envisions reducing tariffs an average of 33 percent and dismantling many non-tariff barriers to trade. The signing was boycotted by most of the developing nations, which protested that the industrial countries had not made the trade concessions promised in 1973 when the trade talks began.

In the United States, a hard fight is expected this summer to win congressional approval of the trade agreement.

TRADE TALKS AND PROTECTIONISM

FIVE YEARS of tough bargaining over the future of the world trade system appears to be drawing to a close. Representatives of the 98 non-communist countries participating in the Multilateral Trade Negotiations (MTN) in Geneva have reached agreement on nearly all outstanding issues. Members of the U.S. negotiating team say they expect to have the entire package of accords "wrapped up" by mid-February.

Anticipating a successful outcome at Geneva, President Carter on Jan. 4 notified the incoming 96th Congress of his intent to sign the package of eight agreements on lowering non-tariff barriers and four agreements on farm trade, tied to an across-the-board cut in tariffs averaging 35 percent. His letter of intent, required by the 1974 Trade Act, will start a prescribed 90-day period of consultation with Congress in advance of his signing. However, it is unlikely that a protectionist-minded Congress will approve implementing legislation without a hard fight, and no one expects its approval until months after the 90 days ends on April 5.[1]

Before the legislation is sent to Congress, a few remaining issues must be settled in Geneva, where the talks resumed Jan. 8. A spokesman for Robert S. Strauss, Carter's special trade representative, has cautioned that the next few weeks are critical. Although the United States has reached "substantially complete" agreement with Japan, it still differs with its European trading partners on two key issues — tariff levels on chemicals and textiles, and certain parts of a proposal for "safeguards" to protect domestic industries against import competition. In addition, the European Community's Council of Ministers, which holds a potential veto over the negotiated accords, has characterized Japan's offers as "inadequate."

Eighty to ninety percent of world trade would be regulated by the agreements if they are signed, as expected, by a score of the leading industrial nations and by two dozen or so of the developing nations. But if the United States, the nine-nation[2] European Community or Japan refuse to ratify them, all of the negotia-

---

[1] Explanations of the agreements were published in the *Federal Register* Jan. 8, together with Carter's letter of intent to House Speaker Thomas P. O'Neill Jr. and Vice President Walter F. Mondale, president of the Senate.

[2] Belgium, Britain, Denmark, France, West Germany, Ireland, Italy, Luxembourg and the Netherlands.

tions would be for naught. Trade experts say that if any of the Big Three balks, the world trade system that has existed for the past three decades would surely degenerate into trade wars and financial crises.

In any event, trade matters will be among the first orders of business in the new Congress after it convenes on Jan. 15. President Carter has said he will press for quick action on extension of his authority to waive countervailing duties on imports subsidized by foreign governments *(see box, opposite)*. A bill to extend the authority died in floor maneuvering on the final day (Oct. 15) of the 95th Congress. As a result, the waiver authority — provided by the Trade Act of 1974 for only a limited time — expired Jan. 3. Without the countervailing duty waiver, the European governments have said they will not approve any agreement produced at Geneva.

Some $600 million in subsidized imports annually have been entering the United States under the waiver.[3] At least two-thirds of that amount are agricultural goods imported from member countries of the European Community. The Community, under its Common Agricultural Policy, spends $13 billion a year subsidizing European agriculture — an amount that averages more than $1,500 for each of the Community's 8.5 million farmers. The subsidy issue has been a sticking point in the trade negotiations for the past five years. However, agreement has been reached on a code governing the use of subsidies and the imposition of countervailing duties. A draft agreement limits the use of subsidies and spells out the conditions under which nations may legitimately counteract such practices. Export subsidies on non-primary products and on primary mineral products are flatly prohibited.

Complexity of Issues in the Tokyo Round

The trade talks have seen difficult times since they were initiated in 1973 at a ministerial-level meeting of the General Agreement on Tariffs and Trade *(see p. 73)* in Tokyo — and hence continue to be designated the "Tokyo Round" even though the actual negotiations have been conducted in Geneva since 1975. Several deadlines have lapsed and the talks have been on the verge of collapse over seemingly intractable disagreements more than once. Originally, the Tokyo Round was expected to end in 1975, but it could not get started until that year. Until Congress passed the 1974 Trade Act and it became effective in January 1975, the United States had no authority to enter into the negotiations. The following November, Western

---

[3] See *CECON Trade News,* November 1978, pp. 1-3. The publication is issued monthly by the Organization of American States and reports on developments affecting Latin American exports.

Countervailing Duties

Countervailing duties are imposed on imports when the U.S. Treasury Department determines that foreign governments are offering "bounties or grants" to exporters, enabling them to sell their goods in the United States at reduced prices. Foreign assistance to exporters may be in the form of grants, loans, tax exemptions or rebates, government-financed export insurance or any of a wide variety of other direct and indirect subsidies.

Additional tariffs, or countervailing duties, are levied against the subsidized exports in the amount of the subsidy. Until Jan. 3, the president was authorized, under terms of the Trade Act of 1974, to waive such additional tariffs while negotiations were under way with foreign governments for the elimination of the subsidies, or when there were pressing foreign policy considerations at stake.

Almost all governments — the United States included — offer subsidies to a variety of exports. There is disagreement among the world's trading nations, however, as to which subsidies are necessary or permissible, and which are properly subject to retaliatory action by trading partners.

leaders meeting at the "economic summit" at Rambouillet, France, reset the deadline to late 1977.[4]

By midsummer 1977, only minimal progress had been made. U.S. and European representatives then agreed to begin "detailed, final negotiations" by Jan. 15, 1978. Strauss said at the time that the talks should be concluded "within 90 days" of the January date. In July 1978, Western leaders met in Bonn and set a new cutoff date, Dec. 15, 1978. Although that deadline also slipped by, U.S. negotiators are cautiously optimistic about meeting the new target date of mid-February. If Congress gets the negotiating package in April, as is currently envisioned, approval of the non-tariff aspects of the trade agreement could be expected by August or September. No congressional action on tariff agreements is needed, since specific authority to negotiate tariff reductions is contained in the 1974 Trade Act. The final deadline, in any event, is January 1980, when the statutory limit on the U.S. negotiating authority runs out.

The Tokyo Round has been more protracted than any of the previous GATT negotiating rounds[5] because of the complexity of the issues involved. Earlier rounds focused rather narrowly on tariff cuts in industrial goods. In the Kennedy Round (1964-67),

---

[4] The conference was attended by President Ford and the leaders of Britain, France, West Germany, Italy and Japan. See "International Trade Negotiations, *E.R.R.*, 1976 Vol. I, pp. 343-362.

[5] There were six earlier negotiating rounds. The most recent, the Kennedy Round of 1964-67, was named for the late president in whose administration the 1962 Trade Expansion Act provided authority for negotiating tariff cuts.

for example, duty reductions of up to 50 percent were achieved on 60,000 items worth $40 billion in world trade. The Tokyo Round deals with proposed tariff reductions on both industrial and agricultural goods, embracing thousands of items, and with non-tariff barriers as well.

Agreements Reached So Far in Geneva

Aside from the two categories of chemicals and textiles, the Geneva negotiators have reached general agreement on tariff cuts. Following the so-called "Swiss formula,"[6] tariff reductions of about 35 percent would be phased in over an eight-year period beginning in 1980. As a result, the average level of U.S. import duties would decline from the current 6-7 percent range to between 3 and 4 percent. Japanese tariffs would drop from 10 percent to 4 percent.

Non-tariff barriers have been more difficult to negotiate; they are often difficult to identify, and their impact on trade may be virtually impossible to quantify. In simplest form, non-tariff barriers consist of direct restraints on imports — such as quotas. The United States places quotas on a broad range of agricultural goods, including sugar and meat, and on textiles. Less easily identifiable barriers include government procurement practices which give domestic producers advantages over foreigners; sanitary, safety and environmental regulations that have a discriminatory effect ·on foreign products, whether intentional or not; discriminatory tax adjustments on imported goods; and government subsidies and similar assistance to exporters. In the view of some experts, currency regulations or manipulations intended to make imports expensive and exports cheap should be added to the list of non-tariff barriers.

Government subsidies have been one of the most controversial matters at Geneva; the achievement of an agreement on a subsidies code is a big accomplishment of the Tokyo Round. A member of Strauss's staff said, "The subsidies code and the disciplines it imposes may well carry the whole MTN [through Congress]." A second critical issue, on which some agreement has been reached, is the use of "safeguards." These are tariff and non-tariff measures applied by governments against imports that threaten to disrupt domestic industries.

A draft code sets out specific rules for the imposition of safeguards and requires countries to demonstrate "serious injury" to domestic industry before taking steps to limit imports. Present GATT rules permit safeguard action only on an across-the-board basis. At the insistence of the European Community,

---

[6] Devised by Swiss negotiators as a compromise between the separate positions of the United States, Japan and the European Community.

the code would permit some selective safeguard actions under carefully defined conditions. Still to be determined are rules governing voluntary restraint agreements or "orderly marketing arrangements" and rules governing the formation of international cartels, and special treatment of developing countries.

In addition to the key agreements on subsidies and safeguards, the Geneva negotiators have drafted codes covering several other non-tariff barriers. One deals with government procurement procedures. It regulates measures used by governments to give domestic suppliers preference over foreign competitors. Trade experts say the liberalized provisions of the procurement code could open up export opportunities totaling nearly $40 billion worldwide.

Another code paves the way for a common international system for determining the value of goods for tariff purposes. A third outlaws trade in counterfeited products, while a fourth will help prevent product standards from being used to manipulate or impede trade. Other draft agreements include rules on import licensing, and trade in civil aircraft, engines and parts. The GATT countries will implement separately a series of agricultural agreements covering trade in wheat, coarse grains, meat and certain dairy products.

Other Trade Questions Before Congress

The 96th Congress holds the key to the free trade-protectionism fight. The Carter administration, like others before it going back to the New Deal, contends that protectionist moves by this country — the dominant partner in world trade — would trigger defensive reactions around the world, generating trade wars, "beggar-thy-neighbor" policies, declines in trade volume and possibly recession. The administration is preparing again to ask Congress to authorize U.S. participation in the International Sugar Agreement. The House on the last day of the 95th Congress refused to ratify the sugar pact, which governs the free market sugar trade of more than 16 million tons a year. The United States signed the agreement when it was drawn up in September 1977, but congressional ratification and implementing legislation are required for U.S. participation.

Using a system of export quotas, the sugar agreement is designed to level off the sharp swings in prices that have characterized the free-market sugar trade in recent years. Without the participation of the United States, the world's leading sugar importer, the pact would collapse and the sugar trade would likely become even more chaotic than it has been. The victims would be the developing-country sugar suppliers, which can least afford instability in the commodity market. A deadline of

Dec. 31 for ratification was recently extended by the International Sugar Council at the request of the United States.[7]

Several trade bills passed by the 95th Congress, but vetoed by President Carter as "protectionist," are expected to be reintroduced early in 1979. One would require the president to withhold U.S. textile and apparel concessions from the Geneva trade talks, a prospect which Strauss has called "devastating." Most observers agree that passage of such a bill would effectively torpedo the Tokyo Round, but there is strong support in both houses. Sen. Ernest F. Hollings, D-S.C., sponsor of the bill, argues that it is necessary to stop the "hemorrhage" of textile imports into the United States and to protect the jobs of America's two million textile workers. Proponents of the bill are expected to try to attach its provisions to legislation extending the countervailing duty waiver authority. Since the maneuver — if successful — is likely to scuttle the Geneva negotiation, the legislative battle could be fierce.

Meat industry interests are expected to reintroduce the Beef Import Act, which President Carter vetoed in November. The act would have set up a "countercyclical" formula for meat import quotas, permitting imports to expand when domestic production fell and to shrink when domestic production rose. It also would have restricted the president's existing authority to raise, lower or suspend quotas. President Carter said he favored the countercyclical formula but opposed limits on his discretionary quota authority.

Protectionist Mood at Home and Abroad

As is evident from the legislative record, there was a strong protectionist mood in the 95th Congress.[8] The mood is expected to carry over into the 96th Congress, challenging President Carter's avowed commitment to free trade. Underlying the protectionist sentiment are such economic issues as balance-of-trade deficits, unemployment, the flight of "runaway" factories to foreign countries, and the declining competitiveness of key sectors of U.S. industry.

American exports have grown steadily in recent years and have hit record highs nearly every month of 1978. The growth of exports, however, has lagged behind that of imports. As a result, the United States has suffered a balance-of-trade deficit for 30 consecutive months. The deficit reached $26.7 billion in 1977 and is expected to exceed $30 billion in 1978. Final figures for the year are still to be calculated. The chronic deficit has contributed to the weakening of the dollar on foreign currency markets.

---

[7] See *CECON Trade News*, December 1978.

[8] See "Job Protection and Free Trade," *E.R.R.*, 1977 Vol. II, pp. 953-972.

U.S. Merchandise Trade Balance
(billions of dollars)

Year	Exports	Imports	Balance
1970	43.2	39.9	3.3
1971	44.1	45.6	- 1.5
1972	49.8	55.6	- 5.8
1973	71.3	69.5	1.8
1974	98.5	100.3	- 1.8
1975	107.6	96.1	11.5
1976	115.0	120.7	- 5.7
1977	120.1	146.8	-26.7

Source: U.S. Department of Commerce

Paradoxically, the fall of the dollar against the Japanes yen and the German mark may strengthen the U.S. trade performance in coming years by making imports more expensive and U.S. exports cheaper overseas. [9]

The primary factor in the deficit is America's enormous oil import bill, now in the range of $40 billion a year. New price increases by the Organization of Petroleum Exporting Countries (OPEC) are expected to add $4 billion to that bill in 1979.[10] Efforts to reduce or slow the growth of American energy consumption have had little effect. The chances are slim that the United States can reduce its oil import bill. In the protectionist view, this makes other imports — particularly consumer goods — fair game for import-reducing measures. Since only about 22 percent of all U.S. imports in 1977 consisted of nonfood consumer goods,[11] import cuts on these goods would have to be very deep to be effective — and shutting off the inflow of cheaper imports could worsen America's inflation. President Carter proposes to attack the trade deficit from another direction. In September 1978, he announced a new federal program to boost exports through direct federal assistance to exporters and a reduction of domestic barriers to export growth.

The U.S. employment picture is as complex as the balance-of-trade situation. The United States, along with most other industrial countries, experienced a sharp rise in unemployment during the 1974-75 recession. The joblessness rate rose from 4.9 percent in 1973 to 8.5 percent in 1975. Recovery has been more rapid in the United States than in most of the other western nations, but the current U.S. jobless rate of 5.8 percent is well above the pre-recession level.

[9] See "Dollar Problems Abroad," *E.R.R.*, 1978 Vol. I, pp. 401-420.

[10] OPEC raised oil prices 5 percent on Jan. 1, the first of four raises scheduled in 1979.

[11] Excluding imports of cars and automotive parts from Canada, which enter the United States duty-free under a 1965 agreement between the two countries. Canadian automotive plants are 97 percent owned by American car makers.

Protectionist forces argue that rising competition from imports is taking jobs away from Americans. Steel and electronic plant closings, and textile industry layoffs, have been widely reported in the press. An AFL-CIO study prepared for the labor organization's annual convention in December 1977 claimed that more than half a million American jobs had been lost in recent years through plant closings and transfer of operations overseas. The big job losses cited were:

Electronics and electrical machinery	150,000 jobs
Textiles and apparel	300,000 jobs
Shoes	70,000 jobs
Primary metals	100,000 jobs

Opponents of protectionism reply that the AFL-CIO figures were incomplete and failed to show the rapidity of the nation's economic recovery. A recent study by the American Importers Association states that "over nine million new jobs have been created since 1975, a peacetime record, and domestic manufacturing unemployment has been cut in half. There are more Americans working today than ever before. . . ." While acknowledging that jobs have been lost in the domestic apparel industry, "employment in the industry as a whole has grown by 100,000 in the past three years." The jobs that disappear tend to be the less productive and lower-paying. "Protecting those inefficient economic activities from import competition freezes the status quo, preventing the shift of capital and labor into more productive channels and better-paying jobs."[12]

The emergence of multinational corporations has added a dimension to the trade competition picture. Manufacturing operations are far more mobile than in earlier years. Corporate managers make decisions on plant location on the basis of "rationalizing production." Stated simply, this means that the corporation will close an obsolete, money-losing plant in the United States if it sees a chance to replace it with a modern, low-cost plant in, say, Taiwan, South Korea or Mexico. The speed with which the multinationals can reallocate production from one country to another often makes it difficult for domestic workers to adjust. Moreover, since many multinationals are, by nature, both importers and exporters of goods, the corporation may support free-trade measures in one sector of the economy, while arguing for protectionism in another.[13]

The pressure for government action to protect domestic industries and preserve jobs is real, not only in the United States but around the world. All the industrial countries face economic

---

[12] American Exporters Association, "Imports, Exports and Jobs," September 1978, pp. vi-vii.

[13] See "Multinational Companies," *E.R.R.*, 1972 Vol. II, pp. 499-518.

problems similar to those of the United States. The more serious the problems, the more intense the demand for protection. World Bank President Robert S. McNamara recently warned that present economic growth rates cannot be sustained "if the protectionist barriers erected by the developed nations against the manufactured exports of the developing countries continue to rise as they have recently."[14] A report by the Organization of American States declares that "an alarming rise of protectionism has occurred in the last several years in the industrialized countries which threatens the development strategies of a number of countries in Latin America and in other regions of the world."[15]

While the industrialized countries are most often accused of protectionism, the practice is widespread in the Third World. To promote their own products and build an industrial base, many developing countries have turned to high tariffs, import quotas and other protectionist devices. Frequently, such negative actions against imports are accompanied by positive measures, such as subsidies, to encourage exports. There is evidence that protectionist measures, once adopted, tend to become entrenched. The argument is advanced by developing countries that high tariffs bring "structural distortions" to the economy. The tariffs cannot be lowered without causing distress to domestic industry. Subsidies then become necessary to "correct the distortions."

The World Bank observes in its "World Development Report" for 1978: "Protectionist measures are common in the developing countries as well. For many, particularly those still in the early stages of industrialization, protection can be justified. But for those that are well advanced in the development process, the adverse effects of industrial protection on economic efficiency and growth become increasingly evident."[16]

Protectionism Vs. Free Trade

THROUGH most of U.S. history, protectionism has prevailed. Partly to encourage struggling new industries in the young nation, Congress imposed moderately high import duties. The heavy cost of the War of 1812 brought a doubling of tariff rates, but even that did not satisfy New England textile

---

[14] Robert S. McNamara, address to the Board of Governors of the World Bank, September 1978.

[15] Organization of American States, "Protectionism Trend in the United States Affecting Latin American Countries," undated, p. 1.

[16] World Bank, "World Development Report, 1978," August 1978, pp. 18-19.

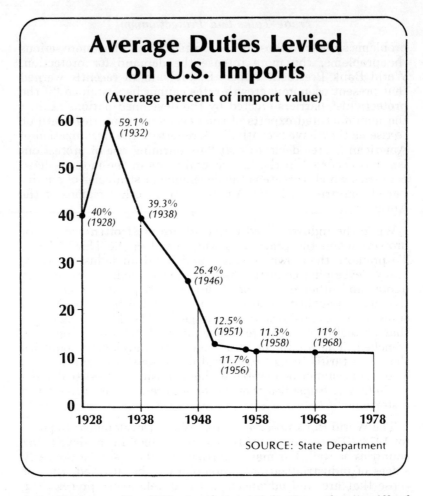

Average Duties Levied on U.S. Imports

(Average percent of import value)

59.1% (1932)

40% (1928)

39.3% (1938)

26.4% (1946)

12.5% (1951)

11.7% (1956)

11.3% (1958)

11% (1968)

SOURCE: State Department

manufacturers. By 1828, to their satisfaction, the "tariff of abominations" established almost prohibitive duties on woolen and cotton goods — to the consternation of the South where growers of cotton, tobacco and rice feared it would kill their profitable sales to England.

For the next half-century, tariff rates see-sawed as first one section and then the other gained influence in Congress, and some of the sectional bitterness that grew out of these tariff fights was considered a contributing cause of the Civil War. America's explosive industrial development after the Civil War, especially after 1890, was attributed by protectionists to the benefits of high tariffs, and by those favoring low tariffs to the country's abundance of natural resources.

As Treasury surpluses grew — customs accounted for half of all federal revenues until the end of the 19th century — sentiment developed for lower tariffs, and early in the new century both major political parties declared themselves in favor of revising the prohibitive rates set by the Tariff Act of 1897. At President Wilson's urging, Congress in 1913 lowered the average rates from about 40 percent to 29 percent. But a new surge of protectionist sentiment drove the rates up again after World War I. That round of tariff-making started as an effort to give greater protection to depressed farm prices in the 1920s, but manufacturers succeeded in protecting many of their products.

The culmination of this maneuvering for protection from imports was the Hawley-Smoot Tariff of 1930, one of the highest ever enacted. It touched off an outburst of tariff-making activity around the world, partly in reprisal, and is often cited by economists as a leading cause of the depression which overtook the world in the 1930s. Economic activity stagnated and by 1932 world trade had sunk to about one-third of the 1929 level.

After this bitter lesson, Congress retreated from protectionism. At the insistence of President Franklin D. Roosevelt and Secretary of State Cordell Hull, it passed the Reciprocal Trade Agreements Act of 1934, the beginning of a worldwide movement for reducing tariffs and other trade barriers. The act, since renewed 11 times, gave the president authority to negotiate trade agreements with individual countries and greatly reduced duties in return for similar concessions on their part. From 1934 to 1961, the value of America's foreign trade increased 15-fold as average U.S. tariffs on dutiable goods dropped from 46.7 percent to 12 percent.[17]

GATT's Founding; 1962, 1974 Trade Acts

In 1947, as part of an effort to ease critical economic conditions abroad after World War II, the United States helped establish the General Agreement on Tariffs and Trade with 22 of its trading partners. GATT represented a break from the previous mode of negotiating with one country at a time. It enabled all of the participating countries to bargain with all of the others simultaneously. Concessions agreed upon by individual negotiating teams had to be extended to all, an arrangement that is known as the "most favored nation" principle.

Year by year, more nations have joined GATT and today its membership embraces most of the non-communist countries in the world. "Looking back on the past three decades," Secretary of the Treasury W. Michael Blumenthal wrote last summer, "that emphasis [on freer trade] seems to have been thoroughly vindicated. In that period, the economic growth of nations has been more rapid and more persuasive than for any such period

---

[17] For background on the course of U.S. trade policies over the years, see the Department of State booklet "The Trade Debate," Publication 8942, issued May 1978.

73

in modern history."[18] The so-called Kennedy Round of GATT gave world trade a strong thrust. The Kennedy Round was made possible by congressional passage of the 1962 Trade Expansion Act authorizing across-the-board tariff cuts of 50 percent rather than commodity-by-commodity negotiations. After three years of bargaining in Geneva, 53 nations accounting for 80 percent of world trade agreed to tariff cuts averaging 35 percent.

The U.S. economy had meanwhile become inflated by its financing of a war in Vietnam and this, with other economic problems both at home and abroad, led in 1971 to President Nixon's devaluation of the dollar, the chief medium of exchange in international trade. Economic conditions were worsened by successive increases in oil prices imposed by OPEC, beginning in the fall of 1973. A world recession followed in 1974-75, intensifying a growing protectionist mood in many countries, including the United States.

Nonetheless, Congress in 1974 passed a new Trade Act signaling this country's intention to work for freer trade as a way of restoring global prosperity. The act authorized the president to negotiate a reduction of duties by as much as 60 percent, the greatest percentage authorization that Congress ever granted. He also was given authority to negotiate the reduction or elimination of non-tariff barriers, subject to congressional approval.

In deference to protectionist sentiment in Congress and the nation, the act required the president to take measures to aid domestic producers injured by imports. If the U.S. International Trade Commission finds that a domestic industry has sustained serious injury, the president must act to restrain imports or provide other assistance to the industry unless he determines that to do so would be contrary to U.S. economic interests.

Concern Over Technology and Productivity

For most of this century, the United States has been the preeminent industrial nation — "the world's first atomic and technological superpower, a Titan towering over the international economy and politics."[19] In recent years chinks have begun to appear in the giant's armor. For a multitude of reasons — ranging from the drain caused by U.S. involvement in a Southeast Asian war to plant obsolescence, declining productivity growth, high energy costs and many more — American dominance of world trade and finance has been eroding steadily.

The United States faces mounting economic challenges from

---

[18] W. Michael Blumenthal, "Steering in Crowded Waters," *Foreign Affairs,* July 1978, p. 734.

[19] "America — Declining Power?" *U.S. News & World Report,* Nov. 27, 1978, pp. 56-62.

such countries as Japan, West Germany and France, which only 30 years ago lay in ruins in the aftermath of World War II. The U.S. share of world manufactured exports, for example, shrank from 24 percent in 1968 to 20 percent in 1977, while the shares of Japan, West Germany and France all increased. Sen. Frank Church, D-Idaho, chairman-designate of the Senate Foreign Relations Committee, said: "Our real competiton comes not from the Soviet Union, which is less competitive than we, but from Western Europe and Japan."[20]

Some experts attribute the decline in competitiveness to the "mind-set" of American businessmen. They see American industry as so beguiled by the size and wealth of the domestic market that it is relatively uninterested in overseas sales. To many American corporations, exports are a fringe benefit. The argument appears to be borne out by the relative importance of trade to the gross national product (GNP) of key industrial nations, as shown in the following table:

Country	Exports* (percentage of GNP)	Imports*
Britain	28	30
West Germany	14	27
Italy	24	25
Canada	24	24
France	20	19
Japan	14	14
United States	7	7

* 1975 figures for France and Italy; other figures for 1976.

Probably more fundamental to America's declining competitiveness in overseas markets (and, in the case of some industries, at home as well) is this country's decreasing lead in technology and· the consequent slump in the productivity of American workers.[21] Output per man-hour grew rapidly for nearly a quarter of a century following World War II but began to fall off in the late 1960s and early 1970s. The comparative productivity gains from 1970 to 1977 for leading industrial countries are shown in the following U.S. Department of Commerce statistics:

West Germany	46%	Canada	25%
France	42	U.S.	21
Italy	38	Britain	17

Productivity performance involves a broad range of factors — management skills, worker training and incentives, manage-

---

[20] Interview, June 9, 1978.
[21] See "Technology Gap: Reality or Illusion," *E.R.R.*, 1978 Vol. II, pp. 945-960.

ment-labor relations, government regulations, technology advance, investment in new equipment. Many experts attribute the recent declines in U.S. productivity to steadily decreasing investment in the research and development of new production techniques and equipment. Recent data compiled by the National Science Foundation shows, for example, that U.S. R&D spending shrank from 2.73 percent of the GNP in 1962 to 2.24 percent in 1977, while the corresponding figures of most other industrial nations — with the exception of Britain — rose.

An intriguing argument is offered by Melvyn B. Krauss, a professor of economics at New York University, in his book *The New Protectionism*. Krauss writes that productivity declines, as well as the increase in protectionist sentiment, may be attributed to the rise of the modern "welfare state." Krauss defines the goals of the welfare state as (1) providing economic security for its citizens by protecting them from change that would hurt their economic positions, and (2) redistributing income (and economic power in general) from capital to labor.

> Simply stated [Krauss continued], the inherent contradiction of the welfare state is that the welfare state requires a high level of productivity to support it, but that the welfare state interventionist policies necessarily reduce productivity levels. Hence . . . the welfare state . . . consists of policies that undermine the factors upon which it critically depends.[22]

New Challenges From Foreign Countries

The principal competition to American industry comes from the advanced industrial nations of Western Europe and Japan. A new congressional study suggests, however, that American manufacturers may expect increasing competition from suppliers in developing countries in the next five to ten years. The study[23] analyzes the export potential of eight "advanced developing nations" — Brazil, Hong Kong, India, Mexico, the Philippines, Singapore, South Korea and Taiwan. The eight countries together account for 29 percent of all U.S. imports from the developing world.

This study identifies 158 product categories in which American industries may be "vulnerable" to competition from foreign suppliers. These include some traditional imports which have long been competitive in the U.S. market, such as electronics equipment, textiles, ceramics and glass, footwear, hats and

---

[22] Melvyn B. Krauss, *The New Protectionism: The Welfare State and International Trade*, New York University Press, 1978, p. 107.

[23] Joint Economic Committee of Congress, "Anticipating Disruptive Imports," Sept. 14, 1978.

The New China Trade

The resumption of diplomatic relations between the United States and China on Jan. 1 appears to open up enormous business opportunities. The trade, finance and investment potential for Americans is expected to amount to several billion dollars a year. Since China is not a member of GATT, the Geneva agreement will not apply to trade between the two countries.

Japanese industrialists and bankers were the first to tap the China market and they remain dominant among foreign traders in China. However, several U.S. companies hold multi-million-dollar contracts with China. They include U.S. Steel, Kaiser Steel, Bethlehem Steel, the Fluor Corp., Coca-Cola and Pan American Airways.

American farmers stand to benefit, too. Agriculture Department estimates are that China will double its annual grain purchases from the United States, which topped 3 million tons in 1978. Total U.S.-China trade last year was $1.3 billion, three times the 1977 level of $374 million. By comparison, U.S. trade with Taiwan in 1978 reached $7.3 billion.

But if there are vast trade opportunities in China, serving a market of almost one billion people, there are also potential dangers. China's supply of low-wage labor threatens to offer new competition to beleaguered American industries such as textiles, shoes and possibly electronics. Chinese and American negotiators open talks Jan. 22 on China's exports of textiles and wearing apparel. The United States hopes China will agree to restraints.

gloves, bicycles, toys and leather products. Also included are several which have not been regarded as competitive threats until recently. Among these are manufactured wood products, hand tools, agricultural machinery, typewriters and office equipment, and cameras and photographic equipment.

The main challenge to U.S. industry from developing countries will not come in the form of a sharp increase in imports, but rather in a rising level of industrial "sophistication" that permits these countries to compete with American products in overseas markets. The study predicted that:

The United States is likely to retain an unchallengeable competitive advantage only in products and techniques that are at the very forefront of technological development or that require a huge integrated market for their creation.

Examples of these are satellite communications and photography, deep-sea mining and the very largest electrical generating and delivery systems. Development of these technologies requires government support for initial research, assistance in the primary stages of marketing, and government purchases of a significant share of the final output.

Strategies for Enlarging Trade

D ESPITE pressures from some members of Congress allied to such industrial interests as steel, chemicals, textiles and shoes, the United States is far from being a protectionist nation. Tariffs are at their lowest levels in more than a century. In the words of economist Paul Samuelson, "America has at long last ceased to be a high-tariff nation."[24] President Carter, like his predecessor, Gerald Ford, has rejected numerous congressional and executive branch attempts to limit imports. Among the items denied import relief in recent months have been copper, stainless steel, ferrochromium, shoes, honey and mushrooms. In addition, President Carter has waived countervailing duties on Mexican steel, leather goods from Colombia and Uruguay, and textiles from Brazil.

Protectionist measures are generally designed to shelter specific products from import competition. In the past four years, hundreds of investigations of foreign products have been undertaken in compliance with U.S. laws covering (1) aid to domestic industries hurt by sudden increases in imports ("escape clause" of the 1974 Trade Act), (2) anti-dumping (1921 Anti-Dumping Act), (3) countervailing duties (1930 Tariff Act), and (4) unfair import practices (1930 Tariff Act). Only a few dozen such investigations have resulted in import controls.

There are other strategies for easing the pressure of import competition and making American producers more competitive. One is to negotiate with foreign suppliers for quotas, or "orderly marketing arrangements." The U.S. government determines what level of imports can be sustained without damaging domestic producers and then negotiates with the principal foreign suppliers to limit the inflow of their goods to specified amounts. There is, or course, an element of protectionism — and coercion — in these arrangements; foreign suppliers liken the bargaining to "negotiating with a gun at your head." Nonetheless, these arrangement regulate U.S. imports of such items as shoes, textiles and meat.

A second strategy is to offer temporary federal aid, called "adjustment assistance," to industries hard-pressed by import competition. The assistance may be in the form of direct payments to workers whose jobs are displaced by imports or by the transfer overseas of manufacturing operations. Or such assistance may be used to establish retraining facilities to upgrade job skills. Still another form of assistance entails loans and

---

[24] Paul Samuelson, *Economics* (eighth edition, 1970), p. 679.

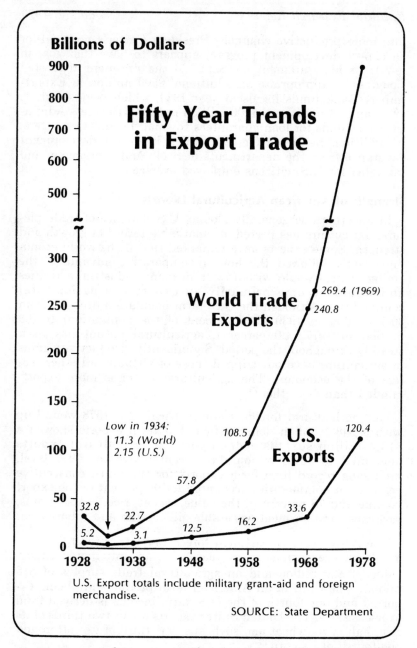

Billions of Dollars

Fifty Year Trends in Export Trade

World Trade Exports

269.4 (1969)

240.8

Low in 1934:
11.3 (World)
2.15 (U.S.)

108.5

U.S. Exports

120.4

57.8

32.8

22.7

33.6

5.2

3.1

12.5

16.2

1928   1938   1948   1958   1968   1978

U.S. Export totals include military grant-aid and foreign merchandise.

SOURCE: State Department

grants to manufacturers so they can modernize their plants. Critics of adjustment assistance say that it often becomes a subsidy to inefficient industry. But supporters contend that it is preferable to outright restrictions on imports.

The goal, of course, is not to shelter inefficient industry, but to encourage the transfer of capital, manpower and resources into more productive channels. President Carter's proposal for an export development program appears to have that goal in mind. In his statement on Sept. 26 the president requested Congress to appropriate an additional $500 million in Export-Import Bank funds for fiscal year 1980, which begins Oct. 1, 1979, and an additional $100 million in Small Business Administration funds for loan guarantees to small business exporters. In addition, he called for $20 million in export development assistance from the departments of State and Commerce, and tax relief for U.S. citizens employed overseas.

Strength of American Agricultural Exports

In an otherwise generally gloomy U.S. balance-of-trade picture, agriculture has posted a remarkable record of growth and strength. Some experts have remarked that if the world economy strictly followed the law of comparative advantage, the United States would withdraw from many industrial activities and would become primarily an exporter of agricultural commodities. Although the U.S. farm population dropped from 30.5 million in 1930 (20.8 percent of the population) to 8.3 million in 1977 (4.0 percent), agricultural output has risen steadily throughout the period. Significantly, productivity gains in agriculture have outstripped those of virtually all other sectors of the economy. The agricultural sector is more export-minded than any other.[25]

Non-agricultural foreign trade in fiscal year 1978 wound up with a $48.2 billion dollar deficit, but farm exports showed a $13.4 billion surplus over imports.[26] Agricultural exports amounted to $27.3 billion, 14 percent above the 1977 level, producing record high farm exports for the ninth consecutive year. Eight commodities accounted for 94 percent of the export volume and 78 percent of the value: wheat, rice, coarse grains, soybeans, protein meal, vegetable oils, cotton and tobacco.

The Agriculture Department forecasts another record performance in the current fiscal year, with an anticipated export value of $29 billion and an agricultural trade surplus of $15 billion. One-third of all American farm products are being exported and one-fourth of the U.S. farm income is derived from overseas sales. The United States exports about two-thirds of its rice, half of its wheat and soybeans, one-third of its cotton and one-fourth of its corn.[27]

Protectionism exists in agriculture just as it does in industry.

[25] See "Farm Policy and Food Needs," *E.R.R.*, 1977 Vol. II, pp. 805-824.

[26] See "How Agri-exports Tilted the Trade Balance," *Monthly Economic Letter*, Citibank, pp. 6-8.

[27] See *Food and Agricultural Policy*, American Enterprise Institute, 1977.

Governments attempt to insulate their domestic markets through high tariffs, variable levies, support payments to farmers, fiscal assistance to exporters and two-tier price systems which maintain fixed price levels at home and fluctuating prices in the world market.

This country's comparative advantage in agriculture is virtually unassailable. Food is a short commodity in world trade. Competition is often keener for supplies than for sales. Nonetheless, American farmers face problems in obtaining access to overseas markets. In Europe, the Common Agricultural Policy levies high tariffs against some U.S. agricultural exports, and provides subsidies to inefficient European producers, enabling them to undercut American exporters. It was once said "America can't squeeze an orange in Japan," but Japan has recently begun to open its market to U.S. citrus fruit and beef. Problems still remain for poultry, soybeans, grapes, walnuts, canned peaches and corn oil. In the developing countries, such non-tariff barriers as import licenses are more formidable than tariffs.

All these issues have been put on the table at Geneva. Trade negotiator Strauss has said: "Key among our objectives is better access for American agricultural products on world markets. This is a condition without which there will be no agreement brought back for the Congress to ratify."[28] Another U.S. representative at the trade talks, Alan Wm. Wolff, has said the United States will "walk away from the table rather than accept something that is contrary to our interests."[29] "Congressional leaders are telling us plainly not to talk about opening any more doors to trade without showing them how we are going to push our exports through them," said Frank Weil, Assistant Secretary of Commerce for industry and trade.[30]

Special Needs of the Developing Countries

In the Tokyo Round, and in various other international forums, the developing countries have frequently asserted that the present structure of the world trade system is tilted against them. They have been seeking a "New International Economic Order" to redress the imbalances. Generally, the developed countries have agreed with the position of the Third World nations. The Tokyo Declaration, which underlies the current Geneva trade talks, pledges to "secure additional benefits for the international trade of developing countries. . . ." An inter-

---

[28] Quoted in *The New York Times,* Dec. 3, 1978.
[29] Alan Wm. Wolff is one of two U.S. deputy negotiators who hold the rank of ambassador (the other is Alonzo McDonald), both under Strauss. Wolff's remarks were made at the Farmland Industries annual meeting in Kansas City, Mo., Dec. 7, 1978.
[30] Quoted in *Business Week,* issue dated Jan. 15, 1979, p. 32.

national trade expert has remarked: "If words were hard coin, the prospects of the developing countries would appear favorable."[31]

The developing countries have been seeking what is called "Special and Differential" (S&D) treatment in the Tokyo Round. They want deep tariff cuts for their leading exports (especially tropical food products) and exemptions from the GATT rules on subsidies and countervailing duties. In addition, they are pressing for an extension and expansion of the Generalized System of Preferences (GSP) under which certain goods from the Third World enter the markets of the United States and other developed countries duty-free.

The current prospects are that the developing countries will receive S&D treatment from some of the industrialized countries only in regard to subsidies and countervailing duties. A code of conduct being negotiated in Geneva is expected to make at least some minimal concessions, relaxing some GATT subsidy restrictions for the poorest of the developing countries or permitting them to phase gradually into compliance with GATT rules. There is no apparent movement toward extension of the GSP, which will expire at different times in the industrialized countries in the early and mid-1980s, or toward granting free access for tropical products in the markets of developed countries. It is possible, however, that the trade representatives may agree to set up a mechanism for continuing negotiations on these issues.

Two problems have prevented more accommodation between the poor and the rich countries in the trade talks. One is the reluctance of the developing countries to agree to reciprocal preferences for the industrialized countries in return for the concessions they seek. The other is the different stages of development within the Third World. The developed countries appear ready to agree that S&D treatment is appropriate for the very poorest countries, such as Mali or Haiti, but are opposed to such concessions for the middle tier of developing countries, such as Brazil or Mexico.

All nations, rich and poor alike, seem to recognize their stake in the successful outcome of the Tokyo Round. The world trading system is an interlocking network, inextricably linking all the world's economies. The world depression of the 1930s was brought on, in large part, by the "beggar-thy-neighbor" policies of the leading industrial powers. Beset with economic problems at home, and pressed by the competition of exports from abroad, each country tried to erect protective walls around its domestic markets.

---

[31] Eric Wyndham White, writing in the *Journal of Commerce*, Dec. 8, 1978, p. 4. White is a former director general of GATT.

Trade Terminology

Adjustment assistance: Aid to industries hurt by imports.

Ad valorem duties: Tariff duties calculated on the basis of the value of goods. (Duties levied on the basis of some physical unit, so many cents a pound or yard, are called specific duties.)

American selling price (ASP): System under which the tariff rate on imported goods, principally benzenoid chemicals, is based on the price of the competitively produced U.S. product rather than on the actual import price.

Anti-dumping regulations: "Dumping" means selling for export at prices lower than those in the exporter's own domestic market. The U.S. Antidumping Act of 1921 provides that if a foreign exporter sells to the United States at prices "less than the fair value," thereby injuring American industry, anti-dumping duties shall be levied on the goods concerned.

Balance of payments: U.S. record of transactions covering receipts from foreign countries on one side and payments to them on the other. The difference represents the balance of payments.

Balance of trade: The relationship between imports and exports. It is only one aspect of the balance of payments.

Bilateral agreement: Agreement between two countries.

Countervailing duty: A charge placed on imports to counteract the subsidies granted to exporters, such as dumping and subsidies.

Duty: Special tax applied to imported goods, based on tariff rates and schedules.

GSP (Generalized System of Preferences): System under which developed countries give duty-free treatment or lower tariff rates to specified imports from developing countries.

Import quota: Government measure limiting total volume or total value of particular goods imported into a country during a specified period. Import quotas frequently are implemented by import licenses issued by governments to individual importers.

Multilateral agreement: Agreement among many countries.

Non-tariff barriers: Term applied to government restrictions, other than tariffs, which distort the flow of international trade.

Tariff: Schedule or system of duties imposed on imported or exported goods; the rate or rates of duty imposed in a tariff.

Since the 1930s, the world's economies have become even more dependent on the international flow of goods and services. The actions of a single country can have a profound effect on all the others. Recession, inflation and high unemployment in the United States also hurt this nation's trading partners. Similarly, economic distress in foreign countries can damage the American economy. The challenge to the Carter administration is to breathe new life into ailing domestic industries without disrupting the liberal patterns of world trade on which all depend.

Selected Bibliography

Books

Cline, William R., et al., *Trade Negotiations in the Tokyo Round: A Quantitative Assessment,* Brookings Institution, 1978.
Food and Agricultural Policy, American Enterprise Institute, 1977.
Krauss, Melvyn B., *The New Protectionism: The Welfare State and International Trade,* published by the New York University Press for the International Center for Economic Policy Studies, 1978.
Rossides, Eugene T., *U.S. Customs Tariffs and Trade,* Bureau of National Affairs, 1977.
Samuelson, Paul A., *Economics* (10th edition), McGraw-Hill, 1976.
Two Centuries of Tariffs, U.S. International Trade Commission, 1976.

Articles

"America — Declining Power?" *U.S. News & World Report,* Nov. 27, 1978.
CECON Trade News, selected issues.
Blumenthal, W. Michael, "Steering in Crowded Waters," *Foreign Affairs,* July 1978.
"How Agri-exports Tilted the Trade Balance," *Monthly Economic Letter,* Citibank publication, December 1978.
Little, I. M. D., "Import Controls and Exports in Developing Countries," *Finance & Development,* International Monetary Fund, September 1978.
"The Resurgence of Protectionism," *Finance & Development,* September 1978.
Tariffs & Trade (biweekly newsletter), selected issues.
White, Eric Wyndham, "LDCs and the Trade Hassle," *Journal of Commerce,* Dec. 8, 1978.
"Strauss's Next Hurdle — the Hill," *Business Week,* issue dated Jan. 15, 1979.

Reports and Studies

American Importers Association, "Imports, Exports and Jobs," September 1978.
Editorial Research Reports: "Technology Gap: Reality or Illusion," 1978 Vol. II, p. 945; "Job Protection and Free Trade," 1977 Vol. II, p. 955; "World's Slow Economic Recovery," 1977 Vol. II, p. 747; "International Trade Negotiations," 1976 Vol. I, p. 343.
Joint Economic Committee of Congress, "Anticipating Disruptive Imports," Sept. 14, 1978.
McNamara, Robert S., "Address to the Board of Governors of the World Bank," Sept. 25, 1978.
Organization of American States, "The United States and the Trend Toward Increased Protectionism in International Trade," November 1978.
Stokes, Bruce, "Worker Participation — Productivity and the Quality of World Life," Worldwatch Institute, December 1978.
U.S. Department of State, "The Trade Debate," May 1978.
World Bank, "World Trade and the International Economy: Trends, Prospects and Policies," Staff Working Paper No. 282, May 1978.

MIDDLE EAST TRANSITION

by

Mary Costello

**Dec. 1
1978**

Editor's Note: The Middle East peace agreement, discussed prominently in this report, did indeed come to fruition with Egypt and Israel's signing of a peace treaty at the White House, March 26, 1979. The main elements of the treaty require a partial Israeli withdrawal from the Sinai, negotiations between the two countries on Palestinian self-rule in the West Bank and Gaza Strip, and make the United States a guarantor of the treaty's terms.

Although Egypt and Israel ended a state of war that formally existed between the two since May 1978, when Israel declared its statehood, the treaty leaves much of the Middle East in turmoil. Egypt incurred the hostility of its Arab neighbors, and an overall Middle East political settlement still seems remote.

MIDDLE EAST TRANSITION

THE peace agreement between Egypt and Israel, hammered out at Camp David in September by President Carter, Egyptian President Anwar Sadat and Israeli Prime Minister Menachem Begin, remains in limbo. The negotiations that followed in Washington in October were expected to be concluded quickly and a peace treaty signed by this time. But the negotiations have been beset by inumerable proposals and counterproposals, hope and despair and what President Carter referred to as a great deal of squabbling over "little, tiny technicalities."

It is uncertain at this time when, where or if the treaty negotiations will resume. On Nov. 21, the Israeli Cabinet accepted a compromise draft treaty proposed by the United States, and Israeli Foreign Minister Moshe Dayan intimated that his country would accept no changes in the draft treaty. "Take it or leave it," Dayan said on Nov. 22. President Sadat reportedly was angered by the rejection of his demands for a timetable for Palestinian autonomy on the Israeli-occupied West Bank and Gaza Strip and may be unwilling to "take" the draft treaty as it now stands.

If a treaty is signed, it will virtually rule out a fifth Arab-Israeli war in the foreseeable future. For without Egypt, the other Arab states would be courting certain defeat by attacking Israel. But the settlement achieved in the Maryland mountains has been criticized by Arab moderates and condemned by Arab hardliners and the Soviet Union. Until at least some of these parties agree to join the negotiations, the comprehensive peace that Carter has advocated since assuming the presidency is likely to remain elusive.

The euphoria which greeted the Camp David agreements in much of the Western world has dimmed considerably, and this disenchantment is expected to be evident when Begin and Sadat receive the 1978 Nobel Peace Prize in Oslo, Norway, on Dec. 10.[1] The presentation has been controversial since it was announced by the Nobel Committee on Oct. 27. Syria immediately denounced the joint award to the "traitor" Sadat and the "ter-

---

[1] Sadat has cast some doubt on whether he will go to Oslo to receive the award. "It may depend to a very small extent on the status of the negotiations," he said on Nov. 25.

rorist" Begin as a "joke." *The Times* of London editorialized on
Oct. 28 that "it is hard not to feel that by making Mr. Sadat
share the award with Mr. Begin, the Nobel Committee have
detracted a good deal from its value." Even the committee
itself, in what can only be described as an understatement, took
note of the difficulties that must be resolved. "Essential negotiations still remain before the idea of peace is anchored in
binding political agreements."

The Camp David accords consist of two parts, a framework for
settling the Palestinian question on the Israeli-occupied West
Bank and Gaza Strip and a framework for an Egyptian-Israeli
peace treaty *(see box)*. Other Arab states, including moderates
like Jordan and Saudi Arabia, have been openly critical of the
West Bank-Gaza formula. Washington expressed its strong
displeasure at Israel's post-Camp David decision to expand
Jewish settlements in the West Bank and its insistence that
East Jerusalem, seized from Jordan in the 1967 war, would
never be returned to Arab control.

The main obstacle to the conclusion of an Egyptian-Israeli
peace treaty has been the linkage between that treaty and the
future of the West Bank and Gaza. The United States and
Egypt contend that the two accords are linked politically and
morally, if not formally. Israel has de-emphasized any linkage,
leading to charges that the Jewish state is interested only in a
separate peace with Egypt and would be quite happy to see the
collapse of the West Bank-Gaza negotiations.

While the Israeli Cabinet approved a vaguely worded reference to the link between the two agreements on Nov. 21, it
categorically rejected any timetable for Palestinian autonomy.
Israeli officials contend that Sadat's insistence on a specific
timetable for elections on at least the Gaza Strip might allow
Egypt to refuse to carry out certain commitments under the
treaty if, for any reason, elections could not be held by that
date. Another problem that emerged during the negotiations
was Israel's demand that its peace treaty with Egypt override
Egypt's military commitment to other Arab states.

Both Camp David frameworks produced a degree of unity
among the other Arab countries. This was apparent in the
reconciliation of Syria and Iraq late in October. The two countries, which have been feuding for years, agreed to work toward a
"full military union" against Israel because of the "great dangers looming over the Arab nation" after Camp David. There
was also more unity than expected at an Arab summit conference held Nov. 2-5 in Baghdad, Iraq.

The conference, attended by 21 Arab states and the Palestine
Liberation Organization (PLO), was widely viewed as a victory

Main Provisions of the Camp David Accords

I. "A Framework for Peace in the Middle East"
  (a) a five-year period of self-rule for Palestinians on the West Bank and Gaza Strip
  (b) withdrawal of Israeli troops to specified locations
  (c) negotiations by Egypt, Israel, elected representatives of the Palestinians and Jordan to determine the status of the area. Israel would have a veto over any Arab proposal on the final status of the area
  (d) a ban on new Israeli settlements during the negotiations (Begin asserted that the ban was limited to the three months' negotiations with Egypt, while Carter, in a press conference on Sept. 28, said that it is "my very clear understanding" that the ban is "related to negotiation for conclusion in the West Bank-Gaza Strip of the establishment of self-government," over a five-year period.)
  (e) security arrangements to be negotiated by the parties
  (f) an exchange of letters between Carter, Sadat and Begin on the status of East Jerusalem (The three leaders were in disagreement on this subject.)

II. "A Framework for the Conclusion of a Peace Treaty between Egypt and Israel"
  (a) a peace treaty between Egypt and Israel is to be signed by Dec. 17
  (b) Israeli withdrawal from all of Sinai to begin within three to nine months after the treaty is signed
  (c) Israeli airfields and, after the Israeli Knesset (parliament) approves, Israeli settlements are to be withdrawn from the Sinai (The Knesset approved the removal of settlements on Sept. 28.)
  (d) the establishment of security zones in the Sinai
  (e) the establishment of normal relations between Egypt and Israel at the end of the first major Israeli withdrawal

for the hard-liners. Among the measures adopted at the meeting were a condemnation of the Camp David accords and the approval of a $3.5 billion-a-year war chest to help subsidize Syria, Jordan and the PLO. It was further agreed that upon the conclusion of an Egyptian-Israeli peace treaty, Egypt's membership in the Arab League would be suspended, the league's headquarters would be moved from Cairo, and all Egyptian firms dealing with Israel would be subject to the Arab boycott. Egypt did not attend the Baghdad conference.

Before the summit ended, a delegation led by Lebanese Premier Salim Hoss was dispatched to Cairo to try to dissuade

President Sadat from signing a treaty with Israel. Sadat refused to see the delegation and Egyptian officials referred to the Baghdad conference as a "comic farce."[2] American officials reportedly saw nothing comic about it and were particularly upset by the support of such moderates as Saudi Arabia and Jordan for the resolutions adopted at the meeting. Since Camp David, Washington has been working to enlist the support of the more moderate Arab states. Without at least their tacit cooperation, there is concern that the upheavals and instability the Camp David conference was called to prevent could well ensue.

Arab Resistance to an Egypt-Israel Treaty

Sadat's hard-line Arab critics maintain that the Camp David agreement is merely the culmination of what Sadat has been aiming at for years and particularly since his visit to Jerusalem in November 1977: a separate Egyptian-Israeli peace. They view the framework for a comprehensive peace involving the Palestinians, Jordan and perhaps Syria as meaningless and intended only to mask the selling out of the Arab cause for what PLO leader Yassir Arafat has called "a handful of Sinai sand." Arab moderates have spoken more in sadness than in anger about Egypt's withdrawal from the Arab-Israeli struggle. In an address to his people on Oct. 10, King Hussein of Jordan said: "Most Arabs still hope that Arab Egypt will not reach the point of no return and isolate itself from its history, its Arabism and even from itself."

Israel had made it known that it was willing to return the Sinai to Egyptian control in exchange for peace long before Sadat's visit to Jerusalem. One of the unanswered questions about Camp David is whether Israel did in fact achieve the separate peace it has sought. There is every indication that most Israeli Jews would welcome a partial settlement that would eliminate, at least for a time, the danger of war and allow the Jewish state to retain control over the West Bank, Gaza and Syria's Golan Heights.

One who would not is journalist Uri Avnery. In an interview published in the London magazine *The Middle East* in October 1978, Avnery said: "As an Israeli, I do not believe that a separate Israeli-Egyptian peace is valuable in the long term, or that it's in Israel's interest. . . . Assume for a moment that we do achieve a separate peace, but that the general turmoil in the Arab world continues, that the Palestinians remain the radicalizing factor in the Arab world and that the Arab-Israeli

---

[2] Many observers speculated, however, that Sadat's tougher position on the linkage issue was a direct result of the Baghdad conference.

conflict continues. Can one really believe that Egypt would stand outside this process?"

Egyptian and American officials have denied categorically that the Camp David frameworks are simply a cover for a separate Egyptian-Israeli peace treaty. Sadat has said that he will negotiate for the Palestinians on the West Bank and Gaza if they or Jordan refuse to participate, and he has stressed the linkage between the two agreements during the negotiations in Washington over the Egyptian-Israeli peace treaty. But Egyptian Foreign Minister Ibrahim Kamel resigned immediately after Camp David; it was reported that he believed Sadat had agreed to a separate peace. And Sen. James Abourezk, D-S.D., a champion of the Arab cause in Congress, told the Senate on Sept. 19: "The dreaded hour has finally arrived, the separate peace between Egypt and Israel, which President Sadat swore would not come from him and for which Israel has hoped for so long a time."

The agreement that President Carter achieved at Camp David is in many respects a return to the "step-by-step" diplomacy engaged in by Henry A. Kissinger when he was secretary of state. Mark Bruzonsky, a Washington writer on Middle Eastern affairs, has said: "Whatever one's view of Camp David's outcome, it is hardly the comprehensive Arab-Israeli settlement Carter loudly preached from inauguration day until the Sadat Jerusalem extravaganza one year ago. At best, the Carter-inspired formula is an uneasy, unstable beginning to what might eventually become a firmer Middle East accommodation. At worst, it is a collapsible gamble at a separate peace — one accomplished in exhausted desperation and one that, if aborted, might create an even more intolerable situation than existed before."[3]

Whether the United States could have secured a more stable and comprehensive agreement than the one achieved at Camp David is debatable. And whether the risks that Sadat faces — isolation in the Arab world, a reduction in subsidies from the oil-rich Arab states and an economic peace dividend that does not meet Egyptian expectations — are worth the settlement he has agreed to may not be apparent for some time. Perhaps the only certainty is that Washington will be increasingly involved, not only in keeping the peace process going but in providing considerably more economic and military assistance to Egypt and Israel.

"Moving from war to peace is going to prove expensive for both Egypt and Israel — as well as the United States," Wolf

---

[3] Mark Bruzonsky, "Assessing Camp David," *Worldview*, November 1978, p. 29.

Blitzer observed in *The Jewish Week* of Washington: "Prime Minister Begin and President Sadat are already making it clear to President Carter that they expect the United States to help meet the financial requirements generated by the proposed peace treaty."[4] While there are no figures yet available on what Washington will be asked to pay, it is certain to be much more than is now being expended on aid to Israel and Egypt.

Problem of the West Bank and Jerusalem

Whether the Camp David accords lead to a comprehensive Middle East settlement or to a separate Egyptian-Israeli peace will depend to a large extent on the participation of Jordan's King Hussein and at least some of the Palestinians living in the occupied West Bank and Gaza Strip. But Hussein is under many constraints not to join the negotiations. From the Arabs, the King would face the wrath of neighboring Syria and the unhappiness of Saudi Arabia, which has long demanded the return of East Jerusalem and its holy places to Arab control.

Furthermore, Jordan's population is about 50 percent Palestinian and these Palestinians are deeply interested in the fate of the West Bank. Israel's recent decision to expand existing settlements in the occupied territories was viewed by both Jordan and the Palestinians as proof that Israel has no intention of ever allowing the Palestinians any meaningful "self-determination." Cynics speculated that Begin approved the settlement expansion and continued to issue statements about the historic right of the Jewish people to the ancient lands of Judea and Samaria — which embrace the West Bank — to discourage Jordan and the Palestinians from participating in the negotiations.[5]

Palestinians living in the West Bank and Gaza, more than one million in all,[6] appear increasingly opposed to an agreement which (1) does not provide for the participation of the PLO or the return of a sizable number of Palestinian refugees, (2) gives Israel a veto over the "final status" of the area and (3) allows Israeli troops to remain and Jewish settlements to be maintained and expanded. Even the few Palestinians who are more sympathetic to King Hussein than to the PLO tend to regard the

---

[4] Wolf Blitzer, "New U.S. Commitments Seen in Wake of Pact," *The Jewish Week*, Oct. 28-Nov. 1, 1978, p. 2.

[5] Others regarded Israel's decision as a response to the meetings of U.S. Assistant Secretary of State Harold Saunders with Jordanian officials and West Bank residents. Saunders, who was sent by the administration to persuade Jordan and the West Bankers to join the negotiations, confirmed U.S. opposition to "illegal settlements in the West Bank" and the present status of "conquered East Jerusalem." Rowland Evans and Robert Novak, in their syndicated column appearing in *The Washington Post* on Oct. 30, said that these statements "infuriated the Israeli government" and convinced Begin to go "public with his long-nourished plan to 'thicken' the settlements."

[6] About 750,000 Palestinians live in the West Bank and over 400,000 in Gaza. Fewer than 500,000 live in Israel itself, 1.1 million are in Jordan, 400,000 in Lebanon, over one million in other Arab states, and 30,000 in non-Arab countries.

agreement for their "self-determination" as an Israeli plot to avoid giving them any real autonomy.

What the vast majority of Palestinians under occupation as well as the PLO want is an independent Palestinian state, and they see little prospect for such an outcome in the Camp David

agreements. However, many Israeli Jews are convinced that Camp David will lead to the creation of such a state. David Landau reported in the English-language *Jerusalem Post* on Oct. 6 that a public opinion poll published in late September showed that 90 percent of those asked "opposed the creation of an independent Palestinian state and yet 50 percent believed that as a result of the Camp David agreements an independent Palestinian state would arise." Still, 75 percent supported the Camp David accords.

The most emotional issue in the very emotional West Bank dispute is the city of Jerusalem, specifically the fate of East Jerusalem — often referred to as the Old City or Arab Jerusalem. This small area, containing places holy to Christianity, Judaism and Islam and inhabited by about 20,000 Arabs, 2,000 Armenians and 1,000 Jews, was seized by Israel in the 1967 war and annexed. The United States has never recognized the annexation.

Proposals like Jerusalem Mayor Teddy Kollek's to create Arab and Jewish boroughs with some measure of self-rule within a united city have been rejected by the Arabs, particularly the Saudis.[7] Arabs are united in demanding that the Old City be under Arab sovereignty. In a press conference on Nov. 1, Prime Minister Begin argued: "Jerusalem is a united city, indivisible, the eternal capital of the State of Israel, morally, culturally and

---

[7] Kollek's proposal was presented in an article, titled "Jerusalem," in the July 1977 issue of *Foreign Affairs* magazine.

historically, and so it will be from generation to generation, forever."

In December 1975, the Brookings Institution released a much-publicized study entitled "Toward Peace in the Middle East." Both Zbigniew Brzezinski, who was to become Carter's national security adviser, and William Quandt, who is today the National Security Council's Middle Eastern expert, participated in the study. The Brookings report concluded that while "no solution will be able to satisfy fully the demands" of either Arabs or Israelis, the Jerusalem "issue must be resolved if there is to be a stable peace."

Public opinion surveys throughout the last decade reveal that the vast majority of Israelis are opposed to returning the West Bank to Arab control and the Golan Heights to Syria. Security considerations are a major factor, perhaps the biggest, in Israeli reluctance to surrender the Golan. Unlike President Sadat, Syrian President Hafez Assad is viewed as an intractable hardliner unprepared to accept the existence of the Jewish state. Israeli settlements established on the Golan are an obstacle to a Syrian invasion of Israel and Syrian bombardment of Israeli villages below. Nevertheless, both Egyptian and American officials have advised Assad that if he were to join the negotiations, Israel would be unable to ignore the precedent established in its agreement to withdraw from the Sinai and remove its settlements there in exchange for peace with Egypt.

So far President Assad has shown no inclination to join the Camp David talks and has been one of the most virulent critics of Sadat and the accords. But there is no guarantee that the Syrian position will not change, particularly if reports that President Assad is suffering from a fatal illness are true. With Egypt's removal from the Arab-Israeli conflict, with 30,000 Syrian troops bogged down in a no-win conflict with Israeli-supplied and -supported Christian militias in neighboring Lebanon, and with the Syrian economy in need of drastic overhaul, Syria's options have been reduced considerably.

Critical Soviet Position in the Middle East

One option for Syria and other opponents of Camp David is closer ties with the Soviet Union. Both President Assad and PLO Chairman Yassir Arafat conferred with Soviet leader Leonid Brezhnev soon after Camp David and received support for their rejection of the agreements. But Syria and the PLO have been under pressure not to accede to the demands of the Algerians, South Yemenis, Libyans and Iraqis to form an alliance with the Russians against the "Zionist-imperialist enemy." The main pressure comes from the oil-rich Persian Gulf states, particularly Saudi Arabia, which subsidize Syria and the PLO and whose enmity toward communism exceeds their antagonism toward Israel.

Nevertheless, Arab hard-liners seem to have little choice but to turn to the Soviet Union for support and weapons, despite rather widespread suspicions about Russian intentions and disappointment with Kremlin assistance. And what Moscow wants — a return to the Geneva Conference at which it would serve as co-chairman with the United States — is bitterly opposed by the radical Arab governments in Algeria, Iraq and Libya. They oppose any direct negotiations with Israel. Ironically, the Soviet desire for a reconvening of the Geneva Conference was the stated American objective until Sadat's visit to Jerusalem a year ago.

The Geneva Conference on the Middle East was first convened in December 1973 but recessed after only two days of ceremonial and propagandistic exchanges. With the prospects of a comprehensive peace involving all parties to the Middle Eastern conflict and the Soviet Union seemingly out of reach, Secretary of State Henry A. Kissinger embarked on his step-by-step "shuttle diplomacy." But Carter, soon after assuming the presidency in January 1977, discarded the step-by-step approach in favor of a comprehensive settlement. This resulted in the Soviet-American statement of Oct. 1, 1977, calling for a Geneva Conference "not later than December 1977" to work out a full resolution of the Arab-Israeli conflict "incorporating all parties concerned and all questions" *(see box)*.

The reaction of Israel and the American Jewish lobby to the Soviet-American statement was swift and visceral. Fearing that it would allow the PLO to participate in the conference, Israeli officials and their American supporters put sufficient pressure on the Carter administration to scuttle the guidelines for Geneva. The Egyptian reaction to the guidelines was also negative. Since 1972, when Sadat expelled 20,000 Russian military advisers from Egypt, Soviet-Egyptian relations had turned increasingly sour. A Geneva Conference, with the Soviet Union as co-chairman, was no more appealing to Sadat than it was to the Israelis, and the unpleasant prospect that the conference might be reconvened is often cited as an underlying reason for Sadat's decision to visit Jerusalem and ask for peace.

While Egypt and Israel appear quite delighted with Soviet exclusion from the Camp David accords,[8] the United States does

---

[8] The chief editor of the semi-official Egyptian newspaper, *Al Ahram*, Ali Hamdi Gamal, wrote on Oct. 20, 1978, that "Soviet hysteria and nervousness" about Camp David stems from Russia's exclusion from the peace process. "The achievement of peace without Moscow's participation means the final disappearance of Soviet influence from the area."

not seem completely comfortable. A number of high-ranking American officials have warned in off-the-record interviews that a stable and comprehensive peace in the Middle East is virtually impossible without Moscow's participation. Before the Camp David accords, Nahum Goldmann, former president of the World Jewish Congress and the World Zionist Organization, reached the same conclusion. "Any attempt to eliminate the U.S.S.R. from the area is, in my opinion, unwise and short-sighted," Goldmann wrote in *Foreign Affairs* this fall.

> The Soviet Union [he continued] is certainly not strong enough to impose a peace agreement in the Middle East, but it is well capable of sabotaging any settlement reached without it. . . . Whatever may be achieved in the direct negotiations undertaken between the Israeli and Egyptian representatives will make necessary a reconvocation of the Geneva Conference, notwithstanding the reluctance of Israel and some Arab states.[9]

Soviet influence is already strong in Syria, Iraq, Libya, Algeria, South Yemen, the PLO and along the periphery in Afghanistan and Ethiopia. The instability in Iran and Lebanon could lead to Russian gains in those countries as well. Eric Rouleau, Middle East editor of the Paris newspaper *Le Monde,* warned that the Camp David accords could lead to further polarization in the Arab world between supporters of the United States and the Soviet Union. "When you divide the Arab world, you make a settlement with Israel much more difficult" and open "the way for strife and possibly military conflict. If this does happen, then it would be preferable to have had no Camp David."[10]

Roots Of Middle East Conflict

THAT PEACE in the Middle East has proved elusive is hardly surprising. The Arab-Isaeli problem involves so many deep-seated conflicts and interests that a truly comprehensive settlement has seemed but a pipe dream for most of the past three decades. The conflict involves the collision of two movements, Arab nationalism and Zionism,[11] and the displacement of large numbers of Palestinian Arabs by foreign-born Jews. It also has strategic, economic and religious significance.

---

[9] Nahum Goldmann, "Zionist Ideology and the Reality of Israel," *Foreign Affairs,* fall 1978, p. 80.

[10] Interview by Mark Bruzonsky in "Begin's Triumph: Carter's and Sadat's Gamble," *The Middle East,* November 1978, p. 64.

[11] Zionism, or Jewish nationalism, began in Europe in the late 19th century with the aim of establishing a home for the Jews "in the land of our forefathers." The name Zionism came from Zion, a hill in Jerusalem on which King David's palace stood. In biblical writing, Zion is a synonym for Jerusalem.

The Middle East is an area of competition between the world's superpowers, the United States and Russia; its oil bears heavily on world economic stability; and finally it is a land sacred to Jews, Christians and Moslems.

European Zionists wanting to establish a homeland in Palestine received their first real encouragement on Nov. 2, 1917, when British Foreign Secretary Arthur Balfour wrote to Lord Rothschild, leader of the British Zionists. That letter, subsequently known as the Balfour Declaration, stated: "His Majesty's Government view with favour the establishment in Palestine of a national home for the Jewish people, and will use their best endeavours to facilitate the achievement of this object, it being clearly understood that nothing shall be done which may prejudice the civil and religious rights of existing non-Jewish communities in Palestine." At the time the declaration was issued, Britain had no legal jurisdiction over Palestine although its military forces were then, in World War I, pushing out the occupying Turks; it was not until July 1922 that the League of Nations approved the British Mandate in Palestine.

Britain sought in the White Paper of 1939 to reassure the Palestinians, who were becoming increasingly restive over the influx of Jewish settlers into Palestine. The White Paper, a policy statement, put restrictions on Jewish immigration and declared that "the object of His Majesty's government is the establishment within ten years of an independent Palestine State." The Jews totally rejected the White Paper and three underground militias, the Haganah, the Stern and the Irgun, began battling British forces. Probably the most publicized of these attacks was the blowing up of the King David Hotel on July 23, 1947. The attack, in which 91 persons were killed, was carried out by the Irgun, then led by Menachem Begin.

By that time, Britain had notified the United Nations that it could no longer continue its role in Palestine. On Nov. 29, 1947, the General Assembly approved a partition plan alloting 5,579 square miles to a Jewish state and 4,421 to an Arab state. Both the United States and the Soviet Union supported the resolution. The Palestinians resorted to arms to block a plan which would give the Jewish minority considerably more land than the Arab majority.[12] In the civil war that followed, the Jews were able to secure the land they were allotted and, when the British mandate expired on May 14, 1948, they proclaimed the establishment of the state of Israel. The United States and the Soviet Union were the first two countries to recognize the new nation.

The next day, the armies of five neighboring Arab nations —

---

[12] According to United Nations estimates, the population of Palestine was 1,972,559 as of Dec. 31, 1946. Of this number, 1,364,332 were Arabs and 608,225 were Jews.

Egypt, Transjordan, Iraq, Syria and Lebanon — invaded Israel. The result was an Arab defeat in the first Arab-Israeli war, bitter feuds among the Arab governments, assassinations and upheavals in several countries, Jordan's annexation of the West Bank, Egypt's seizure of the Gaza Strip and the influx of unwanted Palestinians into other Arab countries. When the shooting finally stopped early the next year, Israel held over 30 percent more territory than it had been assigned under the U.N. partition plan and almost a million Palestinians had fled their homeland. The Arab humiliation and the Palestinian refugee problem made it impossible for any Arab leader to accept, at least publicly, the existence of Israel.

Problems of Refugees and Outside Powers

On Dec. 11, 1948, the U.N. General Assembly adopted Resolution 194 saying that Palestinian "refugees wishing to return to their homes and live in peace with their neighbors should be permitted to do so at the very earliest practicable date and compensation should be paid for the property of those choosing not to return." But Israel refused to repatriate more than a handful of refugees or pay compensation, and Arab countries opposed a repatriation which might be interpreted as recognition of the Jewish state. The failure of the U.N's repatriation effort made it possible for Israel to settle almost a million Jewish immigrants from 40 countries between 1948 and 1960. These years also witnessed the growth of Arab nationalism and a growing involvement by the United States and the Soviet Union in the area.

During the Eisenhower administration (1953-60), American policy in the Middle East was premised on stability and anti-communism. Such a policy involved support, including military support, for conservative Arab governments. Israel's requests for arms were repeatedly turned down and it was forced to turn to France for most of its military equipment. In the early 1960s the United States began to review its weapons ban and after 1967, when France cut off arms to Israel, Washington became Israel's major supplier.

Despite American fears in the late 1940s and early 1950s, Soviet inroads in the Middle East did not really materialize until 1955, three years after Gamal Abdel Nasser seized power in Egypt. Nasser, a nationalist, refused to join the U.S.-sponsored, anti-Soviet Baghdad Pact[13] in 1955 and soon afterward turned to the Soviet bloc for military equipment. Washington responded to Nasser's deepening ties with the Russians by withdrawing an offer of American aid to finance the Aswan

---

[13] Members of the Baghdad Pact were Britain, Iran, Iraq, Pakistan and Turkey. In 1958, Iraq withdrew after its pro-Western government was replaced by one favorable to the Soviets.

Dam. Nasser retaliated on July 26, 1956, by nationalizing the Suez Canal, saying he would use canal tolls to pay for the Aswan project.

Three months later, Israel and the canal's major shareholders, Britain and France, attacked Egypt. Only U.S. and Soviet pressure for U.N. intervention forced the invaders to withdraw. Nasser emerged from the Suez War a hero throughout the Arab world. Angered that no other country had come to Egypt's aid in the 1956 conflict, he used his new prestige to revolutionize and unify the Arab world. To this end, Egypt either instigated or supported revolutions in Syria, Jordan, Iraq, Lebanon, Saudi Arabia and Yemen.[14] By the early 1960s, Nasser's revolutionary ardor had brought the Arab world to almost total disarray. But as Arab leaders have demonstrated before and since, even the most bitter of their quarrels can be patched up with amazing speed.

At a summit conference in Cairo in January 1964, the same leaders who had denounced each other a few weeks earlier embraced and temporarily buried their differences. The reason for the reconciliation was the near completion of Israel's project of diverting the waters of the Jordan River to the Negev Desert. At the conference, Arab leaders agreed to set up a Palestine Liberation Organization to represent the Palestinian people. The early PLO, however, was created and controlled by Nasser and began not so much as the representative of the Palestinians but as a tool of Egyptian policy.

In retrospect at least, the formation of the PLO seemed inevitable. Many of the Palestinians rendered homeless by the creation of Israel survived as best they could in refugee camps administered by the United Nations. Describing the plight of these refugees, Don Peretz wrote in *Israel and the Palestine Arabs* (1958): "Many living in leaky, torn tents were middle-class urbanites who had owned modest but adequate houses in their native land. . . . The self-reliance and individual initiative of former tradesmen and farmers were drowned in the boredom and frustration which the camps bred." This frustration contributed to the growth of Palestinian resistance groups.[15]

Consequences of Israel's Victory in 1967

The PLO did not emerge as an autonomous faction in the Arab world and the Palestinian issue was widely considered a minor, if emotional, problem outside the area until Israel's victory in the June 1967 war. After six days of fighting, the third

---

[14] While the United States opposed most of these revolutions, it intervened militarily in only one. American troops were sent to Lebanon in July 1958 to protect the right-wing government of President Camille Chamoun from a Nasser-supported Moslem rebellion.

[15] See "Palestinian Question," *E.R.R.* 1974 Vol. II, pp. 681-704.

Arab-Israeli war was over and Israel controlled the Egyptian Sinai, the Jordanian West Bank and the Syrian Golan Heights. The 1967 war also increased Israeli dependence on the United States and Arab dependence on the Soviet Union. The Kremlin advanced large amounts of military aid to Egypt and Syria, and Washington moved in to ensure that Israeli military superiority was not undermined. After the war, the Russians severed diplomatic ties with Israel while Egypt and six other Arab states cut off relations with the United States.

After the war, the United Nations, the United States and, according to President Sadat, the Soviet Union stepped up their efforts to resolve the Middle East conflict.[16] On Nov. 22, 1967, the U.N. Security Council unanimously approved Resolution 242. It called for withdrawal of Israeli forces from occupied Arab areas; an end to the state of belligerency; respect for and acknowledgement of the sovereignty, territorial integrity and political independence of every nation in the area; the establishment of "secure and recognized boundaries;" a guarantee of freedom of navigation through international waterways in the area; and a just settlement of the refugee problem. While there have been conflicting interpretations as to whether the document requires Israeli withdrawal from all or just some of the occupied territories, and while the Palestinians object to being relegated to a "refugee problem," Resolution 242 remains the most widely accepted basis for a comprehensive settlement of the conflict.[17]

Oil Power and U.S. Efforts at Settlement

For some time, both the United States and Israel seemed not to appreciate one important change in the Arab world: the death of Egyptian President Nasser in September 1970 and the succession of his vice-president, Anwar Sadat. Sadat moved far closer to conservative Saudi Arabia, called for peace with Israel rather than its destruction, expelled Soviet advisers from his country in July 1972 and sought better relations with the United States. Neither the Soviet expulsion nor Sadat's dispatch of high Egyptian officials to Washington in 1971 and early 1972 received much encouragement from the Nixon administration.

Had the United States responded to these changes, the 1973 Middle East war might never have occurred. Sadat has said that the main reason for the October war was to prevent the world from forgetting about Israel's occupation of Arab lands. There is

---

[16] In a speech to jurists in Cairo on Oct. 10, 1978, Sadat revealed that in early 1972, the Soviet Union had asked him to meet with Israeli Prime Minister Golda Meir in Tashkent to discuss a peace settlement. On Oct. 14, 1978, *Al Ahram* reported that soon after the 1967 war, the Russians advised Nasser to go to Washington and reach "an understanding with the Americans."

[17] American efforts, including the Rogers Plan, submitted by Secretary of State William P. Rogers on Dec. 9, 1969, were based on Resolution 242.

little doubt that the Arabs achieved this objective. Egyptian and Syrian forces fought better than they had previously, inflicted heavy casualties on the Israelis and emerged, if not victorious, at least neither defeated nor humiliated. But it was less the Arab armies than the Arab oil producers, led by Saudi Arabia, that achieved a political victory in the 1973 war.

Arab oil-producing states declared an embargo on exports to the United States after President Nixon announced his intention to ask Congress for $2.2 billion in military aid for Israel during the conflict. Saudi Arabia's price for lifting the embargo was a more active and evenhanded American role in trying to reach a Middle East settlement. The embargo was followed by a quadrupling of oil prices by the Organization of Petroleum Exporting Countries (OPEC) during the fall of 1973 and the following winter. The embargo and the price rise caused Western Europe and Japan to adopt a more pro-Arab stance, and the United States to become evenhanded in its policy.

Largely through the efforts of Secretary of State Kissinger, Egyptian and Israeli military negotiators signed a cease-fire agreement on Nov. 11, 1973. Kissinger's next effort was the reconvening of the Geneva Conference on Dec. 21. The participants were the United States, the Soviet Union, Egypt, Jordan, Israel and the United Nations. Syria boycotted the conference and the PLO, which was not represented, condemned it. The meeting lasted only two days and, according to a former Israeli official, Washington "realized that nothing useful could be achieved from a formal reconvening of such a meeting unless it were for the formal ratification of an agreement already achieved *outside* its format. The format itself was exactly the sort of formalistic stucture that would precipitate confrontation, polarization and futility."[18]

With Geneva and American hopes for a comprehensive settlement in disarray, Kissinger embarked on his "step-by-step approach." He eventually achieved two disengagement agreements in the Sinai in January 1974 and September 1975 and a separation-of-forces accommodation between Israel and Syria in May 1974. While the Camp David accords are often cited as the logical outcome of Kissinger's approach, his focus on partial accommodations resulted in considerable tension within the Arab world. The inter-Arab dissension that resulted was a major factor in the Lebanese civil war.[19] By the time the Arabs reached a rather tenuous peace in Lebanon in late 1976, the step-by-step approach seemed to have reached a dead end, and in both Israel

---

[18] Shlomo Avineri, "Peacemaking: The Arab-Israeli Conflict," *Foreign Affairs*, fall 1978, p. 58. Avineri was director-general of Israel's Ministry of Foreign Affairs in 1976-77.

[19] For Background, see "Arab Disunity," *E.R.R.*, 1976 Vol. II, pp. 785-806, and Congressional Quarterly's *The Middle East: U.S. Policy, Israel, Oil and the Arabs* (1977).

and the United States, the focus shifted to a comprehensive settlement.

The reasons most frequently cited for Sadat's dramatic visit to Jerusalem on Nov. 19, 1977, were the Egyptian President's conviction that in another war the Arabs would suffer a 1967-type defeat, his anger and frustration about involving the Soviet Union in a settlement, as outlined in the joint American-Soviet statement of Oct. 1, his fears of radical upheaval in Egypt and, finally, his belief that a face-to-face encounter between Arabs and Israelis would do much to remove the psychological barriers that separated them. *Time* magazine last summer revealed yet another factor.

Time reported in its Aug. 14 issue that "Israel has always maintained secret contacts with its Arab enemies, largely through Mossad," the Israeli intelligence service. Early in 1977, Mossad learned that "leftist Arab extremists, trained in Libya," were plotting to overthrow the moderate governments in Egypt, Saudi Arabia and the Sudan. In July, the magazine account continued, Prime Minister Begin decided to warn Egyptian, Saudi and Sudanese leaders of the danger and dispatched Foreign Minister Moshe Dayan "on a round of visits to Middle Eastern capitals." According to *Time,* "Dayan met at least twice with Jordan's King Hussein and Egyptian officials and three times with King Hassan II of Morocco." The center of "this diplomatic activity was Morocco, which has had close but secret relations with Israel since 1962."

> Dayan [*Time* continued] assured his Arab hosts that the Begin government was prepared to make more 'generous compromises than previous Israeli governments'. . . . Coming as they did on the heels of Israel's much-appreciated tip to Egypt, Dayan's proposals may well have persuaded Sadat that a dramatic trip to Jerusalem could bring a quick end to the 30-year Mideast impasse. [20]

Hard-line Arab reaction to the Jerusalem visit, despite Sadat's demand in the Israeli Knesset for full Israeli withdrawal from all occupied territories and his refusal to consider a separate peace, was loud and negative. Moderate Arabs tried to straddle the fence without alienating either Sadat or the hard-liners. Washington seemed initially surprised and confused and only later gave its full support to the peace effort. By early spring, there was evidence of growing American impatience with what was commonly termed Israeli "intransigence" and there were ill-disguised attempts to undermine the Begin government.

The Carter administration's desire to appear evenhanded and its unhappiness with Begin were reflected in a decision to sell

---

[20] "Israel's Secret Contacts," *Time,* Aug. 14, 1978, pp. 21-22. Begin became prime minister in May 1977.

warplanes to Egypt and Saudi Arabia as well as to Israel. After an intense lobbying campaign directed from the White House and an equally intense effort against the sale by the American Jewish lobby, Congress agreed to the sale on May 15. By summer, the Egyptian-Israeli negotiations seemed doomed, and there was growing fear in Washington that Sadat would break them off completely and seek peace not with Israel but with the Arab hard-liners. It was at this point that Carter intervened and invited Begin and Sadat to a summit conference at Camp David.

Danger of More Instability

PEACE between Egypt and Israel, if it is achieved, is not likely to decrease — and may actually increase — the dangers of instability and upheaval in the area. [21] While the chaos in Iran and Lebanon was evident long before Camp David became a household word, the upheavals in these two pro-Western nations may be a harbinger of what is in store for the rest of the region. Among Iran's 35 million people, opposition to the U.S.-backed government is widespread. This opposition is centered in the Islamic religious community, which condemns Shah Mohammad Reza Pahlavi's modernization programs. It also includes moderate politicians, leftist intellectuals and students who want an end to the shah's authoritarian rule, and workers who believe that they have received far too few benefits from Iran's oil bonanza.

To cope with the strikes and riots that have paralyzed Iran, the shah recently declared martial law and installed a military government. Washington seems to have had little choice but to support these actions, but this support has increased anti-American sentiment throughout the country. The United States apparently fears that, in the event of the shah's ouster, religious leaders would prove incapable of governing and would be replaced by a radical government strongly influenced by the Soviet Union with which Iran shares a 1,500-mile border. Such an outcome would seriously endanger American interests in Middle Eastern stability and put considerable pressure on the moderate governments in Saudi Arabia and the Gulf sheikdoms. [22]

---

[21] In his speech on Sept. 19, Sen. James Abourezk said that "without Egypt, the military balance will be tipped overwhelmingly in favor of Israel. Too weak militarily to threaten or even to negotiate on an equal basis, the remaining members of the Arab bloc will, in all probability, suffer deep divisions amongst themselves. Radicalism will be greatly encouraged, since it is the only real alternative left."

[22] In an interview with Bill Moyers shown on the Public Broadcasting System Nov. 13, 1978, Carter called the shah "a friend, a loyal ally." Soviet criticism of the shah has been relatively restrained in recent months.

The situation in Lebanon, where Israeli-supported Christian militias have been battling Syrian peacekeeping forces, has been less chaotic since the U.N. Security Council on Oct. 6 approved an American and Soviet call for a cease-fire. Nevertheless, the problems causing the unrest — the domination of the Moslem majority by the Christian minority and the presence of some 400,000 Palestinian refugees —— are no nearer a solution than they were during the bloody civil war of 1975-76. Middle East experts Kai Bird and Max Holland argue that American policy in Lebanon almost ensures a continuation of the sectarian conflict in that country.

> In the grand scheme of things in the Middle East [they wrote], conservative interests, including of course the United States and some of the established Arab regimes that pose as social welfare states, are determined to reimpose on Lebanon a system of government based on religious divisions. This determinatin guarantees renewed sectarian warfare in Lebanon. In the long-run, this American-engineered policy is a setback to the hopes of many that secular states devoid of religious fanaticism can grow in the Arab world. [23]

Until there is a just resolution of the Palestinian issue, the American quest for stability in Lebanon, the Arab world and Israel itself seems doomed to failure. And until the Palestinians have some hope that they will eventually have their own state, they are likely to continue as a radicalizing force throughout the Middle East. Statements by Israeli officials after Camp David ruling out such a state served to dampen whatever slim hope of genuine autonomy that Palestinians in the West Bank and Gaza might have had. But continued occupation of the areas seized in 1967 poses a threat to Israel. There are now almost 500,000 Arabs within the pre-1967 borders and over a million in the West Bank and Gaza. The total Arab population amounts to about 36 percent of the current Israeli population. Demographic trends indicate that within 30 years, there are likely to be more Arabs than Jews within the present boundaries.

There is also a threat of upheaval in Egypt. Unless peace brings some tangible improvement in Egypt's bankrupt economy, there is likely to be increasing opposition to Sadat, Camp David and reliance on the United States. Egypt needs large amounts of foreign capital and it is uncertain whether Saudi Arabia and other oil-rich Arab states will increase or decrease, or even continue, their subsidies to Sadat. The Saudis are obviously not happy with the Camp David agreement, but this unhappiness is tempered by concern that Sadat's ouster could result in a more radical, Nasser-type government in Egypt and an Egyptian-Soviet reconcilitation.

---

[23] "Lebanon's Late and Future War," *The Nation*, July 1, 1978, p. 7.

The desire to "establish some common barriers to further Soviet expansion in the region" was behind the proposal by Sen. Henry M. Jackson, D-Wash. to set up an American aid program for the Middle East modeled on the Marshall Plan for Europe after World War II. Jackson, a strong defender of Israel and critic of the Soviet Union, warned in a speech on Sept. 30: "We must make it plain that those who are unwilling to join with us and Israel and Egypt will lose out on the economic and other benefits of cooperation and mutual assistance." [24] Proposals like Jackson's tend to ignore the fact that several Arab hard-liners have the resources to subsidize opponents of the Camp David accords and that the American people may be unwilling to spend billions of dollars on the Middle East.

Fear of Arabs Renewing the 'Oil Weapon'

A big, and as yet unanswered, question is what steps the Arab oil producers will take to increase pressure on Israel to meet Arab demands for a full peace settlement. The oil embargo and price rises that followed the 1973 war are a strong reminder of the leverage that the Arab oil producers can exercise. By 1978, however, there are numerous constraints on the use of oil power. A large price increase would wreak havoc and possibly precipitate a depression in the industrialized world. While some of the more hard-line Arab states like Iraq have been demanding a doubling of oil prices, there is mounting evidence that Saudi demands for a far smaller increase will be approved when OPEC oil ministers meet in Abu Dhabi on Dec. 16. [25]

Even if, as expected, the Saudis and other oil states continue to cut production, these reductions are unlikely to have much immediate effect on the industrialized world. There is currently an oil glut, and most of the oil producers need the revenues to pay for their vast modernization and industrialization projects. The strike by oil refinery workers in Iran reduced the glut considerably, but that strike apparently has fizzled.

Nonetheless pressure from the oil producers cannot be ruled out. Saudi Arabia, which has almost a quarter of the world's proven reserves and provides almost 25 percent of America's oil imports, could put considerable pressure on countries supporting Israel if it chose to do so. And if the shah of Iran were replaced by a ruler less sympathetic to Israel, the Jewish state might find itself faced with serious oil shortages. It is believed that Israel currently depends on Iran for at least half of its oil.

---

[24] Address to members of the Coalition for a Democratic Majority in New York. President Sadat has called for a "Carter Plan," based on the Marshall Plan, which would give Egypt "$10 billion to $15 billion" over the next five years.

[25] The Lebanese newspaper *Al-Anwar* reported on Nov. 1, that oil prices will be raised by 15 percent to cope with high inflation and the drop in the value of the dollar. The Kuwaiti newspaper *As Siyahah* reported on Nov. 5 that Arab oil producers had agreed to limit the price rise to 10 percent. Many expect a smaller increase.

The *Near East Report* revealed recently that "in addition to concern over its oil supply, Israel is concerned by the violence in Iran because of its quiet trade and military ties to the shah and out of fear for Iran's 80,000 Jews. Opponents to both the left and right of the shah are more receptive to the Arab cause and less well disposed to the Jewish community. But it is oil that is the biggest problem. As if the potential cutoff from Iran weren't enough, Israel will soon be turning over oil fields in the Sinai to Egypt. [26]

Egypt has agreed in principle to sell Israel the 200,000 barrels of oil a day that is currently being pumped from the Israeli-occupied Sinai fields, but this supply could be cut off if relations between the two countries deteriorated. Under a secret addendum to the 1975 Sinai II agreements, the United States is committed to guaranteeing enough oil to Israel to meet "normal" requirements if Israel's supplies were cut off. In the short-term, at least, this could create problems for both Washington and Jerusalem. In the longer term, the development of oil fields in Mexico and, to a lesser extent, off the China coast, the North Sea and Alaska's North Slope is likely to lessen world dependence on Arab oil.

Chances for a Comprehensive Peace Pact

The prospects of Camp David evolving into the comprehensive settlement that President Carter has long advocated do not look particularly promising at this time. "There can be no stable peace" until the Palestinian problem and Israel's relations with Jordan, Syria and Lebanon are resolved, former U.N. Ambassador Charles W. Yost wrote in *The Christian Science Monitor* on Oct. 6. "With the Palestinians and Syrians frustrated and bitterly angry, and with radical Arabs and the Soviet Union ready to fuel their anger and Jordan and Saudi Arabia unwilling for sound reasons to disavow them, neither Israel nor Egypt would be secure."

> The U.S. [Yost continued] would be foolish merely to press King Hussein and the Saudis to do what they cannot do — deliver Palestinian support of the Camp David agreement as written and as interpreted by Mr. Begin. If he will not deal with Palestinians in the liberal fashion which has any chance of producing a settlement, we shall have to do so. And to do so, we shall have to deal with various sorts of Palestinians, including the PLO.

Under the 1975 Sinai II disengagement agreement, the United States promised Israel that it would not negotiate with the PLO until the organization explicitly recognized Israel's right to exist.

---

[26] "Israel Could Be First to Feel Impact of Shah's Troubles," *Near East Report*, Nov. 8, 1978. *Near East Report* is published by pro-Israeli lobbyists in Washington.

There have been reports that some form of recognition may be forthcoming at the Palestine National Council meeting in Damascus in December. The PLO policy-making body is also expected to call unconditionally for the establishment of an independent Palestinian state in the West Bank and Gaza at that meeting.

The great majority of Israeli Jews seem adamantly opposed to the creation of a Palestinian state, and the United States, fearful that such a state would be dominated by the more radical factions in the PLO and would turn to the Soviet Union for support, has shown little enthusiasm for a new state between Israel and Jordan. But to date, Washington has been unsuccessful in its efforts to find more "moderate" Palestinian leadership on the West Bank.

Walid Khalidi, a Palestinian who was born in Jerusalem and currently is a research fellow at the Harvard Center for International Affairs, has written that the only solution to the Palestine problem, and hence to the entire Middle East conflict, is "a sovereign Palestinian state." Khalidi discounts Israeli and American fears that such a state would pose a mortal danger to Israel. "Any PLO leadership would take the helm in a Palestinian state with few illusions about the efficacy of revolutionary armed struggle in a direct confrontation with Israel. They would be acutely aware of its costs."[27]

Another impediment to a comprehensive settlement based on the Camp David accords is the strong opposition of the Soviet Union. Marshall Shulman, special adviser to Secretary of State Cyrus R. Vance on Soviet affairs, told the House International Relations Subcommittee on Europe and the Middle East on Sept. 26: "The Soviet Union has sought to become an active participant in Middle East negotiations through the convening of a Geneva conference, and it has bitterly expressed its frustrations at the course of events that followed President Sadat's trip to Jerusalem, leading to the Camp David summit meeting."

The improvement in Soviet-American relations in recent months and the desire of both nations to conclude a strategic arms limitation treaty (SALT) may encourage the two superpowers to cooperate in finding a comprehensive solution to the Arab-Israeli conflict. Without such cooperation, the outlook for the Camp David agreements is at best a fragile and unstable Egyptian-Israeli peace and at worst an intensification of the chaos and upheavals that have wracked the area for more than three decades.

---

[27] Walid Khalidi, "A Sovereign Palestinian State," *Foreign Affairs*, July 1978, pp. 701, 713.

Books

Cohen, Saul B., *Jerusalem: Bridging the Four Walls,* Westview, 1978.

Jiryis, Sabri, *The Arabs in Israel,* The Institute for Palestine Studies, 1977.

Mangold, Peter, *The Great Powers and Middle East Politics,* Lexington Books, 1977.

Quandt, William B., *Decade of Decisions, 1967-1976,* University of California Press, 1977.

Rostow, Eugene V., *The Middle East: Critical Choices for the United States,* Westview, 1977.

Sadat, Anwar, *In Search of Identity: An Autobiography,* Harper & Row, 1978.

Safran, Nadav, *Israel: The Embattled Ally,* Harvard University Press, 1978.

Sheehan, Edward R. F., *The Arabs, Israelis and Kissinger,* Reader's Digest Press, 1976.

Stevens, Richard P., *American Zionism and U.S. Foreign Policy,* Pageant Press, 1962.

The Middle East: U.S. Policy, Israel, Oil and the Arabs, Congressional Quarterly Inc., 1977, third ed.

Articles

Ball, George W., "America's Interests in the Middle East," *Harper's,* October 1978.

Bird, Kai and Max Holland, "Lebanon's Late and Future War," *The Nation,* July 1, 1978.

Bruzonsky, Mark, "Assessing Camp David," *Worldview,* November 1978.

Commentary, selected issues.

Eliot, Alexander, "What Shall Become of Jerusalem the Golden?" *The Atlantic,* October 1978.

Foreign Affairs, selected issues.

Foreign Broadcast Information Service, Department of Commerce, "The Middle East and North Africa," selected issues.

Foreign Policy, selected issues.

Journal of Palestine Studies, selected issues.

Kohut, Andrew, "American Opinion on Shifting Sands," *Public Opinion,* May-June 1978.

The Middle East, selected issues.

Morgenthau, Hans J., "An Unsteady Mideast Framework," *The New Leader,* Oct. 9, 1978.

Rosen, Steven J., "What the Next Arab-Israeli War Might Look Like," *International Security,* spring 1978.

Reports and Studies

The Brookings Institution, "Toward Peace in the Middle East," December 1975.

Department of State, "Annual Review of U.S. Middle East Policy," July 1978.

Editorial Research Reports, "Arab Disunity," 1976 Vol. II, p. 787; "Israeli Society After 25 Years," 1973 Vol. I, p. 315; "Middle East Diplomacy," 1975 Vol. I, p. 349; "Middle East Reappraisal," 1973 Vol. II, p. 949; "Palestinian Question," 1974 Vol. II, p. 683; "Saudi Arabia's Backstage Diplomacy," 1978 Vol. I, p. 23.

CHINA'S OPENING DOOR

by

Mary Costello

**Sept. 8
1 9 7 8**

Editor's Note: President Carter's commitment to establish "normal relations with China," in fulfillment of the 1972 Shanghai communiqué (p. 123), came about on Jan. 1, 1979. The president had unexpectedly announced to a national television audience two weeks earlier, on Dec. 15, that the two countries would send ambassadors to each other's capitals in the new year.

Moreover, acquiescing to Peking's longstanding demands, he said the United States would sever relations with the Nationalist Chinese government on Taiwan and let America's defense treaty with Taiwan expire.

Deputy Premier Teng Hsiao-ping of the People's Republic visited the United States, Jan. 28-Feb. 5. By extending his visit beyond Washington to the industrial centers of Atlanta, Houston and Seattle, he dramatized his country's quest for U.S. technological aid and its drive for modernization.

CHINA'S OPENING DOOR

A CENTURY AGO, the European powers were busy carving out economic spheres of influence in China. To ensure that China remained territorially intact and "open" to all outside interests, the United States, in 1899, asked the European governments to agree to an Open Door policy in China. The Chinese, who never forgot the humiliation they suffered at the hands of foreigners, now are beginning to open a few doors of their own. The leaders who came to power after Mao Tse-tung died on Sept. 9, 1976, seem determined to modernize China and bring it out of its relative isolation.

Mao's successor, Communist Party Chairman and Premier Hua Kuo-feng, has paid dutiful lip service to Maoist theory and practice. But Hua's insistence on the need to upgrade agriculture, industry, education, defense and particularly science and technology is in many respects a reversal of Mao's doctrines of "uninterrupted revolution" and "self-sufficiency." Hua told a national conference on finance and trade in Peking on July 7, 1978, that China should "learn everything that is advanced from other countries."

The Fifth National People's Congress (NPC), held in Peking from Feb. 26 to March 6, 1978, adopted an ambitious eight-year development plan. Among other things, the plan called for a tripling of steel production, a 40 percent increase in grain production, an annual industrial growth rate of 10 percent a year and the development of over 100 large industrial projects.

Hua Kuo-feng appears determined to avoid repetition of the chaos and anarchy that followed the Mao-inspired Great Proletarian Cultural Revolution of 1966 (see p. 120) Shortly after Mao's death, the so-called Gang of Four were arrested for their activities during and after that upheaval; since then, the four radicals have been labeled "ultra-rightists" and blamed for nearly every problem confronting China.[1]

China's new leaders have not challenged Mao's anti-Soviet policies and, in fact, have sought to improve relations with nations opposed to Russian "imperialism." Foreign Minister

---

[1] The Gang of Four includes Mao's widow Chiang Ching, former director of the People's Liberation Army (PLA) Political Department Chang Chun-chiao, journalist Yao Wen-yuan and former Deputy Premier Wang Hung-wen. The Japanese newspaper *Asahi Shimbun* reported in August that the Gang of Four would be put on trial later this year.

Huang Hua told a United Nations disarmament conference on May 29, 1978, that the Soviet Union, "flaunting the label of socialism, is more aggressive and adventurous than the other superpower; it is the most dangerous source of a new world war and is sure to be its chief instigator."

Chinese foreign policy is based both on the desire to contain Soviet influence and the need for outside aid in modernizing China. According to Chinese spokesmen, Peking's recent feud with communist Vietnam is due to Hanoi's harsh treatment of Chinese living in Vietnam. Others, including President Carter's National Security Adviser Zbigniew Brzezinski, contend that the conflict is a result of Vietnam's increasingly close relations with Moscow. China, which supports the repressive and reclusive regime in Democratic Kampuchea (Cambodia) in its border war with Hanoi, withdrew its aid and advisers from Vietnam in July.

Peking also is challenging the Soviet Union closer to home. Last month, Chairman Hua visited Romania (a member of the Soviet-controlled Warsaw Pact), Yugoslavia and Iran. This was Hua's second trip outside China since he came to power two years ago.[2] He is expected to visit France, and possibly West Germany, later this year.

Members of the North Atlantic Treaty Organization (NATO) and the European Economic Community (EEC) have been warned repeatedly about the Russian threat and approached for military and technological equipment. Earlier this year, Japan and China signed an eight-year, $20 billion trade agreement and, on Aug. 12, concluded a peace and friendship treaty. Peking also has become more and more active in Africa, Asia and the Middle East *(see p. 117)*. While U.S.-Soviet relations have deteriorated in the past year, contacts between Washington and Peking have increased considerably. High-level government officials and delegations of U.S. businessmen, farmers, scientists, scholars and tourists are visiting China in increasing numbers. In addition, American oil company executives have been invited to Peking to discuss exploration and development of China's vast offshore oil reserves *(see box p. 658)*. Former President Nixon, who initiated the U.S.-China dialogue *(see p. 655)*, is expected to visit Peking in the next few months.

Considerable attention has been given to the handful of men who currently lead China's estimated 930 million people.[3] Some analysts believe that those in control are more or less in agreement about the need to modernize China quickly and contain the

---

[2] Hua visited North Korea in May 1978. Chairman Mao made only two trips abroad in 27 years as head of state; he visited Moscow in 1949 and 1957.

[3] As of July 1, 1978. This estimate was compiled by the Population Reference Bureau from United Nations figures and other data. No exact figure is available since China has not conducted a national census.

Soviet Union. But others perceive certain strains and potential conflicts among the leaders. A major and as yet unanswered question is how far and for how long the current leadership can carry on programs of de-Maoification while basing those same programs on Mao's dictates.

Potential Conflicts Among New Leaders

In theory, at least, the most powerful figure in China is 58-year-old Hua Kuo-feng. Hua serves as head of the Chinese Communist Party, Premier of the country and Commander in Chief of the People's Liberation Army (PLA). Not even Mao at the height of his power held all three posts. But until his recent trip to Eastern Europe, Hua was a relatively obscure figure outside China. Far more colorful and, to many observers, far more influential is 74-year-old Teng Hsiao-ping, First Vice Premier, Vice Chairman of the Party and Chief of the General Staff. Hua was little known and generally regarded as a compromise candidate when Mao chose him as Premier after Chou En-lai's death in January 1976. He became Party Chairman after Mao's death. Hua, who reportedly impressed Chou with his administrative ability and Mao with his loyalty, is often pictured as trying to balance the factions wanting faster modernization with those demanding a more orthodox or Maoist approach. Teng Hsiao-ping, outspoken by Chinese standards, is widely viewed as a pragmatist and a progressive.

Hua Kuo-feng

Twice purged by Mao as a "capitalist roader," Teng "has shown himself eager to shed the deadweight of Maoist policies in order to launch a rapid modernization program," Victor Zorza wrote. "Hua, who owes his present position to Mao's belief that he would preserve Maoism, pays lip service to modernization but would obviously prefer to make haste more slowly."[4] Teng is also eager for closer relations with the United States and has been increasingly critical of the Soviet Union.

Reports of a bitter dispute between Hua and Teng have appeared in both the Western and Soviet press. Hua apparently tried to squelch these rumors in his remarks about modernization at the finance and trade conference on July 7. Nevertheless, the rumors persist. David Bonavia wrote that "the implications of a falling out between Teng and Hua are so serious for China's political stability that there is a natural reluctance on the part of

---

[4] Victor Zorza, "The de-Maoization of China," *The Guardian*, May 7, 1978, p. 9.

many observers to believe in it until harder evidence is available.
However, the last great political struggle, which culminated in
the overthrow of the Gang of Four in 1976, was couched in such
abstruse terms for most of its duration that no scrap of evidence
pointing to high-level conflict can ever again be safely ignored."[5]

The Trilateral Commission noted in a recent report that while
the supporters of modernization seem to
have emerged victorious over the
ideologues, there still are obstacles to be
overcome. "As recently as April 1976,"
the commission said, "Hua had still condemned and deposed Teng for advocating
the very views that are now proclaimed as
official, and he only turned against the
'radicals' in the short and sharp struggle
for the succession after the death of
Mao."

Among the difficulties the modern-
izers face, the commission noted, are
Teng Hsiao-ping
"the anti-pragmatic indoctrination which the younger generation received in the course of the Cultural Revolution," the loss
of "technical or scientific training" during and after that upheaval and the "still doubtful stability of the restored Party institutions."[6]

Stress on Productivity and Development

In his speech to the National People's Congress last March,
Hua Kuo-feng urged his people to "make China a great and
powerful socialist country with modern agriculture, industry,
national defense and science and technology by the end of the
century." To meet the ambitious goals Hua called for, "stability
and economic progress have again become China's first order of
business."[7]

In addition to the emphasis on rapid modernization, Chinese
leaders also are trying to make life easier for their people. The
principal Chinese policy journal, *Red Flag,* noted in its June 1978
issue: "As a result of the country's technical and economic
backwardness and its large population, the amount of capital
and consumer goods China is now able to produce for each individual is very small.... China must control the growth of its

---

[5] "Hint of Distant Thunder," *Far Eastern Economic Review,* June 23, 1978, p. 20.

[6] Jeremy R. Azrael, Richard Lowenthal and Tohru Nakagawa, "An Overview of East-West
Relations" (1978), pp. 13-14. The Trilateral Commission is a private group set up in 1973 to
foster cooperation among the nations of Western Europe, Japan and North America. Both
President Carter and Zbigniew Brzezinski served on the commission.

[7] Beau Grosscup, "Mao's Lost Vision," *The Progressive,* March 1978, p. 38. Grosscup
teaches politics at Ithaca College in New York State.

population to accumulate more funds for construction to improve people's life."[8]

According to Population Reference Bureau estimates, the per capita GNP in China now is $410 a year, up from $350 in 1977. Most Chinese workers were given pay increases in the last year; for many it was the first raise in more than two decades. And to increase productivity, the new constitution adopted a "policy of combining moral encouragement with material reward...in order to heighten the citizen's socialist enthusiasm and creativeness in work." Mao had condemned material incentives as "bourgeois."

These pay increases and incentives are likely to spur the demand for consumer goods that already is evident for items like television sets, fashions, particularly women's skirts,[9] bicycles, watches and sewing machines. More books are available, including works by Shakespeare who was banned during the Cultural Revolution as a "reactionary bourgeois." Traditional operas, films and theater productions are replacing the stilted ideological fare of the Cultural Revolution and even some churches are being allowed to reopen.

---

[8] The Fifth National People's Congress called for an annual population growth rate of less than 1 percent by 1981.

[9] During the Cultural Revolution, skirts and dresses were frowned upon and most women wore baggy trousers.

There are some risks in the modernization program. The foreign technology and experts it will require, educational improvements, the enrollment of thousands of students in Western universities and the ever-increasing number of tourists visiting China[10] — all could be destabilizing factors. Modernization also will be expensive. Tourist revenues and development of offshore oil will help defray some of the enormous costs but far more revenue will be needed. In another repudiation of Maoist dogma, China has let it be known that it will now accept direct loans from abroad and approve joint ventures with foreigners. Both long were considered incompatible with China's desired "self-sufficiency."

Modernization of the estimated four-million-member People's Liberation Army likewise will be costly. China currently spends about $17 billion a year, or 10 percent of its gross national product, for defense. But its military equipment is considered antiquated and training has been more ideological than practical. John Fraser noted recently that "it seems clear now that the legendary Maoist concept of a 'people's war' — in which China's principal strategic asset was its vast population — is in for some fundamental adjustments. Army and government officials are scouring the globe looking for appropriate military weapons."[11]

Anti-Soviet Emphasis in Foreign Policy

The attempt to upgrade China's armed forces is due in large measure to the perceived threat from the Soviet Union and the growing animosity between Russian-supported Vietnam and Peking. Contrary to some expectations at the time, the Sino-Soviet feud has intensified since Mao's death. According to some estimates, about 40 percent of all Russian forces and over half the Chinese army are deployed along the disputed 4,300-mile Sino-Soviet border.

The ostensible reason for the Sino-Vietnamese dispute is Hanoi's treatment of the estimated 1.7 million Chinese living in Vietnam. Peking claims that these ethnic Chinese, some 160,000 of whom already have fled to China, were persecuted by the Vietnamese. The problem came to light in March when Hanoi cracked down on what it termed rich capitalists in the south, most of whom were Chinese. But far more important to both sides in the conflict is Vietnam's longstanding distrust of China and Peking's fear about the creation of an impregnable Moscow-Hanoi sphere of influence in all Southeast Asia.

---

[10] China expects about 100,000 visitors in 1978 and double that number in 1979. Under 50,000 tourists visited China in 1977.

[11] John Fraser in *The Globe and Mail* of Toronto, Canada, June 13, 1978. The Chinese Communist Party is estimated to have about 35 million members.

Peking has good reason for concern.[12] There have been rumors that Vietnam may allow the Russians to take over former U.S. military bases in the country. Hanoi has by far the best trained and equipped army in Southeast Asia, has made neighboring Laos a virtual satellite and is waging a bloody border war with Cambodia. Under these circumstances, China seemed to have little alternative but to ally itself with Cambodia, where the regime of Pol Pot has massacred many and cut itself off from virtually all contact with the outside world.[13]

In recent years, Peking has improved its relations with virtually all the non-communist nations in Asia, even though this has meant curtailment of support for communist guerrilla movements in those countries.[14] China has gone out of its way to assure its new-found Asian friends that the large communities of overseas Chinese (*hua-chiao*) living in these countries are not agents of Peking. Since Mao's death, Chinese leaders have been trying to attract overseas Chinese investment and convince the *hua* to return to China for as long as they wish and help with the country's modernization program.

Both modernization and Soviet containment are behind China's increased contacts with Japan, Western Europe and the United States. During his visit to Peking in May, Zbigniew Brzezinski let it be known that while the United States was not prepared to supply China with military weapons, it did not object to these sales to Peking by Western Europe.[15]

Peking, in turn, has warned the United States and anyone else who will listen to take stronger actions in countering Soviet "aggression," particularly in Africa and the Middle East. China has increased its aid to conservative African states like Zaire and has strengthened its ties with such anti-communist Mideast nations as Saudi Arabia, Iran and Oman. And on Aug. 9, oil-rich Libya, one of Moscow's closest allies in the Arab world, agreed to establish diplomatic relations with China. Hua Kuo-feng's visit to Romania and Yugoslavia last month and to North Korea in

---

[12] There have been recent indications that Vietnam is not particularly happy about its dependence on the Soviet Union and wants to establish diplomatic relations and trade ties with the United States. Washington and Hanoi are expected to hold talks on these issues during the U.N. General Assembly session this fall. Observers also are waiting to see what the United States does when the trade embargo on Vietnam expires on Sept. 14.

[13] The Chinese may be embarrassed by Cambodian extremism, but that did not prevent them from attacking Sen. George McGovern, D-S.D., who on Aug. 21, proposed international military intervention against the Pol Pot regime.

[14] Early this year, Vice Premier Teng Hsiao-ping visited Thailand, Burma and Nepal. Indian Foreign Minister Atal Bihari Bayapyee is scheduled to go to Peking in October. This will be the first important official visit between the two countries since Premier Chou En-lai went to New Delhi in 1961.

[15] The Soviet Union has registered strong objections to western military sales to Peking. A statement issued on Aug. 26, 1978, by the Kremlin's ruling Politburo warned that such military sales to Peking would doom any chance for the conclusion of a U.S.-Soviet Strategic Arms Limitation Treaty (SALT).

May underlined Peking's support for communist regimes trying to pursue policies independent of the Soviet Union.

China Since Communist Takeover

STRAINS between ideological purity and modernization have existed since the communists seized control in China on Oct. 1, 1949. Mao and his followers quickly set about transforming Chinese society. Collectivist goals and centralized control were implemented under the direction of a disciplined Communist Party elite. "Primary emphasis was placed on recovery rather than on rapid expansion of production," A. Doak Barnett wrote. "In general, the regime achieved its initial goals in an impressive fashion and in a relatively short period of time."[16]

In 1953, China embarked on its first five-year plan. Based on the Soviet model, priority was given to rapid industrialization and the development of heavy industry. Material incentives were offered to increase productivity, and management by professionals took precedence over mass mobilization. Despite an overall rate of growth of about 7 percent a year, several problems were obvious by 1957. China had become dependent on Soviet loans which soon would have to be repaid, agricultural output was lagging, rural areas had been seriously neglected and unemployment was rising. In addition, Mao appeared to be increasingly concerned about the growth of the bureaucracy and what he termed "elitism."

Chinese foreign policy after 1949 was premised on ideological antagonism to imperialism and capitalism, both of which were associated primarily with the United States. But evidence that has come to light recently indicates that the anti-American rhetoric and policies might have been avoided. State Department documents released Aug. 13, 1978, show that Chou En-lai had contacted U.S. officials in Peking in the spring of 1949 and asked them to transmit a message to "the highest American authorities." In the message, Chou proposed that Washington help China stay out of the Soviet orbit. The secret offer from Chou was rejected.[17]

On the day the communists took power, Chou issued a

---

[16] A. Doak Barnett, "Uncertain Passage" (1974), p. 121. Barnett was born in China and is now a senior fellow at the Brookings Institution, which published this study.

[17] The rejection was viewed as a victory for hard-line State Department China experts, led by Foy Kohler, then U.S. Ambassador to the Soviet Union, and a defeat for the so-called "China hands," who wanted to encourage liberals within the Chinese Communist Party.

declaration inviting all countries to establish ties with the new regime "on the basis of equality, mutual benefit and mutual respect for territory and sovereignty." The Soviet Union was the first country to recognize China but without specifically accepting Chou's three principles. By that time, the Cold War had begun, and American policy was to isolate China. With no major power to turn to, China signed a 30-year alliance with the Soviet Union in early 1950.

The outbreak of the Korean War in June 1950 and China's involvement on the side of North Korea brought a U.S. commitment to the Nationalist Chinese government of Chiang Kai-shek on the island of Taiwan. It also increased Peking's dependence on the Soviet Union and its isolation throughout the non-communist world. To counter this isolation, China in 1954-55 began to tone down its revolutionary foreign policy utterances and to stress its desire for "peaceful coexistence" with other countries. Chou En-lai set the tone at the Bandung Conference of Asian and African countries in Indonesia in April 1955. The so-called Bandung period, which lasted until 1957-58, saw the signing of a Sino-Indian agreement on Tibet, Peking's sponsorship of non-alignment and the promotion of trade with foreign countries.

Criticism of Mao After Great Leap Forward

Mao's concern about the bureaucracy and "elitism," his determination to achieve a classless society and his disillusionment with the Soviet model of development resulted in the Great Leap Forward of 1957-58. During this period economic planning was decentralized, material incentives were replaced by political slogans to rally the masses, agricultural development in rural areas was given top priority, urban workers and professionals were sent to the countryside, university examinations were abolished and self-reliance and self-sufficiency were stressed. The experiment, which was opposed by Chou En-lai, was a failure and China's already low standard of living fell sharply.[18]

Mao himself criticized the Great Leap in a speech delivered on Jan. 30, 1962. "We adopted the general line of 'going all out, aiming high and achieving greater, faster, better and more economical results in building socialism,' " Mao said. But, he continued, "we hadn't the time to work out a complete set of specific principles, policies and measures suited to our conditions" and "the cadres and masses couldn't get any systematic education and policy."[19]

---

[18] See "China Under Mao," *E.R.R.*, 1968 Vol. II, p. 572.

[19] Reported by John Fraser in *The Globe and Mail*, July 4, 1978. Mao's speech was publicized widely in the Chinese press on June 30 and July 1, 1978. Fraser suggests that the current leadership allowed the speech to be disseminated to make Mao "the central prop" in its modernization drive.

In late 1957 and early 1958, there was a change in China's foreign policy. The spirit of "peaceful coexistence" that Chou had proclaimed at Bandung was replaced by calls for militancy and revolution against all "imperialists," particularly the United States. The Chinese had been outraged by Premier Nikita S. Khrushchev's address to the Twentieth Soviet Party Congress in February 1956 in which the Soviet leader condemned many of Stalin's policies and enunciated the doctrine of "peaceful coexistence" with the West to avoid nuclear war. China had not been consulted on the new Soviet line and began to attack it.

Moscow further antagonized China by refusing to offer Peking any support in "liberating" Taiwan or in the Sino-Indian conflicts of 1959 and 1962.[20] In 1959, the Kremlin also repudiated a promise it had made two years earlier to give China nuclear assistance. Amidst a barrage of charges from Peking that Russian leaders were prostituting themselves before the United States, Moscow in 1960 withdrew its technical advisers from China, demanded repayment of debts and drastically reduced its exports. Peking responded by allying itself with Albania which broke with the Soviet Union in 1961 over the Kremlin's "revisionism."

Although both China and Russia supported North Vietnam against the United States, competition rather than cooperation guided Sino-Soviet policy in Southeast Asia in the mid-1960s. As the war in Vietnam widened, each side accused the other of conspiring with the United States to defeat the Vietnamese communists. Moscow said Peking obstructed the transport of Russian war materials across China, while Peking charged Moscow with collaborating with Washington to sell out Hanoi. By 1966, all inter-party relations between Russia and China had ended.[21]

Excess and Upheaval in Cultural Revolution

The same year, Mao embarked on the Great Proletarian Cultural Revolution whose effects plagued China for over a decade.[22] The Cultural Revolution was intended to revolutionize the country and to oust or denigrate Communist Party leaders and bureaucrats who, Mao believed, had become "capitalist roaders." Although Mao's prestige still suffered from the failure of the Great Leap Forward, he was able to mobilize the masses and secure the support of the army.

Mao was successful in launching the Cultural Revolution, but he proved unable to control it. "The Cultural Revolution was a

---

[20] The disputes involved armed conflicts in border areas that both countries claimed belonged to them. See "India-China Border War," *E.R.R.* 1962 Vol. II, p. 755.

[21] See "Sino-Soviet Relations," *E.R.R.* 1977 Vol. I, p. 83.

[22] It was not until the Eleventh Party Congress in August 1977 that the Cultural Revolution officially was declared over.

time of controlled anarchy, when many social structures were torn down or severely weakened," economist Jan P. Prybyla wrote. "The work of tearing down was assigned to various sections of the popular masses, mainly to those young people whose career aspirations were being blocked by the increasingly rigid and stratified status quo."[23]

The most publicized of Mao's revolutionary followers during the Cultural Revolution were the Red Guards, mostly university students who were eager to confront "reactionary" bureaucrats and academics. The Red Guards were launched at a rally which Mao attended in Peking on Aug. 18, 1966. Their zeal for purifying China and communist ideology soon turned to violence. They entered private homes and confiscated "bourgeois" items and artifacts, destroyed street signs with Western names, denounced prominent suspects, threatened individuals with violence and disrupted inter-city transportation. By early 1967, the cultural Revolution looked as if it might get out of hand and result in the collapse of orderly government in China.

To restore some semblance of order, Mao turned to the army to keep the peace and to Premier Chou En-lai to run the government. According to Swedish journalist Hans Granqvist, who was visiting China at the time, it was Chou who "almost singlehandedly...held China together."[24] Among other things, Chou insisted that the schools be reopened, that priority be given to economic recovery and that adult control in the factories be reinstated. In both domestic and foreign policies, he stressed the kind of pragmatism and flexibility that was anathema to supporters of the Cultural Revolution.

China's current leaders have refrained from any direct criticism of the Cultural Revolution. Instead, the excesses of the period have been blamed on "deviationists" and, since Mao's death, on the Gang of Four. Outright condemnation of the Cultural Revolution would imply criticism of Mao and China apparently is not yet ready to castigate the "Great Helmsman." And despite the chaos that resulted from the Cultural Revolution, there were some benefits. It increased popular political participation, put an end to the privileges of the Communist bureaucracy and created greater equality between the city and the countryside.[25]

Rapprochement With the United States

While the excesses of the Cultural Revolution had diminished considerably by early 1968, the radicalism it unleashed plagued

---

[23] "The Chinese Economy After the 'Gang of Four,' " *Current History,* September 1977, p. 70.

[24] Hans Granqvist, *The Red Guards: A Report on Mao's Revolution* (1967), p. 154.

[25] Susan Shirk, "Has China Changed?" *Foreign Policy,* spring 1973, p. 93.

the Communist Party and the government for several more years. According to the Trilateral Commission, the pragmatists did not achieve a clear victory until August 1977, when Hua Kuo-feng outlined China's modernization program and condemned the Gang of Four at the Eleventh Party Congress. Hua's speech "constitutes a sharp break with the Maoist concept of 'uninterrupted revolution' in general and with the traditions of the Cultural Revolution in particular and is clearly intended to end the uncertain wavering between two opposite policy lines," the commission stated.[26]

In the immediate post-Cultural Revolution period, Mao turned to the army to restore order and stability. At the Ninth Party Congress in 1969, Defense Minister Lin Piao was designated the only Vice Chairman and Mao's successor, and the military was given a major voice in the Communist Party and the government. But the stability became increasingly precarious as Mao and Chou grew concerned about Lin Piao's ambitions. Lin was killed in a plane crash in Outer Mongolia on Sept. 12, 1971; the circumstances surrounding his death remain a mystery. According to the official Chinese version, Lin was plotting to overthrow and assassinate Mao and, when the plan failed, died trying to escape to the Soviet Union.

Lin Piao's fall from grace was due in part to his advocacy of improved relations with the Soviet Union. During the 1960s, tensions between the two communist giants increased and there were a number of incidents along the Sino-Soviet border. The most serious of these occurred on March 2, 1969, when Chinese troops attacked a Russian patrol along the Ussuri River. The Kremlin hinted that it might be forced to use nuclear weapons against China. Former White House chief of staff H.R. Haldeman wrote that the Soviet Union approached President Nixon on several occasions in 1969 to propose a joint U.S.-Soviet attack on China's nuclear facilities. Nixon turned the Kremlin down and warned that "a Soviet nuclear strike might bring the Russians into confrontation with the United States."[27]

Growing Sino-Soviet hostility and the buildup of Russian forces along the border led China out of the self-imposed isolation of the Cultural Revolution. Under Chou's direction, contact between China and foreign countries was encouraged. By 1975, China had established formal diplomatic relations with over 100 countries, or more than double the number recognized in 1968. The most publicized development after 1969, however, was Peking's rapprochement with the United States.

---

[26] "An Overview of East-West Relations," *op. cit.*, pp. 12-13.

[27] H.R. Haldeman, *The Ends of Power* (1978). China detonated its first atomic bomb in 1964.

In the spring of 1971, Peking invited members of a U.S. table tennis team competing in Japan to visit China. "Ping-Pong Diplomacy" was followed by a secret mission to China by National Security Adviser Henry A. Kissinger in July 1971 and by President Nixon's visit the following February. During that visit, Nixon and Chou En-lai signed the Shanghai Communiqué which stated that "the normalization of relations between the two countries is not only in the interest of the Chinese and American people but also contributes to the relaxation of tensions...in the world."

There is evidence that the Sino-American rapprochement produced considerably more enthusiasm in the United States than it did in China. The still-vocal radicals opposed any contact with the leading "imperialist" power, military leaders argued against the Mao-Chou initiative and, after years of anti-American propaganda, the Chinese people were apparently stunned by the sudden change. That Mao was able to surmount this opposition was evidence of his control over the country.

Outlook For Big Power Relations

THE NORMALIZATION of Sino-American relations still awaits full implementation six and a half years after the Shanghai Communiqué was signed. President Carter has reiterated his commitment to "normal relations with China" in the last few weeks.[28] There have been rumors that the administration intends to proceed toward full normalization after congressional elections this November. If such rumors are true, there is likely to be an intense debate in this country about what conditions the Chinese would insist upon and whether the benefits of meeting these conditions would outweigh the costs. A central question involves the impact that full Sino-American diplomatic ties would have on Sino-Soviet relations and on what remains of U.S.-Soviet détente.

"The political choices associated with normalization are onerous and potentially divisive for both China and the United States," Richard H. Solomon has written. "The compromises required to defuse the Taiwan issue touch highly emotional questions in both countries. At stake for the Chinese is a basic issue of sovereignty, and for the Americans the integrity of defense com-

---

[28] At a press conference on Aug. 18 and in an interview with the editors of *U.S. News & World Report* published Aug. 21. In that interview, the president said that "one of our goals, ultimately, is to have normal relations with China, but the pace of that progress has to be a mutual thing. The Chinese and we are patient."

mitments and the welfare of a long-time ally. Part of the challenge facing each government is to justify to its people the risks and compromises necessary to reach an agreement in terms of global interests and gains to national security that are indirect and may not be evident for years to come."[29]

The most serious impediment to normal relations is the Republic of China or Taiwan. Peking insists that before full diplomatic ties can be established, Washington must withdraw all of its military forces from the island, break off diplomatic relations with the Chinese Nationalist government and renounce the 1954 military security treaty with Taiwan. The United States maintains that these conditions can be met only if China commits itself to a peaceful settlement of the issue. But so far Peking has been unwilling to give up the option of forceful reunification.

Vice Premier Teng Hsia-ping did tell a U.S. congressional delegation led by House Asian and Pacific Affairs Subcommittee Chairman Lester Wolff, D-N.Y., in July that China is willing to negotiate directly with the government of Taiwan over the future of the island. Taiwan's President Chiang Ching-kuo rejected the offer on the ground that "negotiation with the communists is tantamount to suicide."[30] But delegates from both countries attended an international science conference in Tokyo in late August; this was the first time since the communist takeover in 1949 that representatives of China and Taiwan attended the same meeting.

A. Doak Barnett has written that "the act of upgrading ties with China is not intrinsically of crucial importance, but it will probably be impossible to deal with many more important problems until this occurs; and unless it occurs, even the present minimal relationship between Washington and Peking might deteriorate." He went on to say that "if full normalization is not achieved, Peking could well reassess its policies and move in new directions in its policy toward either Washington or Moscow or both, with consequences that could damage U.S. interests. Even protracted delay is likely to create new risks."[31]

While there is virtually no possibility of a return to the intimacy that characterized Sino-Soviet relations in the late 1940s and early 1950s, a limited rapprochement is still possible. To

---

[29] Richard H. Solomon, "Thinking Through the China Problem," *Foreign Affairs*, January 1978, p. 325. Solomon, director of the Rand Corporation's research program in international security policy, served on the staff of the National Security Council from 1971 to 1976.

[30] Most of the 15 million Taiwanese and two million Chinese on the island oppose reunification with the mainland. In the past few years, more Taiwanese have been brought into important positions in the government and Taiwan is now the 22nd largest trading nation in the world. Despite the prosperity, the number of nations recognizing Taiwan has fallen from over 100 to 23 since 1972.

[31] A. Doak Barnett, *China Policy: Old Problems and New Challenges* (1977), pp. 122-123.

date, China's post-Mao leadership has rejected Russian offers to resolve bilateral differences and shown no interest in a peace and friendship treaty that the Soviets proposed earlier this year. Instead, the Chinese have continued and intensified their anti-Soviet rhetoric and hinted that they will abrogate the 30-year mutual assistance treaty between the two countries when it expires in 1980. The Russians, in turn, have stepped up their verbal assaults on "the Peking inciters of war" and the "great Han chauvinists."

Prospect of Closer Ties With Soviet Union

Nevertheless, there are believed to be factions in both countries that would like to end the growing Sino-Soviet animosity. A relaxation in tensions could come when Russian Communist Party leader Leonid Brezhnev, now 71 and reportedly in ill health, passes from the scene. A change in Chinese attitudes or leadership might also spur some sort of Sino-Soviet détente. Chinese leaders "seem to have considered and to have rejected the possible advantages of such a rapprochement," Donald S. Zagoria wrote. "Probably the most important factor is that the new Peking leadership is still divided and would require a united leadership to undertake such a substantial change in foreign policy as a limited accommodation with Russia."[32]

The pragmatism and stress on modernization that have characterized the post-Mao leadership could either increase Russian fears of China becoming a superpower or contribute to a reduction in Sino-Soviet tensions. For all the rhetoric about the inevitability of war with Russia, Peking cannot afford a large-scale conflict, with the damage that Soviet nuclear power would likely inflict on the country, and proceed with its ambitious modernization program. Similarly, the Russians would be deterred from starting a war by the threat of Chinese nuclear retaliation and by the danger of tying down their armed forces for an indefinite time in a land conflict with the most populous nation on earth.

Barring any unexpected turn of events, Chinese-Soviet antagonism short of war is likely to continue for the foreseeable future. Washington could well play a significant role in keeping the hostility within reasonable bounds. Some administration spokesmen, notably Zbigniew Brzezinski, advocate "playing the China card" against the Kremlin, while Secretary of State Cyrus Vance reportedly favors a more balanced approach to both countries. Those favoring closer relations with Peking argue that American national interests require at least a tacit alliance with China. But retired Foreign Service officer O. Edmund Clubb

---

[32] Donald S. Zagoria, "The Soviet Quandary in Asia," *Foreign Affairs*, January 1978, pp. 308. Zagoria is a professor of government at the graduate center of New York City University.

China's Oil

Chinese leaders are hoping that oil revenues will pay for an increasing part of their ambitious modernization program. Lacking the expertise to begin development of its offshore resources, China recently played host to representatives of four American oil companies — Pennzoil Col, Exxon Corp., Phillips Petroleum Co. and Union Oil Co. of California. Hobert Rowen predicted in *The Washington Post* on Aug. 11, 1978, that the development of offshore oil "is likely to lead to an investment of $25 billion to $50 billion by American companies in the shared development of Chinese oil."

Estimates on how much oil China has vary widely. J. Hugh Liedtke, chairman of Pennzoil, contends that "there may be as much oil in China as in the Middle East, but production problems under existing technology may make it more difficult to recover." Some petroleum geologists attending an international symposium in Honolulu in August estimated total offshore and onshore recoverable reserves of 50 billion to 75 billion barrels. Others argued that China's likely reserves were only about half that much or about the same as Alaska's North Slope.

China is believed to have produced about 700 million barrels of oil in 1977, some of which was exported, primarily to Japan. A few weeks ago, Peking offered its oil for sale on the American market. According to Central Intelligence Agency estimates, China's petroleum exports will be almost 300,000 barrels a day until 1982 and a half million barrels a day by 1985.

warned in a letter to the editor of *The New York Times* on Aug. 8, 1978, that an "American strategem designed to enlist the Chinese 'enemy of our enemy' " might be counterproductive. "The Soviet Union might benefit more than the United States from such a policy," Clubb said.

Question of Continued Stability in China

Predictions about Chinese foreign and domestic policies are dangerous since there are no assurances that Peking's current opening to the world or its drive for modernization will continue. There has been speculation about serious disagreements within the leadership, particularly between Hua Kuo-feng and Teng Hsiao-ping. Hua remains a relative unknown despite the publicity surrounding his recent trip to Eastern Europe and Iran. He lacks Mao's stature and prestige, has shifted in the past decade from a defender of ideological purification to a more pragmatic stand and lacks a strong base of support in the army and the Communist Party.

Last year, the Trilateral Commission summed up three possibilities for China's political future. The first, "which is clearly the more likely, would see a coalition of party leaders and pragmatic bureaucrats maintaining the hold on power that they achieved in the wake of Chairman Mao's death." The second contingency is that the radicals "might restore their strength and influence — leading either to a renewed coalition between the pragmatists and the radicals or to an outright radical victory." The third and least likely outcome "is that the military might gain a political victory."[33]

There is evidence that many Chinese do not share Teng Hsiao-ping's enthusiasm for rapid modernization. "The reason is simple," John Fraser noted in *The Globe and Mail* on July 24, 1978. "There is not sufficient trust that things won't get bad again. A cadre assigned to urge people to be more open in their criticisms, a teacher ordered to upgrade the quality of education, a worker urged to increase his workload with a wage bonus for an initiative, a bureaucrat encouraged to cut through red tape and make a decisive decision on his own — all these people are understandably worried that their initiative today will leave them marked and dangerously exposed when the next rectification campaign comes along."

Another destabilizing factor is the existence of thousands of young people whose education was interrupted and whose revolutionary enthusiasm was unleashed by the Cultural Revolution. The monotony of low-level jobs in an economy stressing production is unlikely to inspire the kind of exhilaration that the upheavals of a decade ago did. There also is likely to be increasing dissatisfaction among present-day students who are not able to qualify for the limited number of university openings as well as among those who are sent abroad to study and are exposed to Western values and lifestyles. Dissatisfied youth need look no further than Mao's words and actions to justify a revolt against bureaucrats, pragmatists and "capitalist roaders."

China's future is fraught with uncertainties. The pace of modernization at home could be too slow or too fast, provoking expectations that cannot be met or undermining the central authority of the Communist Party. Greater contact with the rest of the world, particularly developed nations, could result in disappointment and frustration if other nations fail to deliver what the Chinese expect of them. The major task for the post-Mao leadership will be to keep the opening door under control. The task will not be an easy one.

---

[33] "Collaboration With Communist Countries in Managing Global Problems" (1977), pp. 32-33.

Selected Bibliography

Books

Leys, Simon, *Chinese Shadows,* Viking, 1977.

Oksenberg, Michel and Robert D. Oxnam, *Dragon and Eagle: United States-China Relations Past and Future,* Basic Books, 1978.

Peyrefitte, Alain, *The Chinese: Portrait of a People,* Bobbs-Merrill, 1977.

Sutter, Robert G., *Chinese Foreign Policy After the Cultural Revolution, 1966-1977,* Westview Press, 1978.

Whiting, Allen S. and Robert F. Dernberger, *China's Future: Foreign Policy and Economic Development in the Post-Mao Era,* McGraw-Hill, 1977.

Articles

Clubb, O. Edmund, " 'Great Order' Under Hua Kuo-feng," *The Nation,* April 8, 1978.

Cooper, John F., "Taiwan's Strategy and America's China Policy," *Orbis,* summer 1977.

Current History, September 1978 issue.

Far Eastern Economic Review, selected issues.

Grosscup, Beau, "Mao's Lost Vision," *The Progressive,* March 1978.

Pye, Lucian W., "The Puzzles of Chinese Pragmatism," *Foreign Policy,* summer 1978.

Scalapino, Robert A., "The Struggle for Mao and the Future," *Orbis,* spring 1977.

Shirk, Susan L., "Human Rights: What About China?" *Foreign Policy,* winter 1977-78.

Solomon, Richard H., "Thinking Through the China Problem," *Foreign Affairs,* January 1978.

Zagoria, Donald S., "The Soviet Quandary in Asia," *Foreign Affairs,* January 1978.

Reports and Studies

Azrael, Jeremy R., Richard Lowenthal and Tohru Nakagawa, "An Overview of East-West Relations," The Trilateral Commission, 1978.

Barnett, A. Doak, "China and the Major Powers in East Asia," The Brookings Institution, December 1977.

——"China Policy," The Brookings Institution, April 1977.

——"Uncertain Passage: China's Transition to the Post-Mao Era," The Brookings Institution, 1976.

Clough, Ralph N., Robert D. Oxnam and William Watts, "The United States and China: American Perceptions and Future Alternatives," Potomac Associates, 1977.

Editorial Research Reports, "China After Mao," 1974 Vol. I, p. 103; "China Under Mao," 1968 Vol. II, p. 565; "Sino-Soviet Relations," 1977 Vol. I, p. 83.

Hosoya, Chihiro, Henry Owen and Andrew Shonfield, "Collaboration With Communist Countries in Managing Global Problems," The Trilateral Commission, 1977.

Rothenberg, Morris, "Whither China: The View From the Kremlin," Center for Advanced International Studies, 1977.

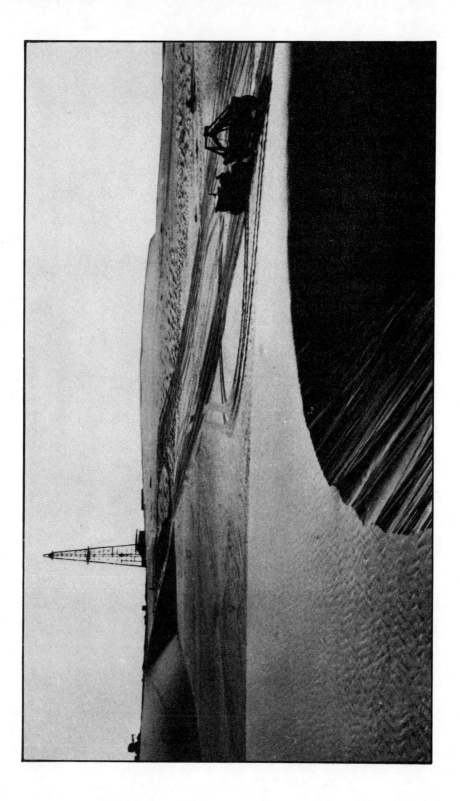

OIL IMPORTS

by

Kennedy P. Maize

**Aug. 25
1 9 7 8**

Editor's Note: New developments since this report was written in the summer of 1978 have made Americans more acutely aware of their dependence on foreign oil — and the consequence of this dependence. The revolution in Iran all but dried up a big source of America's oil imports and led other OPEC countries to raise prices and cut back production (as a means of maintaining higher prices). By spring, gasoline shortages had occurred in California and a few other parts of the country, while the price at the pumps rose steadily upward.

OIL IMPORTS

A T THE ECONOMIC summit meeting in Bonn in July, President Carter pledged to raise oil prices in the United States to world levels and to reduce U.S. oil imports. Carter's pledge was strongly praised by the other summit participants — Chancellor Helmut Schmidt of West Germany, President Valéry Giscard d'Estaing of France and Prime Ministers Takeo Fukuda of Japan, James Callaghan of Britain, Pierre Elliott Trudeau of Canada and Giulio Andreotti of Italy. In return, the six foreign leaders agreed to try to stimulate their economies in order to improve markets for U.S. exports.

For months preceding the summit meeting, the foreign leaders had denounced the Carter administration's failure to curb the U.S. addiction to imported oil. America's continued dependence on foreign oil has been blamed for the nation's sagging balance of trade, the slide of the U.S. dollar in world money markets, rising worldwide inflation and a host of other economic ills.[1]

Whether President Carter can deliver on his pledge is a matter of speculation at home — and of intense interest to America's trading partners abroad. Given the problems the president has had in trying to move his national energy plan through Congress, some observers have concluded that he may have overstated what the United States can actually accomplish. In 1977 imports averaged 8.7 million barrels a day, providing almost half of the oil the country consumed. Oil imports decreased 13 percent in the first seven months of 1978, but many energy analysts regard that as a temporary situation and foresee a resumption next year of the long-term rise in imports (see p. 139).

Between 1973 and 1978 oil prices rose from just below $3 per barrel to well above $13. The burden of higher oil prices has fallen most heavily on Western Europe and Japan which do not have America's coal, oil, natural gas and uranium reserves to help cushion the blow. Last year, for example, imports accounted for 47.5 percent of oil consumption in the United States, 91.7 percent in Western Europe and 99.7 percent in Japan.

Foreign leaders would like the United States to share the burden of conserving oil and gas. "To the Europeans and

---

[1] See "Dollar Problems Abroad," *E.R.R.*, 1978 Vol. I, pp. 401-420.

Japanese," *Business Week* magazine noted recently, "American actions — or lack of them — on energy policy appear a power play designed to improve the U.S. position in world trade at their expense."[2] Because the dollar is the world's reserve currency, the United States, according to some economists, can afford to spur its own growth by buying large amounts of imported oil even at the expense of the devaluation of the dollar. The result was costly energy in the United States and a devalued dollar, making U.S. goods cheaper and more competitive on foreign markets, hurting the foreign economies.

To help cope with rising energy costs the governments of Western Europe and Japan adopted restrictive monetary and fiscal policies to slow the growth of their economies. "By last year," *Business Week* reported, "not only Germany but Japan as well were running an enormous balance-of-payments surplus while the so-called 'convalescing' major industrialized countries — France, Italy and Britain — had brought their current accounts into precarious balance."

In response to U.S. pressure, West Germany, Japan and the other countries represented at the Bonn summit agreed to promote economic growth in non-inflationary ways. But the foreign leaders emphasized that efforts to stimulate their economies were linked to American efforts to curb energy use. "The Europeans argue with some validity that if they set reasonable growth paths and the U.S. does not curb its energy use, they will be confronted by either oil shortages or rising energy prices or both in a few years," an unidentified administration economist told *Business Week*.

Senate Barrier to Carter's Bonn Pledge

At Bonn, the president specifically pledged to reduce U.S. oil imports from a projected 11.5 million barrels a day to 9 million by 1985. This represented a retreat from his National Energy Plan, introduced in April 1977, which called for a 4.5 million barrel a day reduction in oil imports by 1985. As steps along the way, Carter pledged at Bonn that U.S. oil imports in 1978 and 1979 should be less than in 1977. To achieve these goals Carter said the United States would:

> Increase coal production by two-thirds. (The president's 1977 plan called for a doubling of coal production by 1985.)

> Maintain economic growth at a higher rate than the growth in energy demand, with oil use growing more slowly than overall energy consumption.

> Increase the price of oil produced in the United States to the world level by the end of 1980.

---

[2] "New World Economic Order," *Business Week*, July 24, 1978, p. 71.

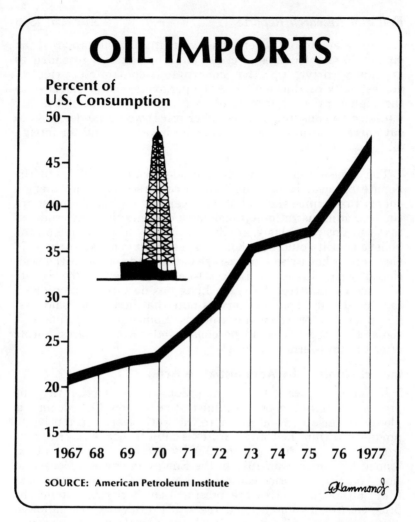

OIL IMPORTS

Percent of U.S. Consumption

50
45
40
35
30
25
20
15

1967 68 69 70 71 72 73 74 75 76 1977

SOURCE: American Petroleum Institute

Carter did not specify how he would accomplish these goals, but administration spokesmen since have said that he hoped to achieve them through his energy program now before Congress. But after more than 16 months of consideration in both houses of Congress, no element of the plan has been enacted into law *(see box, p. 144).* Both the House and Senate passed versions of Carter's energy program last year[3] but the Senate went far afield from the president's approach in two key areas — natural gas regulation and energy tax policy. Conference committees settled other issues but bogged down over gas and taxes. House Speaker Thomas P. O'Neill Jr., D-Mass., has continued to insist that the House will not act on any part of the energy package until it can act on all sections at once.

---

[3] See *1977 CQ Almanac,* pp. 708-746.

A key element of Carter's energy program was a proposed tax on purchases of domestic crude oil. The tax was intended to gradually drive up the government-controlled price of domestically produced oil — $9.55 per average 1977 barrel — to the higher price of foreign oil, with the proceeds of the tax refunded to consumers. The higher prices would be designed to cut energy consumption and thereby lower demand for foreign oil.

The House approved Carter's crude oil tax in 1977, but the Senate refused. House and Senate conferees have not met on energy taxes since the end of last year and all but the most optimistic administration officials now concede that the crude oil tax[4] will not pass this year. But supporters of the crude oil tax believe that it could be taken up again next year, after the 1978 elections. A key to Senate passage of the crude oil tax is the position of Sen. Russell B. Long, D-La., chairman of the Senate Finance Committee. Although Long has declared the crude oil tax "politically dead," observers note that he has not said that he opposes it on economic grounds. Some interpret this as a signal that the tax could be considered when Congress meets after the mid-term elections.

Import Controls by Administrative Action

If Congress does not pass the crude oil equalization tax, the president might choose administrative action to redeem his pledge to raise U.S. oil prices to the world level. Currently, oil produced within the United States is subject to federal price controls. They were imposed in 1971 by President Nixon and extended by Congress in 1975 in the Energy Policy and Conservation Act. But the price control authority in the act expires next May, although it gives the president authority to extend the price controls two additional years. If President Carter allowed the controls to expire, domestic oil prices would be set by market conditions and undoubtedly would rise.[5]

It is considered highly unlikely that President Carter will allow the oil price controls to expire. The chief beneficiaries of the subsequent price increases would be the large oil companies. This would likely be unpopular politically and lead to complaints of "windfall profits" similar to those that surfaced during the 1973-74 energy crisis.[6]

---

[4] The Senate Finance Committee killed the other Carter tax proposals, which had passed the House. They were a tax on industries and utilities which use oil and gas, and a tax on "gas guzzler" cars. The full Senate restored a version of the user taxes and the House-Senate conference restored a version of the gas guzzler tax.

[5] See "Possible Solution to Carter's Summit Pledge," *Congressional Quarterly Weekly Report*, July 22, 1978, p. 1881.

[6] See "Oil Antitrust Action," *E.R.R.*, 1978 Vol. I, pp. 101-120.

A third way to raise oil prices would be presidential imposition of fees on oil imports. Carter often has threatened to levy fees of up to $5 per barrel on imported oil if Congress does not pass his oil tax. Carter repeated the warning at a news conference Aug. 17. The president has the authority to order such a move under the 1962 Trade Expansion Act. Import fees would drive up the purchase price for domestic refiners who buy foreign oil. The Department of Energy's entitlements program requires that the cost of acquiring oil be balanced among all domestic refiners; so a boost in the price of foreign oil eventually would force higher costs all around. A $5 per barrel fee on imported oil would cost motorists about seven additional cents a gallon at the gasoline pumps.

The Senate voted June 27 to bar Carter from imposing such fees. It attached the ban to the fiscal 1979 Treasury, Postal Service and general government appropriations bill.[7] White House press secretary Jody Powell said Carter viewed the Senate vote as "just another unfortunate demonstration of the desire to duck a tough problem and of why we're still the only industrialized nation in the world without a national energy policy." Before the ban provision becomes law, it must survive a House-Senate conference. The House did not provide for a ban in its version of the appropriations bill and House Speaker O'Neill has said that the House Democratic leadership will oppose it in the final bill.

President Carter encounters additional problems trying to fulfill his promise to reduce U.S. oil imports by 2.5 million barrels a day by 1985. When Carter first introduced his energy plan in April 1977, he predicted that it would save the nation 4.5 million barrels of oil a day by 1985. Department of Energy analysts now contend that total energy savings from the energy bills likely to emerge from Congress will only amount to about 1.9 million barrels a day.

Effect of Alaskan Oil; Import Reductions

Even without Carter's energy program, U.S. oil imports have been declining since the first of the year. For the first seven months of 1978, oil imports accounted for 42 percent of all oil consumed in the United States; during the same period last year, imports accounted for 47 percent of total oil consumption. The American Petroleum Institute reported in June[8] that U.S. crude oil imports were down 13.1 percent in the first six months of 1978. Crude oil imports during this period averaged 5.8 million barrels a day compared to an average of 6.7 million barrels a day during the first six months of 1977. The trend continued in July; crude oil imports last month were 13 percent lower than in July 1977.

---

[7] See *Congressional Quarterly Weekly Report,* July 1, 1978, p. 1659.

[8] American Petroleum Institute, "Estimated U.S. Supply/Demand Situation," p. 2.

Alaskan Oil Dilemma

The biggest question about Alaskan oil today is: What to do with it? When pipeline construction began in 1973, it was assumed that the oil would be absorbed in the western states. But reduced growth of energy demands, the opening of California's Elk Hills Naval Petroleum Reserve and increased imports from Indonesia have led to an overabundant supply of oil on the West Coast. Eastern and midwestern states sorely need the oil but are far from West Coast ports.

Some oil company executives and government officials have proposed selling Alaskan oil to Japan in exchange for diverting Middle Eastern oil, now purchased by Japan, to the U.S. East Coast. This swap would save both countries millions of dollars in shipping costs. It also would improve the U.S. balance of trade with Japan and improve the value of the dollar in relation to the yen. But it would require an act of Congress, since the 1973 Alaska Pipeline bill specifically prohibited the export of Alaskan oil except in extraordinary circumstances. Selling Alaskan oil abroad would be "politically unthinkable," according to Rep. Mark W. Hannaford, D-Calif.

Department of Energy officials hope that increasing demand for oil will dry up the excess supply. In the meantime, the irony of the situation has not been lost on opponents of the administration's energy plan.

A downward trend also was detected in imports of refined petroleum products. During the first six months of 1978, imports of refined petroleum products fell 12.2 percent below the same period in 1977. There have been other hopeful signs as well. According to the American Petroleum Institute, domestic crude oil production was up 8.8 percent during the first half of 1978; in June alone production rose 10.9 percent above June 1977 production. The institute attributed most of the increase to the flow of Alaskan crude oil into the lower 48 states through the Alaskan pipeline. But the influx of oil from Alaska is not expected to increase over current levels. The pipeline already is carrying its full capacity of crude oil. In the future, increasing demand will more than make up for the extra oil coming from the North Slope of Alaska *(see box)*.

On the demand side, the picture has been mixed. Demand for petroleum products during the first six months of this year was up 2.4 percent over the first six months of 1977, according to the American Petroleum Institute. That was the smallest oil increase recorded for the January-June period since 1975, when the country was just emerging from a recession. But last month the demand for petroleum products rose 4 percent over July 1977 levels. Leading the increase was a 7.7 percent jump in the demand for gasoline.

Oil Imports

Most energy analysts find little reason for optimism in the recent decline in oil imports. Department of Energy projections for the remainder of the year show an upturn in oil imports, particularly in the fourth quarter. Regardless of the final outcome for 1978, there seems to be general agreement that oil imports will go up again in 1979. "This import decline we have seen will start leveling off in the second half [of 1978] and will disappear altogether in 1979," John H. Lichtblau, executive director of the Petroleum Industry Research Foundation, said recently.[9] Some energy specialists have predicted that oil imports in 1979 will exceed the 1977 record high of 8.7 million barrels a day.

Economic Growth as Key to Oil Demand

Most energy analysts consider economic growth, and the consequent growth in energy demand, as the crucial elements in determining the need for imported oil. According to a recent study by the Petroleum Industry Research Foundation, if energy demand in the United States grows at an annual rate of 3.8 percent — slightly above the 1960-1976 rate of 3.7 percent — the United States would be importing 12 million barrels of oil a day by 1985. If energy demand grows at an annual rate of 3 percent, the United States would be importing 9.4 million barrels of oil a day in 1985.[10]

If energy demand only grows at the 3 percent rate, it appears that the Carter goal of 1985 imports of 9 million barrels a day is achievable. But if growth in demand runs at nearer the historical rates, it is unlikely that U.S. imports could be reduced to 9 million barrels a day as a result of the programs that appear likely to pass the Congress. Many analysts suggest that fulfilling the Bonn summit goals may be more a matter of what happens to the economy over the next seven years than what happens to a legislative package on Capitol Hill.

On April 18, 1977, two days before he presented his energy program to Congress, President Carter addressed the American people in a nationwide television broadcast. In somber tones, he exhorted Congress and the American people to join forces in staving off an impending energy crisis. What was demanded of the people, he said, was the "moral equivalent of war." The president gave a bleak diagnosis of the nation's energy ills. "Each new inventory of world oil reserves has been more disturbing than the last," Carter said. "World oil production can probably keep going for another six or eight years. But sometime in the 1980s it can't go up any more. Demand will overtake production."

---

[9] Quoted in *The Wall Street Journal*, Aug. 9, 1978.

[10] Petroleum Industry Research Foundation, "The Outlook for World Oil into the 21st Century with Emphasis on the Period to 1900," May 1978, pp. 1.10-1.11.

The president's gloomy forecast was influenced by a report prepared by the Central Intelligence Agency.[11] The CIA postulated three central conclusions: first, that domestic production of energy by the United States, Canada, Japan and Western Europe combined will fall short of their own 1985 energy demand by the equivalent of almost 34 million barrels of oil a day; second, that the Soviet Union's oil industry "is in trouble" and the Russians consequently will be forced to compete for oil imports; and third, that Saudi Arabia alone can provide the margin of extra oil necessary to meet the world's 1985 demand, but whether the Saudis will do so is questionable.

Many analysts still support the CIA conclusions. Daniel Yergin, a member of the Energy Research Project at Harvard University, for example, recently concluded: "By 1985 or 1986 or 1987, if present trends continue, we'll be staring at an energy crisis far worse than the one we went through in the early 70s. And then our present boredom with the energy problem and with the Carter administration's efforts to cope with it, will seem like complacent sleep."[12]

In recent months, however, several studies have been published that conclude that an energy shortage is, at the worst, quite a long way off. One of those was the recent Petroleum Industry Research Foundation report, which concluded: "...[A]n oil shortage before the late 1980s is unlikely...[and] an oil shortage before the end of the century is a possibility but not a probability." The report said that a gradual transition from oil to non-oil sources over the next 25 to 30 years "is more likely than an extended oil shortage of crisis proportions."[13] According to newspaper accounts, a report being prepared by the Trilateral Commission in New York will arrive at similar conclusions.

U.S. Oil Policy Development

TWENTY YEARS AGO an energy crisis seemed unthinkable. Most estimates of domestic and global energy supplies foresaw an almost endless sea of oil. During the late 1950s a series of increasingly optimistic estimates of U.S. domestic oil reserves emerged from a variety of public and private sources, including

---

[11] Central Intelligence Agency, "The International Energy Situation: Outlook to 1985," April 1977.

[12] Daniel Yergin, "The Real Meaning of the Energy Crunch," *The New York Times Magazine*, June 4, 1978, p. 32. A new book by Yergin, *Coming to Terms: the Energy Crisis As It Really Is*, is scheduled for release this fall.

[13] Petroleum Industry Research Foundation, *op. cit.*, p. s-1.

the U.S. Geological Survey, the Chase Manhattan Bank, the Exxon Corp., and Resources for the Future, a private research organization.

Even during the 1950s a few petroleum geologists and economists were predicting the approaching exhaustion of U.S. oil reserves. But according to economist John Blair, their analyses, published in academic journals or congressional hearings, were ignored or soon forgotten. "Warnings of an impending shortage were highly inconvenient to a government embarked on a program designed to enlarge the oil producers' profits by excluding what were then low-cost foreign imports," Dr. Blair wrote in 1976.[14]

Government geologist M. King Hubbert was among the first to predict that U.S. oil reserves would diminish more rapidly than was generally believed. In a report published in 1956 Mr. Hubbert stated that the nation's oil production would rise steadily until 1970 and then begin a sustained and irreversible decline. His prediction proved astonishingly accurate. After decades of steady annual increases, domestic crude oil production peaked in 1970 at 9.6 million barrels a day. Since then crude oil production in the United States has declined. U.S. oil production rose during the first six months of 1978 because of the influx of oil from Alaska *(see p. 138)*.

As domestic oil production leveled off and then declined, the United States came to rely more and more on imported oil. Between 1969 and 1972 the United States expanded its oil imports by 52 percent, with most of the increment coming from the Middle East.[15] In 1972 the United States received 850,000 barrels of Arab oil a day, which represented 17.9 percent of all U.S. oil imports.

Energy Crisis and Project Independence

Few Americans realized how dependent the nation had become on Arab oil until the supply was cut off during the fourth Arab-Israeli war, which broke out on Oct. 6, 1973.[16] The Arab oil embargo lasted five months — until March 18, 1974 — and resulted in the loss to the United States of about two million barrels of oil per day. Measures taken to cope with the oil shortage included Sunday bans on gasoline sales, reduced speed limits, increased prices, restrictions on emergy usage, cutbacks in auto production and reductions in heating fuels.

Coinciding with the embargo was a sharp increase in the price of Middle Eastern oil. Other members of the Organization of

---

[14] John Blair, *The Control of Oil* (1976), p. 4.

[15] See Dana Adams Schmidt, *Armageddon in the Middle East* (1974), p. 215.

[16] See "Middle East Reappraisal," *E.R.R.*, 1973 Vol. II, pp. 947-966.

Petroleum Exporting Countries (OPEC)[17] quickly followed suit and within a year the price of oil had more than quadrupled. In January 1973 the posted price[18] for Persian Gulf crude — the standard reference in the oil trade — was $2.59 a barrel; a year later it had shot up to $11.65.

The immediate response of the U.S. government to the oil embargo was to rally the nation in support of a crash program aimed at removing dependence on foreign oil in a few years. President Nixon launched the campaign in an address to the nation on Nov. 7, 1973. "Let us set as our national goal...that by the end of this decade we will have developed the potential to meet our own energy needs without depending on any foreign sources," he said. Nixon called his program "Project Independence." He likened it to two other successful American ventures — the Manhattan Project for developing an atomic bomb and the Apollo Project for putting a man on the moon.

Hardly had the ring of Nixon's words died out when leaders both inside and outside of government began to question the wisdom and practicality of total self-sufficiency in energy. One government estimate indicated that to reach energy self-sufficiency by 1980, the United States would have to replace the equivalent of 12 million barrels of imported oil per day. This would require increased domestic energy production equal to 7.3 million barrels of oil per day and energy savings of 4.7 million barrels per day. Most experts found this goal unrealistic.[19] The lifting of the Arab oil embargo in March 1974 removed some of the incentive for Project Independence. And increasingly the Nixon White House and the nation were distracted by the more immediate crisis of Watergate.

The energy situation became intertwined with the grave economic problems President Ford inherited on taking office in August 1974. Though the Arabs had lifted their oil embargo, they and the other oil producing nations refused to lower the posted price for oil. The continuing high oil prices played havoc with the international monetary system and contributed heavily to the deepening worldwide recession. President Ford told a Detroit audience Sept. 23 that "it is difficult to discuss the energy problem without unfortunately lapsing into doomsday language.... Exorbitant [oil] prices can only distort the world economy, run the risk of worldwide depression and threaten the breakdown of world order and safety."

---

[17] OPEC was established in September 1960. Current members are Algeria, Ecuador, Gabon, Indonesia, Iran, Iraq, Kuwait, Libya, Nigeria, Qatar, Saudi Arabia, the United Arab Emirates and Venezuela.

[18] In contrast to the actual price, the posted price is an artificially high price set by oil-exporting countries for boosting their royalties from Western-owned oil companies.

[19] See *Congressional Quarterly Weekly Report*, June 8, 1974, p. 1463.

Throughout 1975 President Ford and Congress wrangled over the best way to solve the nation's energy problems. The president based his plan to cut energy consumption and stimulate domestic energy production on higher fuel prices. The cornerstone of his proposal was a three-part move to allow fuel prices to rise by:

Increasing the import fee on every barrel of foreign oil by $3, added in three $1 steps.

Lifting federal price controls on the cost of two of every three barrels of domestically produced oil.

Ending federal price controls on the wellhead price paid for new natural gas.

The Democratic leadership of the House and Senate rejected the president's price-based approach. They argued that Ford's proposals would have an unduly harsh impact on American consumers and the recessionary economy. Instead they advocated a tax-based approach, increasing gas taxes to encourage conservation and providing tax incentives to spur energy production.

Evolution of Carter's Energy Program

By the end of the year, both approaches had been rejected. The Energy Policy and Conservation Act of 1975, which emerged from Congress in mid-December, continued controls of oil prices for at least three years and authorized a national strategic oil reserve to help protect against a future oil embargo. Reluctantly signing the measure in the face of an intense industry effort to persuade him to veto it, President Ford said he hoped that the bill was "a beginning...a foundation upon which we can build."

During the 1976 presidential campaign, candidate Carter criticized both the Nixon-Ford administrations and Congress for not establishing a comprehensive national energy policy. "I think almost every other developed nation in the world has an energy policy except us," Carter said Sept. 23, 1976, during the first televised presidential debate in Philadelphia. "We've got to have a firm way to handle the energy question." Upon becoming president, Carter ordered a small team of energy planners to construct a comprehensive national energy program in 90 days; the deadline was met. The primary goal of Carter's "National Energy Plan," unveiled in April 1977, was to cut America's appetite for oil and natural gas and to use energy more efficiently. His answer was an exceedingly complex package of regulatory and tax measures.

The Carter plan would have empowered the federal government to (1) require industries to make products that met mandated standards of energy efficiency; (2) tell businesses to burn certain fuels but not others; (3) sponsor massive programs en-

Carter's National Energy Plan—
The Score in Congress

Proposed	House	Senate	Status
Crude oil equalization tax	Passed	Rejected	Stuck in conference, unlikely to pass this session.
Natural Gas Pricing—extend price controls with higher price ceiling	Passed	Rejected	Conferees approved compromise for phased deregulation, not yet approved by either house. Compromise may fail and may face Senate filibuster.
Standby gasoline tax	Rejected	Rejected	
Gas guzzler tax	Passed	Rejected: substituted ban on building "gas guzzlers"	Conferees agreed to a weakened "gas guzzler" tax. Outlook uncertain.
Coal conversion	Passed	Passed weaker version	Conferees approved, passed Senate, waiting House action.
Utility rate reform	Passed	Passed weak version	Conferees approved a weaker version, not yet passed either house.
Home insulation tax credits	Passed	Passed	Conferees approved as part of tax bill still requring action. Outlook uncertain.
Home appliance energy standards	Passed	Passed	Conferees approved; not yet passed either house.

couraging property owners to insulate their buildings; (4) levy stiff taxes against cars that used too much gasoline, against businesses that burned oil or natural gas, and against purchasers of domestically produced oil.

Carter's ambitious energy plan soon became bogged down in political realities. There is no single, simple answer why his energy program foundered, but an analysis by Congressional Quarterly[20] identified a number of contributing factors:

---

[20] See *1977 CQ Almanac*, pp. 708-709.

It was a plan tackling inherently difficult political problems that was drafted virtually in secret by non-political technicians.

Its drafting was rushed and consequently the plan suffered from technical flaws, which undermined confidence in it.

It was the object of intense and negative lobbying by a broad range of powerful special interest groups.

It was poorly presented to Congress by Carter's lobbyists.

It lacked a constituency.

Despite those drawbacks, the Carter energy program managed to pass the House virtually intact Aug. 5, 1977. Then it moved to the Senate, where it was butchered. In addition to the basic problems previously listed, at least four other problems arose:

There was a complete loss of momentum between the time of House passage and Senate consideration, caused principally by the August 1977 recess and the troubles of Bert Lance, then Carter's budget director.

The two Senate committees handling the Carter energy plan had a different predisposition toward energy policy than their two counterpart committees in the House.

The Senate was guided by a different style of leadership than was the House, due in part to the nature of the Senate and in part to the nature of Senate Majority Leader Robert C. Byrd, D-W.Va.

The administration misread the Senate, hoping it would come through somehow for the president as had the House.

The administration is optimistic that it can overcome these problems. But the energy bill that finally emerges from Congress likely will be much different from the energy program President Carter proposed more than 16 months ago.

Factors in Future Policy

C ARTER'S sole success in energy legislation has been the creation of the mammoth Department of Energy (DOE). When the president on March 1, 1977, proposed a government reorganization, he said: "Nowhere is the need for reorganization and consolidation greater than in energy policy. All but two of the executive branch's Cabinet departments now have some responsibility for energy policy, but no agency...has the broad authority needed to deal with our energy problems in a comprehensive way."

In naming a secretary of energy to direct the new department,

Carter chose James R. Schlesinger, who had served under Presidents Nixon and Ford as chairman of the Atomic Energy Commission, director of the Central Intelligence Agency, and secretary of defense. Though abrasive, he was reputed to be a tough, intelligent manager who made things work.

The new department has been under fire almost since Carter signed its enabling legislation Aug. 4, 1977. Most of the early criticism focused on the inability of the department to guide the energy legislation through Congress. But recently new criticism has surfaced. Most of it is directed at Schlesinger's apparent inability to make the unwieldy agency function smoothly. Among other problems cited are the continuing failure of the agency to fill its top leadership jobs. For most of the year after it was created, DOE did not have a general counsel, an inspector general or three key assistant secretaries — for defense programs, environment, and conservation and solar applications. This has resulted in some bureaucratic and legal snarls, including a General Accounting Office opinion, disputed by the Justice Department, that the interim acting chiefs in those jobs did not have legal authority because they had not been confirmed by the Senate.

DOE sometimes responds to its critics by pointing its finger at the Senate. Schlesinger's nominee for general counsel, Lynn Coleman, waited eight months before his nomination was confirmed by the Senate. Coleman was a partner in a Houston law firm with oil industry clients, a fact that troubled some senators who delayed action on his nomination. The nomination of Omi Walden as assistant secretary for conservation and solar applications was delayed for six months while her role in fuel allocations in Georgia during 1973-74 was investigated. She had been director of the Georgia energy office when questionable practices were alleged to have occurred. She was cleared, and confirmed for the post.

Because of the staffing problems, and because the regulations it administers are complex, the department is not able to work as rapidly as many would like. *The Wall Street Journal,* for example, castigated it in a recent editorial for taking too long to review a request by Cities Service to build a natural gas pipeline from Wyoming to Kansas and Missouri. The Journal suggested that DOE change its name to DONE, the Department of No Energy. "Clearly the true function of that labyrinthine, super-expensive department is to prevent Americans from having energy."[21]

Schlesinger has acknowledged the validity of some of the criticism of his department. In his defense, he speaks of the vast

---

[21] *The Wall Street Journal,* Aug. 7, 1978.

amount of time he must spend lobbying Congress for passage of the energy legislation. "No question about it," he has said, "the dual track we've been pressing ahead on has resulted in some distraction from our underlying objectives. Most of my time has to be devoted to the legislative goals, and less of it to the internal management matters that I prefer. We have a great deal of room for improvement."[22]

Conflicting Scenarios for the Middle East

Events in places such as Riyadh, Baghdad and Tehran may ultimately have more significance for American oil consumers than events in Congress. Because OPEC and Saudi Arabia in particular control so much of the world's oil,[23] they remain in a position to effectively ration the supply of petroleum and manipulate its price. The key to the question of how much oil will be available in 1985 and how much it will cost may well rest on the ability and willingness of the Middle East to produce the oil the West needs.

The CIA's predictions of a world energy crisis by 1985 *(see p. 140)* are based on gloomy forecasts of what OPEC policies will be in the next few years. The CIA predicted that production from low-reserve countries such as Iran would decline during the 1980s. It also predicted that high-reserve countries — principally Saudi Arabia — would also restrict production in order to conserve oil, in essence banking it for later sale as a hedge against inflation and dollar fluctuations.

This scenario has drawn substantial criticism recently. Robert S. Pindyck, for example, an economist at Massachusetts Institute of Technology, has termed it "unconvincing," arguing that "Saudi Arabia and some of her high-reserve neighbors could as much as double their capacity, particularly if there is a revenue incentive to do so." He went on to say that "as long as these countries are dedicated to pursuing their economic interests, they should increase their capacity, and exploit their oil resources at the optimum price. To do otherwise would be to waste the economic value of their resources."[24]

A recent General Accounting Office report took a line somewhat between that of Pindyck and the CIA. The report concluded that "Saudi Arabia's dominance among oil exporters is expected to increase in the years to come.... However, continued increases in Saudi Arabia's oil production cannot be taken for

---

[22] Quoted in *Time*, June 19, 1978, p. 67.

[23] Of the 16.6 billion barrels of oil produced in the non-communist world in 1976, 11.9 billion barrels (72 percent) were produced in OPEC countries. Saudi Arabia alone produced 3.1 billion barrels. See Department of Energy, "International Petroleum Annual 1976," June 1978. pp. 20-21.

[24] Robert S. Pindyck, "OPEC's Threat to the West," *Foreign Policy*, spring 1978, p. 43.

granted by the United States. Its capability and willingness to increase production is dependent on many complex and interrelated technical, political, security and economic factors."[25]

The Petroleum Industry Research Foundation did not directly deal with the use of oil as a political weapon, but commissioned Dankwart A. Rustow of the City University of New York to consider the question. Rustow concluded that "economic factors are likely to remain the crucial determinants of the price and availability of oil for the remainder of this century. The political factors that played such a prominent role in the petroleum crisis of 1973-74 are likely to have less of an effect in the future...."[26]

Significance of Iraqi, Mexican Reserves

Major new oil discoveries could render the pessimistic predictions of the CIA, Yergin, and others meaningless. And it appears likely that some discoveries in Iraq and Mexico are indeed major. Iraq has been producing oil since about 1914, but has never been one of the world's big producers. Its current production of 884 million barrels a year is less than one-third of Saudi Arabia's 3.1 billion, but there has been evidence for some time that Iraq may have reserves far in excess of 34 billion barrels. In 1976 the late John Blair described CIA reports that Iraq had "fantastic" untapped reservoirs of oil.[27]

Because Iraq's government is very secretive, little is known about the true dimensions of oil in the country, but some recent estimates of its reserves have been on the order of 100 billion barrels. If true, its potential would be second only to Saudi Arabia (with 154 billion barrels of proved reserves) in OPEC. Iran, now No. 2, has 62 billion barrels of proved reserves.[28] Iraq also appears to be moving away from the Soviet political orbit and observers suggest that the government may wish to exploit its oil strength in coming years.

Recent discoveries in southeastern Mexico in the states of Tabasco and Chiapas may turn Mexico, now a very minor oil producer, into another Saudi Arabia. Pemex, the government-owned oil company, has recently speculated that Mexican proved reserves may soon be set at 120 billion barrels. Current figures credit Mexico with only about 17 billion barrels of proved reserves, and production of 327 million barrels annually.

---

[25] General Accounting Office, "Critical Factors Affecting Saudi Arabia's Oil Decisions," May 12, 1978, p. i.

[26] Petroleum Industry Research Foundation, *op. cit.,* p. a-18. In an earlier article, "Oil Crises of the 1980s," *Foreign Affairs,* winter 1977-78, pp. 494-516, Rustow generally supported the CIA analysis of Saudi production cutbacks by around 1985.

[27] Blair, *op. cit.,* p. 19.

[28] Figures from Department of Energy. Proved reserves are the oil recoverable from known reservoirs and under existing economic and operating conditions.

The new discoveries appear to be spectacular. In an industry where the success rate in explorations is only about 9 percent — nine oil strikes for every 100 holes drilled — Mexico is finding oil in 63 percent of its wells in the two states. George Grayson, a political scientist at the College of William and Mary who has a special interest in Mexico, has written: "Pemex claims proven, probable and possible reserves of 120 billion barrels. No doubt this puffing is designed to secure foreign investment, credit and political support. Still, a number of foreign geologists and petroleum engineers consider 17 billion barrels to be an implausibly low figure and believe that reserves really exceed 60 billion barrels."[29]

Mexico's potential as an oil producer is doubly enticing to the United States. Not only is Mexico a neighbor, it is not a member of OPEC. U.S.-Mexican relations have often been hostile but the economies of the two countries are closely tied.[30] American funds and technology are already very much in evidence in Mexico's oil development.

The modern world turns on oil. Its availability and the price that nations must pay for it have understandably dominated world councils in recent years. That situation is likely to continue. Regardless of the success of the United States in redeeming President Carter's pledges at the Bonn economic summit this year — and success is far from assured — oil will not vanish from the agenda of global concerns.

---

[29] George Grayson, "Mexico's Opportunity: The Oil Boom," *Foreign Policy,* winter 1977-78, p. 73.

[30] See "Mexican-U.S. Relations," *E.R.R.,* 1977 Vol. II, pp. 701-720.

Selected Bibliography

Books

Blair, John M., *The Control of Oil*, Pantheon Books, 1976.

Exploring Energy Choices, Ford Foundation, 1974.

Fried, Edward R. and Charles L. Schultze, eds., *High Oil Prices and the World Economy*, The Brookings Institution, 1975.

Mitchell, Edward J., ed., *Dialog on World Oil*, American Enterprise Institute, 1974.

———*U.S. Energy Policy: A Primer*, American Enterprise Institute, 1974.

Tanzer, Michael, *The Political Economy of International Oil and the Underdeveloped Countries*, Beacon Press, 1969.

Vallenilla, Luis, *Oil: The Making of a New Economic Order*, McGraw-Hill Book Company, 1975.

Articles

"A Department in Disarray," *Time*, June 19, 1978.

Grayson, George W., "Mexico's Opportunity: The Oil Boom," *Foreign Policy*, winter 1977-78.

"New World Economic Order," *Business Week*, July 24, 1978.

Phillips, Kevin P., "The Energy Battle: Why the White House Misfired," *Public Opinion*, May/June 1978.

Pindyck, Robert S., "OPEC's Threat to the West," *Foreign Policy*, spring 1978.

Sheils, Merrill, "Mexico's Oil Bonanza," *Newsweek*, Aug. 14, 1978.

"Two at the Summit," *Newsweek*, July 24, 1978.

Yergin, Daniel, "The Real Meaning of the Energy Crunch," *The New York Times Magazine*, June 4, 1978.

Reports and Studies

American Petroleum Institute, "Estimated U.S. Supply /Demand Situation," July 19, 1978.

Central Intelligence Agency, "The International Energy Situation: Outlook to 1985," April 1977.

Department of Energy, "International Petroleum Annual 1976," June 1978.

Department of State, "The United States and World Energy," November 1977.

Editorial Research Reports, "America's Coal Economy," 1978 Vol. I, pp. 281-300; "Dollar Problems Abroad," 1978 Vol. I, pp. 401-420; "Oil Antitrust Action," 1978 Vol. I, pp. 101-120.

General Accounting Office, "Critical Factors Affecting Saudi Arabia's Oil Decisions," May 12, 1978; "The Federal Government Should Establish and Meet Energy Conservation Goals," June 30, 1978.

Petroleum Industry Research Foundation, "Outlook for World Oil into the 21st Century," May 1978.

Resources for the Future, "Oil and Gas Resources — Welcome to Uncertainty," March 1978.

The Trilateral Commission, "Energy: Managing the Transition," final published version scheduled for September 1978.

Brown, Lester R., "Redefining National Security," Worldwatch Institute, 1977.

AFRICAN POLICY REVERSAL

by

Richard C. Schroeder

**July 14
1 9 7 8**

Editor's Note: Since this report was written, black and white Rhodesians have elected a government headed by a black prime minister, Abel T. Muzorewa, but in which 28 of 100 seats in the new parliament are reserved for whites.

A 1978 U.S. law requires President Carter to lift American economic sanctions against Rhodesia upon his determination that a government had been installed in the country by free elections and showed a willingness to negotiate with the black guerrilla organization, the Patriotic Front.

The elections were held in April 1979 and he had made no determination when the Senate on May 15 adopted a "sense of Congress" resolution declaring (1) that the elections were indeed free, (2) that the new multiracial government satisfied U.S. demands for black majority rule, and (3) that the sanctions should be lifted.

By withholding such a determination, Washington could put pressure on the new Rhodesian government to negotiate with the guerrillas — a course of action pleasing to most of black Africa. While the Senate did not legally bind the U.S. government to act, the lopsided vote (75 to 19) forced the Carter administration to give utmost consideration to taking prompt action.

The vote was a rebuff to the new policy the administration has been following in black Africa, which is discussed in this report.

AFRICAN POLICY REVERSAL

THE Organization of African Unity (OAU) will open its 15th annual meeting in Khartoum, the capital of the Sudan, on July 19. The meeting may be the most critical since the OAU was set up in Addis Ababa, Ethiopia, in May 1963. A proposal to create a pan-African peacekeeping force to intervene in African border disputes and forestall foreign intervention is backed by the United States and several of its allies, especially the former French colonies. But countries with close ties to the Soviet bloc have assailed it as a "neocolonial" plot. The OAU's Liberation Committee, in a preliminary meeting June 23 in Dar es Salaam, Tanzania, denounced the plan and demanded that "the imperialists, their lackeys and their mercenaries in Africa" keep hands off the continent and let the African nations solve their own problems.

The issue of foreign involvement in Africa[1] was brought to a head in May when 1,300 Belgian paratroopers and 600 French Foreign Legionnaires were flown — in U.S. planes — into Zaire's Shaba (formerly Katanga) province to repel an invasion by Katangese rebels based in Angola. The rebels seized Kolwezi, capital of copper-rich Shaba and held it for several days. The death toll reached at least 855, according to a body count by the International Red Cross, of which more than half were civilians, including 136 Europeans. The Belgian and French troops removed the city's 2,250 European residents and drove the invaders back into Angola. These troops were replaced in early June by a contingent of Moroccans, also airlifted in U.S. planes.

A year earlier, the same Katangese rebels had invaded Shaba, but were stopped short of Kolwezi by French-supported Moroccan and Zairian troops after more than a month and a half of fighting. At that time, U.S. involvement was limited to supplying 18 transport planes to carry supplies for the French operation. The Carter administration was silent on the issue of Cuban or Soviet support for the invaders. In May of this year, however, the administration responded vigorously, both in offering aircraft and supplies, and in denouncing Cuban responsibility for training and arming the Katangese.

Kolwezi was only one of a number of places where foreign

[1] See "Africa and the Big Powers," *E.R.R.*, 1976 Vol. II, pp. 641-660.

forces have intervened in conflicts between African countries or tribal groups in recent years. In 1975, Cuban soldiers intervened in a civil war in Angola; by most accounts, 23,000 are still in the country, aiding in the continuing fight against anti-government guerrillas.

Late last year, Cuba and the Soviet Union began a buildup of forces in Ethiopia, helping that country stem an invasion from neighboring Somalia. By State Department estimates, there are at least 17,000 Cuban fighting men in Ethiopia, battling insurgents in the Ogaden and Eritrea regions. France also has a huge military presence in Africa, with a total of 10,000 troops in several former colonies, and French soldiers actively fighting a revolt in Chad, a former French colony.

What troubles many African leaders is the potential for still further foreign intervention in African national and tribal wars. "Since African national boundaries were drawn by colonial powers without regard to geographic or ethnographic considerations, irredentism threatens every nation."[2] The most obvious trouble zones are Rhodesia and Namibia (Southwest Africa), where guerrilla forces are being trained by Cuban, Soviet and Eastern European advisers. But the threat of explosive conflict hangs over South Africa, Kenya and several other sub-Saharan nations as well.[3]

U.S. Response to the Invasion of Shaba

During the 1976 presidential campaign President Carter stressed his interest in reducing U.S.-Soviet tensions over Africa. Shortly before the election, he said:

> I think that the United States' position in Angola should be one which admits that we missed the opportunity to be a positive and creative force for good in Angola during the years we supported Portuguese colonization. We should also realize that the Russian and Cuban presence in Angola, while regrettable and counterproductive of peace, need not constitute a threat to the United States' interests, nor does that presence mean the existence of a Communist satellite on the continent.[4]

One of Carter's first presidential appointments was that of Rep. Andrew Young, D-Ga., a civil rights leader, as U.S. ambassador

---

[2] Peter Vanneman and Martin James, "Soviet Thrust into the Horn of Africa: The Next Targets," *Strategic Review*, spring 1978, p. 39. *Strategic Review* is published by the United States Strategic Institute, a non-governmental "think tank" in Washington, D.C., devoted to the study of national security problems. Dr. Vanneman, chairman of the political science department of the University of Arkansas, was an adviser to the president of Tanzania in 1966-67. James is a research assistant to Sen. Henry Bellmon, R-Okla.

[3] See Walter F. Hahn and Alvin J. Cottrell's *Soviet Shadow Over Africa* (1977). Hahn is deputy director of the Institute for Foreign Policy Analysis at Cambridge, Mass.; Cottrell is director of research at the Georgetown University Center for Strategic and International Studies, Washington, D.C.

[4] Quoted by Gerald J. Bender in "Angola, the Cubans and American Anxieties," *Foreign Policy*, summer 1978, pp. 5-6. Bender, former congressional aide, is visiting assistant professor of political science at the University of California, San Diego.

AFRICA

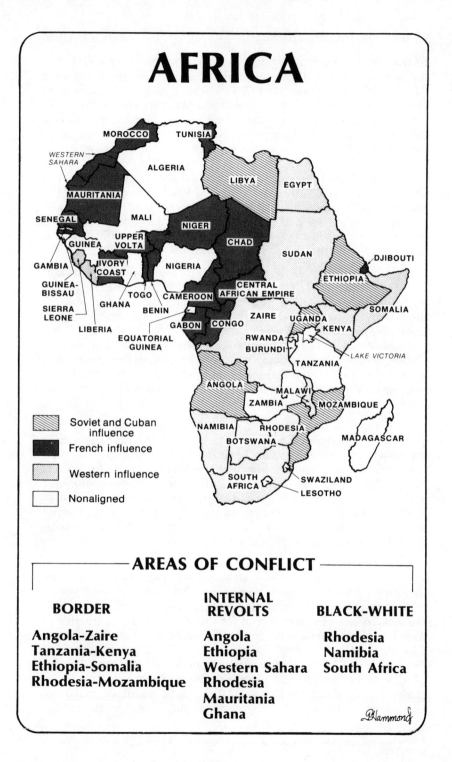

Legend:
- Soviet and Cuban influence
- French influence
- Western influence
- Nonaligned

AREAS OF CONFLICT

BORDER

Angola-Zaire
Tanzania-Kenya
Ethiopia-Somalia
Rhodesia-Mozambique

INTERNAL REVOLTS

Angola
Ethiopia
Western Sahara
Rhodesia
Mauritania
Ghana

BLACK-WHITE

Rhodesia
Namibia
South Africa

155

to the United Nations. Young was given special responsibilities for overseeing the formulation of a new U.S. policy toward Africa, particularly southern Africa where black majorities were challenging white minority governments and colonial rule in several places. For the first time, a representative of this country's 23 million black people had an influential role in shaping American policy toward the continent of their ancestry. Young was outspoken — to the point of creating controversy at home and abroad — in his criticism of white minority regimes. Early in the Carter administration, at least, it seemed that the United States would discard the "big power" politics of confrontation in Africa that had characterized previous administrations and would concentrate instead on the ethnic, political and economic problems of the African nations themselves.

Gradually, however, Carter and his assistant for national security affairs, Zbigniew Brzezinski, seemed to become preoccupied with the growing Soviet and Cuban presence in and influence over such African states as Angola, Mozambique and Ethiopia. In late 1977, Carter indicated that the progress of U.S.-Cuban reconciliation depended on the swift withdrawal of Cuban troops from Angola, a suggestion which was brusquely turned down by Cuban leader Fidel Castro, who said: "This has nothing to do with Carter nor with the United States. Our relations with Africa are not negotiable."

By early this year, the Carter administration was expressing alarm over Cuban and Soviet activities in Ethiopia. Brzezinski warned that strategic arms limitation talks (SALT) between the United States and Russia were threatened by the incursions in the Horn of Africa, and on Feb. 16, during a news conference with black journalists, Carter declared that the United States would "consider it a very serious breach of peace, endangering even worldwide peace" if Cuban-supported Ethiopian troops should invade Somalia.[5]

Then early in May, the administration apparently took a sharp turn away from the restraint that had characterized its handling of African affairs. On May 1, Adm. Stansfield Turner, head of the Central Intelligence Agency, visited Sen. Dick Clark, D-Iowa, to unveil a secret plan for "destabilizing" the regime of Angolan leader Agostinho Neto. The plan was based on covert CIA aid to the National Union for the Total Independence of Angola (UNITA), a rebel group entrenched in southern Angola. Clark's agreement to the plan was deemed necessary since, as chairman of the Senate Foreign Affairs Subcommittee on Africa, he was the author of a congressional measure preventing the

---

[5] For background on the Ethiopian war, see "Ethiopia in Turmoil," *E.R.R.*, 1974 Vol. II, pp. 905-924.

president from sending military aid to Angola.[6] Clark concluded that the aid would be illegal even if channeled through a third country. and the matter was dropped.

After the Shaba invasion. Carter charged Cuba with complicity in the affair. saying that "the Cubans have played a key role in training and equipping the Katangans who attacked." Castro vehemently denied the charge. saying he had advance knowledge of the planned invasion and tried to stop it by applying pressure on the Angolan government. He called the accusation "an absolute. total complete lie." and said "it was manufactured in Brzezinski's office."

On May 27. following a meeting with Carter. Soviet Foreign Minister Andrei Gromyko also challenged the president's assertion. saying "the information which the President has at his disposal is not correct — that is our assessment...." Gromyko's undiplomatic observation provoked U.S. protests. but it was seemingly backed up by Andrew Young, who declared in a *U.S. News & World Report* interview: "I don't think anyone can be sure of everything that's going on there — not even the Cubans or the Angolans. I think that even the president's information has been greatly limited by the restrictions on intelligence-gathering inside Angola. and the fact that it's difficult to gather adequate intelligence."[7]

Abrupt Reversal of Hard-Line Approach

Carter continued on the offensive into early June. releasing a summary of CIA evidence purporting to show Cuban involvement in the Zaire invasion, and linking Cuban activity in Africa to the Soviet Union. He had told a news conference in Chicago on May 25: "It's a joke to call Cuba non-aligned. They have military alliances with the Soviet Union; they act at the Soviet Union's direction; they're economically dependent on the Soviet Union; they act as a surrogate for the Soviet Union." He repeated the charge in a speech to the graduating class at the U.S. Naval Academy on June 7, saying "the non-aligned movement is being subverted by Cuba, which is obviously closely aligned with and dependent upon the Soviet Union for economic sustenance and for political and military guidance and direction." Carter added: "The Soviet Union can choose either confrontation or cooperation. The United States is adequately prepared to meet either choice."

The hard-line approach generated considerable criticism within the administration and in Congress, as well as among some of this country's allies which believed the verbal assaults

---

[6] For congressional restrictions on foreign military and economic aid, see *Congressional Quarterly Weekly Report*, June 3, 1978, pp. 1410-1412.

[7] *U.S. News & World Report*, June 12, 1978, p. 25.

on Cuba and Russia threatened détente and the negotiation of a strategic arms agreement. Senator Clark complained that "in the last few weeks we have made the Cubans into the third superpower."[8] Sen. George McGovern, D-N.D., said he found "the vehemence of the reaction hard to understand and completely out of line with what the president himself has often told us are his priorities."[9] Sen. Frank Church, D-Idaho, the prospective chairman of the Senate Foreign Relations Committee in the next Congress, said he was concerned by the president's harping on the theme "the Russians are coming." Church said: "The SALT negotiations are much more important than the Cuban or Russian connection in Africa."[10]

Stung by such criticism, the administration late in June slipped out of the Cold War rhetoric as quickly as it had slipped into it two months earlier. Speaking to the U.S. Junior Chamber of Commerce (Jaycees) at Atlantic City and testifying before the House International Relations Committee, Secretary of State Cyrus R. Vance adopted a conciliatory line. In Atlantic City, he said, "We believe it could be helpful to increase our consultations with the Angolan government and begin working with it in more normal ways, in order to improve the prospects for reconciliation between Angola and Zaire, as well as for achieving a peaceful settlement in Namibia." Despite the fact that the United States has never recognized the government of Angola and has no diplomatic mission in Luanda, one day later Vance dispatched a senior member of the U.S. Mission to the United Nations, Donald F. McHenry, to Angola for talks with President Neto.

Policy Split in the Carter Administration

The move was as surprising as it was sudden. Graham Hove, a *New York Times* Washington correspondent, wrote on June 23 that "there have been few reversals in the recent conduct of American foreign policy that seemed as abrupt or complete as this one." Unexpected or not, the initiative appeared to bear fruit. On his return to the United States on June 24, McHenry reported to Vance that Angolan officials had expressed an interest in "stabilizing" the Angola-Zaire border. Neto reportedly indicated Angola would restrain the Katangese rebels within its jurisdiction, in return for Zairian efforts to check Angolan guerrillas who make across-the-border raids from bases in Zaire. As if to underscore the diplomatic shift, Fidel Castro on June 27 told a group of American mayors visiting Havana that he was willing to meet with President Carter personally to discuss out-

---

[8] Quoted by Sanford J. Ungar in "The Real Reasons for Our Africa Role," *The Washington Post*, June 18, 1978. Ungar is managing editor of *Foreign Policy* magazine.
[9] George McGovern, "Alarmism on Africa," *The Washington Post*, July 1, 1978.
[10] Interview, June 9, 1978.

standing differences between Cuba and the United States. But, he added, Carter must take the initiative.

Some Washington observers see in the "double reverse" on African policy signs of a serious schism in high administration circles. Brzezinski is regarded as the architect of the hard-line stance and the author of the CIA destabilization plan presented to Clark, while Vance and Young are identified as the leaders of the moderate approach.[11] In this scenario, Vance and Young emerged victorious.

Not all agree with this interpretation, however. Liberal columnist Carl Rowan writes: "The reality is that there never have been any clear lines of difference between Brzezinski and Vance on what U.S. African policy should be. This administration was bequeathed not only a can of worms involving Angola and Zaire, but a set of Kissinger dogma and assumptions that involved more personal pique than wisdom. So Vance, Brzezinski, President Carter and other U.S. officials have been fumbling, groping frustratedly for an African policy that makes sense."[12]

Whether or not there actually was a Brzezinski-Vance showdown on Angola, several factors contributed to the administration's retreat from its brief foray into Cold War rhetoric. There was formidable congressional and public opposition to anything that smacked of Vietnam-style involvement in Africa. At a White House meeting with Carter, Rep. E. (Kika) de la Garza, D-Texas, is reported to have declared that people in his district did not even know where these African countries are and would never support American intervention. Columnist Joseph Kraft called Carter a "tyro" — novice — in foreign policy, and wrote that "the sensible thing for Carter would be to follow two previous presidents not overly versed in foreign policy — Truman and Eisenhower — who placed prime reliance on the secretary of state."[13]

Carter may also have been taken aback by the intensity of reaction from African leaders. The president reportedly received three confidential messages from Tanzanian President Julius Nyerere, one of Africa's most influential leaders, asking him to back down a bit. Interviewed June 25 on the ABC television program, "Issues and Answers," Nyerere characterized Carter as "an honest person" misguided by "hysterical" voices telling him the United States "can prove its toughness to the Soviet Union" in Africa. "This," said Nyerere, "we don't like."

[11] See, for example, I.F. Stone's "Carter, Africa & SALT," *The New York Review*, July 20, 1979, pp. 22-27.

[12] Carl T. Rowan, "A Sound American Policy on Africa," *The Washington Star*, June 28, 1978.

[13] Joseph Kraft, "The Foreign Policy Tyro," *The Washington Post*, June 13, 1978.

A final and possibly determining factor may have been the realization by the administration that Zaire was the wrong place for the United States to make a stand. By the accounts of most observers, the regime of President Mobutu Sese Seko is one of the most corrupt and brutal in Africa.[14] In 13 years of iron-fisted rule, Mobutu has ruthlessly suppressed all opposition, quarreled with most of the neighboring African states and led the country to the brink of bankruptcy. Mobutu has been negotiating for a billion-dollar emergency aid package with the International Monetary Fund and Western nations,[15] and is under pressure from the United States and other countries to ease his harsh rule.

Foreign Involvement in Africa

A VAST storehouse of raw materials, Africa is coveted by the developed nations of both the East and West.[16] Its balkanized tribal politics offer a tempting invitation for foreign meddling and influence-seeking. An expert on African affairs describes the political situation this way:

> Africa is highly unstable because it is experiencing a period of profound historic change — the kind of change one saw in Western Europe in the seventeenth and eighteenth centuries when, with the rise of the nation States, there were conflicts over borders and everything else.
>
> Just as Europe and America had their periods of unstable government, corrupt governments, military governments, of conflict and slaughter, and so on, such periods are going to exist in Africa as well. And just as some areas of Europe and North America developed stability sooner than others, and aspired to real development, and showed a higher respect for human rights than others, so too will some areas of Africa.[17]

The majority of African nations emerged from colonial rule only after World War II. They exhibit the classic symptoms of arrested political development and severe economic underdevelopment. With the poorer nations of Asia and Latin America, they share such ills as archaic societies, one-crop economies, overworked land, unfavorable climates, endemic disease and overpopulation. Virtually all of black Africa — countries with black majority rule — is caught between rising

---

[14] See, for example, Christoph Gudel's "Report from Central Africa — Zaire: Teetering on the Brink," *Swiss Review of World Affairs,* June 1978, pp. 19-22.
[15] See "Zaire Economic Therapy for a Basket Case," *Business Week,* July 3, 1978, p. 34.32.
[16] See "Nation Building in Africa," *E.R.R.,* 1973 Vol. I, pp. 353-372.
[17] Colin Legum, "The Stakes in Africa" (interview), *Atlas World Press Review,* July 1978, p. 19. Legum is African affairs specialist of the London *Observer* and author of two recent books on Africa, *The Year of the Whirlwind* and *Conflict in the Horn of Africa.*

rates of population growth and the pressures of poverty and unemployment. Unless these governments can somehow satisfy the
aspirations of the people for better lives, the potential for explosive violence will be very high. A Westerner wrote almost a
decade ago: "They [the black African nations] constitute in a
sense the ghettos of the world, and, like ghettos within a modern
nation, have...the capacity to pollute the atmosphere with bitterness,, lawlessness and unpredictability."[18]

Western nations have lent considerable support for African
development efforts in recent years. World Bank lending to sub-
Saharan Africa, for example, reached $964.3 million in 1977.[19]
But, ironically, Western concern has focused more on the
political and strategic threats of communist influence in Africa
than on the more fundamental root of unrest — poverty. To
many observers, this fear of communist domination of newly independent African states is overstressed. African nationalism,
they point out, has its own distinct characteristics, grounded in
tribal and racial politics.

A leading scholar wrote a few years ago: "Communism is no
immediate threat to Africa. If ever the Africans turn to communism it will be due to the stupidity of the white settlers. What
the majority of Africans know about communism is what their
imperialist rulers have told them of the red bogey. Even the
handful of West African intellectuals claiming to be communists
are of a kind that orthodox Marxists would find it difficult to
recognize as true disciples of Marx, Lenin and Stalin."[20]

Castro's Incursions on Soviet Behalf

Virtually from the beginning of his rule in Cuba, Fidel Castro
has envisioned himself as a Third World leader. His early support for revolutionary movements in the Americas was an unset-
tling political factor in the early- and mid-1960s, and a source of
friction not only with the United States, but with a majority of
Latin American nations as well. Cuban adventurism in this
hemisphere brought about the expulsion of the Castro
government from the Organization of American States in 1962
and an economic embargo of the island in 1964. The embargo
was ended in July 1975.[21]

Not so well known is Cuba's longstanding involvement in
African countries. As early as 1963, four years after Castro's coming to power, Cuban troops fought on the Algerian side in a
border war with Morocco. By 1964, according to U.S. intelligence
reports, revolutionaries from several African countries were

---

[18] Waldemar A. Nielsen, *The Great Powers and Africa* (1969), p. 5.
[19] World Bank *Annual Report, 1977.*
[20] George Padmore, *Pan-Africanism or Communism* (1972), p. 355.
[21] See "Cuban Expansionism," *E.R.R.*, 1977 Vol. I, pp. 373-392.

receiving insurgency training in Cuba. Surreptitious Cuban intervention, including the personal involvement of Castro's lieutenant Ernesto "Che" Guevara in Congo-Kinshasha (now Zaire) in 1964-65, has been amply documented[22] as has Cuban assistance to the left-wing government of neighboring Congo-Brazzaville (now the People's Republic of the Congo) from 1966 onward.[23]

By 1967, Cuba was providing technical assistance and training to Angolan guerrillas, then fighting the Portuguese colonial Army. When Portugal granted Angola its independence in 1975, Cuba stepped up its aid to the Popular Movement for the Liberation of Angola (MPLA), which was struggling for control of the country with two other liberation groups, both supported by the United States. A Cuban expeditionary force helped MPLA leader Agostinho Neto defeat his rivals, although significant guerrilla activity continues, in the south and from bases in Zaire.

Cuba's most recent commitment in Africa is to Ethiopia. Cuban troops helped stem a Somali invasion of Ethiopia in the country's Ogaden desert and are now reportedly aiding in suppressing a rebellion in Eritrea province along the Red Sea. During a visit to several African countries in March 1977, Castro attempted to mediate the border dispute between Somalia and Ethiopia, both allies of Cuba and the Soviet Union. His effort failed. When the invasion began in mid-summer, Cuba and the Soviets abandoned Somalia and went to the aid of Ethiopia.

Cuban technicians and military advisers are active in a half a dozen or more African countries and in South Yemen on the Arabian peninsula, where President Salim Robaya Ali was killed in a coup on June 26 and replaced by a pro-Soviet faction. Robaya Ali had opposed Ethiopia's subjugation of Eritrea and was reportedly seeking closer relations with Saudi Arabia.

Kissinger's Initiative in Southern Africa

All administrations since John F. Kennedy's have hewed to a succinct policy line of "Africa for the Africans." Different presidents and secretaries of state, however, have defined in varying ways who the Africans are. Generally speaking, the United States in the 1960s and the early 1970s "tilted" toward the white regimes of southern Africa and shied away from close relations with radical regimes in the black African states. The first break in that tradition came toward the end of the Ford administration when Secretary of State Henry A. Kissinger, moving to head off a racial crisis in Rhodesia, took the first tentative steps toward rapprochement with black African countries.

---

[22] See George W. Grayson's "Cuba's Developing Policies," in *Current History*, February 1977, pp. 49-51.

[23] Robin Hallett, *Africa Since 1875* (1974), p. 485.

African Policy Reversal

In April and May 1976, Kissinger visited six black African nations — Kenya, Tanzania, Zambia, Zaire, Liberia and Senegal — to line up support for a negotiated settlement in Rhodesia. This "shuttle" diplomacy produced a 10-point U.S. proposal based on majority black rule and economic and political guarantees for Rhodesia's white minority. "Of all the challenges we have before us," Kissinger said, "of all the purposes we have in common, racial justice is one of the most basic." He added that the United States does "not recognize the [white] Rhodesian minority regime." He affirmed U.S. support for the eventual independence of Namibia and called for a "peaceful end to institutionalized inequality" in South Africa.

Kissinger's policy shift drew fire from political conservatives in the United States, some of whom have said the shift contributed to Ford's defeat in the 1976 presidential election. In Africa, Kissinger's new stance was strongly criticized by white leaders. Rhodesian Prime Minister Ian Smith called Kissinger an "uninformed meddler" and South African Prime Minister John Vorster wryly observed that Kissinger had talked only with black Africans.

Whether Kissinger, if he had remained in office, could have resolved all or even some of southern Africa's crises is questionable. He did maneuver Smith into an agreement to transfer power to a multiracial government, which led, in the course of the next two years, to the present transitional four-man executive council. Current plans call for the election of a black majority government in Rhodesia before the end of this year. But the underlying split between black radicals on the one hand and black and white moderates on the other continues; the country is still plagued by ferocious internecine guerrilla warfare.

Some African specialists regarded Kissinger's program as a change in tactics rather than a fundamental shift in U.S. policy.[24] There is some evidence that Kissinger's basic views on the continent had not changed since he drafted National Security Study Memorandum 39 (NSSM 39) for President Nixon in 1970. NSSM 39 was dubbed the "tar baby memo" by critics. Its central recommendations read as follows:

> The whites are here to stay and the only way that constructive change can come about is through them. There is no hope for the blacks to gain the political rights they seek through violence, which will only lead to chaos and increased opportunities for the communists.

> We can, by selective relaxation of our stance toward the white regimes, encourage some modification of their current racial and

---

[24] See, for example, Neil O. Leighton's "A Perspective on Fundamental Change in Southern Africa: Lusaka — Before & Beyond," in *Africa Today*, July-September 1976, p. 17. Leighton is assistant professor of political science at the University of Michigan at Flint.

colonial policies and through more substantial economic assistance to the black states (a total of about $5 million annually in
technical assistance to the black states) help to draw the two
groups together and exert some influence on both for peaceful
change...."[25]

Indeed, even after his 10-point proposal, Kissinger continued bitterly to oppose the MPLA in Angola as communist-dominated,
and when it took power he vetoed Angola's application for U.N.
membership in June 1976.

Symbolism of Andrew Young's Diplomacy

Despite the limitations, Kissinger's African initiatives paved
the way for further openings by the Carter administration. The
appointment of Andrew Young, a black, as U.N. ambassador
with special African responsibilities, was a signal that
"diplomatic negotiations would no longer be conducted to please
the South Africans."[26] Young launched a strenuous round of
African visits, calling on the principal black African leaders, including representatives of radical dissident groups. He called for
majority rule in South Africa, "something that had previously
not been part of U.S. policy makers' rhetoric or goals."[27]

Young also made a special effort to solidify U.S. relations with
Nigeria, a country neglected by Kissinger because of its strong
support for Angola's MPLA. Nigeria is Africa's most populous
country, with 68 million people,[28] and is the second largest supplier of crude oil (after Saudi Arabia) to the United States. Since
the end of the Nigerian civil war (1967-1970), the country's
economy has been growing more rapidly than any other in black
Africa, and Nigeria's prestige and influence in the continent
have expanded apace. Largely through Young's efforts,
President Carter included Nigeria in his four-nation overseas
trip in the spring.[29]

As a symbolic gesture to black Africans, Carter pressed for and
obtained congressional repeal of the Byrd Amendment, which
permitted U.S. purchases of Rhodesian chrome in disregard of
U.N. sanctions against the Smith regime. Dozens of nations
have surreptitiously traded with Rhodesia since the U.N. ban
went into effect in 1965. Nevertheless the Byrd Amendment had
been a barrier to better U.S.-African relations.

The political right in the United States, chagrined by the

---

[25] *Ibid.,* p. 17.

[26] Richard E. Bissell, "United States Policy in Africa," *Current History,* December 1977,
p. 194. Bissell is managing editor of *Orbis* magazine and author of two recent books on
African international relations.

[27] Michael A. Samuels, "The Evolving African Policy of the United States," *Vital
Speeches,* Sept. 15, 1977, p. 723. Samuels is executive director of the Third World Studies
Center for Strategic and International Studies.

[28] Mid-1978 estimates of the Population Reference Bureau Inc., Washington, D.C. A
Nigerian census in 1973 recorded a population of 79,758,969 but has been challenged as being
inflated.

[29] Between March 28 and April 3, Carter visited Venezuela, Brazil, Nigeria and Liberia.

amendment's repeal, was further disturbed by an Andrew Young remark that Cuban forces represented a "stabilizing influence" in Angola. Carter's human rights campaign has run into trouble on the ground that it applied only to minority white regimes in Africa, and not to such repressive black governments as those of President Idi Amin in Uganda, Emperor Bokassa I of the Central African Republic, and General Mobutu in Zaire. There is also a keen awareness that, for all the energy and talk expended, the Rhodesian crisis is not much closer to settlement than it was two years ago when Kissinger undertook his southern African "shuttle" diplomacy.

U.S. Interests in the Continent

SOVIET and Cuban activity in Africa is viewed by many — but not all — in Washington as a challenge to American interests on a broad range of issues in many parts of the world. In his June 7 speech at Annapolis, President Carter linked Soviet behavior in Africa with the détente and SALT. This global approach to regional problems is believed by many observers to be similar to the policy perspectives of Henry Kissinger in the previous administration.

In the current debate over future American policy in Africa, the globalist view is generally identified with the National Security Council[30] and particularly Brzezinski, while the area approach is linked to the State Department as represented by Vance and Young. The current U.S.-Soviet engagement in Africa is obviously too complex to reduce to simple global vs. regional formulas, but it is apparent that Africa — much to the dismay of African leaders — is a prime area of East-West competition. Each side is using African hot spots to test the other's will and intentions, and each side is maneuvering to deny strategic raw materials to the other while gaining access for itself.

Attraction of Mineral Wealth and Trade

In the long run, Africa's raw material potential may be the most important factor in the competition of the superpowers for influence in the continent. The United States has long counted on white-ruled South Africa as a secure source of strategic minerals, including uranium, chrome, cobalt, gold and diamonds. But there is increasing awareness that black Africa, too, is rich in commodities and minerals. The oil riches of

---

[30] Council members are, by law, the president and vice president and the secretaries of state and defense. Its advisers, also designated by law, are the chairman of the military joint chiefs of staff, the CIA director, and presidential assistant for national security affairs.

Nigeria, the copper deposits of Zaire and the vanadium mines of Gabon may be only a faint portent of the subsoil wealth of black Africa.

Geologically speaking, this is the least explored and exploited of the world's major regions — the oceans excepted. In an ironic twist, one task of Cuban troops in Angola is to guard the employees and installations of Gulf Oil Corp. in the enclave of Cabinda, which is separated from Angola by a narrow strip of Zaire. Gulf produces 122,000 barrels of oil a day from its Cabinda wells; taxes and royalties from the installations provide 60 to 80 percent of the income of the Angolan government.

Africa represents a growing market for goods, particularly for Western Europe, but also for the United States as well. Nigeria's relative affluence has whetted its appetite for this country's goods;[31] as other African countries develop, and especially if petroleum or mineral deposits are found, the market will expand rapidly.

There are also strategic and military factors that come into play. The South Africans, for example, have long stressed the importance of the sea route around the Cape of Good Hope, an importance which has increased rather than diminished in recent years with the use of oil supertankers too large to transit either the Suez or Panama Canals. The United States is not in open competition with the Soviet Union for African bases, but it does seek port privileges, aircraft landing rights and overflight permission. A concomitant aim of the Soviet Union is to deny such access to U.S. commercial and military vessels and planes.

Finally, according to Carter administration pronouncements, the United States has an abiding interest in the human rights situation in Africa — including not only political freedoms but the human right to be fed, clothed and housed decently. Unfortunately, both political and material rights are severely restricted in a majority of African countries, both black and white. Freedom is a scarce commodity in such countries as Zaire, Uganda and the Central African Republic. And in most of the black African countries, vast numbers of people suffer malnutrition, disease and privation in urban slums and primitive rural villages.

Among the extracontinental powers, the United States and the Soviet Union have the biggest stakes in Africa. American companies have invested more than $4 billion in the continent, and are active even in areas where Soviet influence is dominant. Am-

---

[31] U.S. exports to Nigeria rose from $114 million in 1972 to $958 million in 1977. However, U.S. imports from Nigeria — mostly oil — have expanded much faster, growing from $271 million in 1972 to almost $6.1 billion in 1977.

bassador Young remarked recently, "You bleed the Cubans and you destroy Gulf Oil in Angola," a reference to the petroleum company's important holdings in Cabinda. The Russians, for their part, are major suppliers of weapons and equipment to numerous African rebel groups and "client" governments, such as in Angola and Ethiopia. The Soviet Union shipped $500 million in war materiel to Ethiopia in the latter half of 1977, according to U.S. intelligence sources, after supplying former ally Somalia with $1 billion in arms during the previous seven years.

Closely allied to the Soviet Union in Africa and often, in President Carter's description, acting as a "surrogate" for the Russians is Cuba. It is estimated in Washington that 43,000 Cuban troops are now in 14 African countries. Some, as in Angola and Ethiopia, are front-line combat forces. Others are training and equipping revolutionary cadres for action against white-controlled governments. In Mozambique, for example, several hundred Cuban "technicians" work with Rhodesian rebels at base camps along the border.

Cuba's motives for involvement in Africa are the source of debate among experts. Clearly, the island is heavily in debt to the Soviet Union and may be expected to follow the Soviet policy line as closely as possible. The Soviet subsidy to Cuba — in the form of direct aid, technical assistance, cut-price oil supplies, and sugar purchases at prices well above free market levels — is believed to be more than $2 billion a year. Another impelling factor may be Fidel Castro's vision of himself as a leader of Third World freedom fighters. This latter consideration guarantees that, while Soviet and Cuban interests in Africa often converge, they are not always identical. In Ethiopia, for example, Castro has long supported the cause of independence for Eritrea. He is resisting pressure from the Soviet Union and the government in Addis Ababa to support Ethiopia's military efforts to crush the Eritrean rebels.

Other Powers: France, Belgium and China

On the U.S. side, this country's most formidable ally in Africa is France, formerly a major African colonial power. It has been suggested that France is becoming America's "surrogate" in Africa, a counterweight to Russia's use of Cuban troops in the continent.[32] In recent months, French forces have moved into combat not only in Zaire, but in Western Sahara (formerly Spanish Sahara) against Algerian-backed Polisario guerrillas, and in Chad against Libyan-supported guerrillas intent on overthrowing the government of President Felix Malloum. Press reports commonly state the number of French troops in the con-

---

[32] For elaboration of this view, see *The Economist*, May 13, 1978, pp. 57-58. See also "Our French Connection in Africa" in *Foreign Policy*, winter 1977-78, pp. 160-166.

Africa's Volatile Politics

Two sudden and unexpected changes of government underscore the turbulence of African politics. Ghana's military strong man, Gen. I. K. Acheampong, in power for the past six years, abruptly resigned the presidency on July 5, reportedly under pressure from his fellow military officers. He was replaced by Lt. Gen. Fred Akuffo, Acheampong's deputy on the six-man Supreme Military Council and the nation's defense chief.

Acheampong faced mounting criticism for his handling of the country's deteriorating economic situation. Inflation in Ghana is running at a rate of 150 percent a year; in recent months, there have been protest demonstrations and riots by students and the political opposition.

On July 10, the Mauritanian army deposed President Moktar Ould Daddah, who had ruled the nation since it won independence from France in 1960. Ould Daddah was replaced by Gen. Mustapha Ould Mohammed Salek, army chief of staff. The Mauritanian military was said to be disturbed with the course of a protracted war against the Polisario Liberation Front, an Algerian-based guerrilla force fighting for the independence of Western Sahara, a former Spanish colony partitioned between Mauritania and Morocco in 1976.

tinent at 10,000, but some observers suggest that a "careful count" might show a considerably larger French presence.

There are other NATO members with obvious economic and political stakes in Africa. Belgium, as a former colonial power, still has business investments in Zaire valued at $1 billion or more. The Brussels government maintains contact not only with the Mobutu regime in Kinshasa but also with the Front for the National Liberation of the Congo, the group that staged the invasion of Shaba province in May. Belgium is reportedly ready to accept a Liberation Front government, if the front comes to power either in Shaba or throughout Zaire.[33] Among other former European colonial powers, West Germany, Spain, Portugal and Britain all have extensive economic and political interests in Africa. State Department officials say that on the communist side, East Germany and Czechoslovakia are supplementing Soviet weapons supply and military training programs in Angola, Mozambique, Ethiopia and Guinea-Bissau.

One other outside power — China — is less active than it was a few years ago. Peking, along with Washington, backed the UNITA and FNLA guerrillas in Angola in opposition to the Soviet-supported MPLA. China quietly withdrew its aid when it became apparent that the MPLA would gain control of the country. In the early 1970s, China was, in fact, the primary rival of the Soviet Union for influence in black Africa. The Chinese

[33] I. F. Stone, *op. cit.*, p. 26.

provided 27 African nations with $1.8 billion in aid; among other projects built with Chinese aid was the Tanzam Railway, linking Zambia with the Indian Ocean at Dar es Salaam, Tanzania. Since the middle of this decade, the Chinese, preoccupied with internal problems, have scaled down their African presence.

Perspectives for Africa's Own Leadership

The pervasive influence of foreign powers in Africa is the product of the economic and political weakness of the African states themselves. The Organization for African Unity (OAU) has proved ineffective in mediating African national and tribal disputes. The rudimentary stage of development of many black African states prevents them from mounting any credible challenge to the incursions of foreign powers. The outside nations, for their part, are forced into an activist African role, either from humanitarian motives (as was at least partly the case in the Shaba invasion), or from fear of a rival winning an advantage. Until very recently, the most powerful sub-Saharan African country has been South Africa. The threat of South Africa's economic and military strength has served as an effective brake on any major black African initiative, particularly in southern Africa. South African leaders, and some Western strategists as well, have viewed that nation as the primary guarantor of southern African stability and as the only viable counterpoise to communist influence.

That situation is now changing. The humiliating defeat of South African forces by Cuban troops in Angola eroded part of South Africa's reputation for military excellence. The rise of Nigeria as a formidable economic (although not yet military) power, and the political involvement of Lagos in southern African affairs, have, for the first time, raised the possibility that black Africa can put some muscle into the OAU. Concurrently, the Carter administration's policy shift away from support for the white-dominated government of South Africa has conferred a new international legitimacy on the African nationalist movement.

The current stalemate in Rhodesia implies, to many observers, that black guerrilla forces will prevail against the transitional white-black government. After Rhodesia the next major, and violent, struggle for black domination is likely to come in South Africa. The prospect is for mounting conflict throughout southern Africa and the growing involvement of several African nations and outside powers. The prospect is welcomed by some OAU members and dreaded by others. The creation of a pan-African peacekeeping force, as proposed to the OAU, would not forestall the expected clash, but it would be an important first step toward continent-wide cooperation for political stability and economic development in the trying years ahead.

Selected Bibliography

Books

Hahn, Walter F. and Alvin J. Cottrell, *Soviet Shadow Over Africa*, Center for Advanced International Studies, University of Miami, October 1977 (2nd printing).
Hallett, Robin, *Africa Since 1875*, University of Michigan Press, 1974.
Kahn, E.J. Jr., *The First Decade*, W.W. Norton, 1972.
Nielsen, Waldemar A., *The Great Powers and Africa*, Praeger, 1969.
Padmore, George, *Pan-Africanism or Communism*, Doubleday, 1972.

Articles

Bender, Gerald J., "Angola, the Cubans and American Anxieties, *Foreign Policy*, summer 1978.
Bissell, Richard E., "United States Policy in Africa," *Current History*, December 1977.
Grayson, George W., "Cuba's Developing Policies," *Current History*, February 1977.
Gudel, Christoph, "Report from Central Africa — Zaire: Teetering on the Brink," *Swiss Review of World Affairs*, June 1978.
Legum, Colin, "The Stakes in Africa" (interview), *Atlas World Press Review*, July 1978.
Leighton, Neil O., "A Perspective on Fundamental Change in Southern Africa: Lusaka-Before & Beyond," *Africa Today*, July-September 1976.
Nyerere, Julius, "Why We Reject Our Rescuers," *The Nation*, July 8-15, 1978.
Samuels, Michael A., "The Evolving African Policy of the United States," *Vital Speeches*, Sept. 15, 1977.
Stone, I.F., "Carter, Africa, & Salt," *The New York Review*, July 20, 1978.
Vanneman, Peter and Martin James, "Soviet Thrust into the Horn of Africa: The Next Targets," *Strategic Review*, spring 1978.
Young, Andrew (interview), *U.S. News & World Report*, June 12, 1978.

Reports and Studies

Clark, Dick, *U.S. Corporate Interests in Africa*, Subcommittee on African Affairs, Senate Committee on Foreign Relations, January 1978.
Crocker, Chester A. and Penelope Hartland-Thunberg, *Namibia at the Crossroads: Economic and Political Prospects*, Center for Strategic and International Studies, Georgetown University, 1978.
Editorial Research Reports, "Cuban Expansionism," 1977 Vol. I, p. 373; "Africa and the Big Powers," 1976 Vol. II, p. 643; "Southern Africa in Transition," 1975 Vol. I, p. 245; "Ethiopia in Turmoil," 1974 Vol. II, p. 907; "African Nation Building," 1973 Vol. I, p. 355.
Samuels, Michael A. and the Review editors, *White Paper: The Horn of Africa*, The Washington Review of Strategic and International Studies, May 1978.

DOLLAR PROBLEMS ABROAD

by

William V. Thomas

**June 9
1978**

DOLLAR PROBLEMS ABROAD

IN ECONOMIC TERMS, the 1970s are likely to be remembered as the period when the once "almighty" dollar fell on hard times. Its domestic purchasing power is half what it was in 1965; its value in gold is one-fifth what it was just six years ago. Since the end of World War II, non-Communist countries have pegged their economies to the dollar. But in the face of mounting U.S. trade deficits and spiraling inflation, the dollar's role as an international currency is being challenged as never before.

That topic is expected to be high on the agenda at the economic summit meeting next month in Bonn.[1] Prior to the Bonn conference, leaders of the European Economic Community (EEC — "Common Market") will gather in Bremen, West Germany, on July 6 to discuss the creation of a monetary union linking the principal European currencies to the Deutschmark — one of the world's two (along with the Japanese yen) strongest currencies today. The Bremen conference will be preceded by a meeting of EEC finance ministers in Luxembourg on June 19.

The dollar's immediate problems are related to this nation's sagging balance of trade. The U.S. State Department reported in April that America's trade deficit increased from $9 billion in 1976 to $31 billion in 1977. Imports rose by nearly $28 billion during that time, while exports increased less than $6 billion.[2] Many economists foresee a similar deficit in 1978. They attribute these deficits to: (1) the high U.S. oil import bill — about $40 billion in 1977 — and (2) the reluctance of American businesses to seek foreign markets for their goods. Sales abroad are needed to support domestic employment, restrain trade protectionism and help bring this nation's income from abroad into balance with its foreign spending — on trade, investments, tourism, and military and foreign aid.

Another reason for the dollar's decline is the nature of the U.S. economic commitment around the world. Economist Sidney Lens has written: "In the last dozen years the United States has exacted from its allies a sort of reverse lend-lease. It rang up

---

[1] The meeting will be held July 16-17 and will bring together leaders of the United States, West Germany, Japan, Britain, France, Italy and Canada. The first economic summit was held in Paris in 1975, the second in Puerto Rico in 1976 and the most recent in London in 1977.

[2] See "U.S. Export Expansion Program," U.S. Department of State, April 1978.

ever-increasing balance-of-payments deficits to pay — in part — for such military adventures as the Vietnam war and for a worldwide network of military bases. In the settlement of those deficits, central banks of foreign nations were flooded with dollars which — until 1971 — were redeemable for gold. But since 1971, when the dollar was divorced from gold, these gluts of U.S. currency can only be redeemed for U.S. goods. And there is no way America's trading partners can absorb enough U.S. imports to use up their accumulated dollars."[3]

Foreign countries are stockpiling more dollars than they can spend. And as U.S. imports continue to exceed exports, the amount of dollars held abroad increases. The U.S. Treasury estimates that dollar holdings abroad total $132.6 billion.[4] Meeting in Mexico City in April, officials of the International Monetary Fund (IMF) declared that world economic recovery is imperiled because the United States is incurring huge payment debts while a few other industrial nations — Japan and West Germany in particular — pile up big surpluses. Outgoing IMF Director H. Johannes Witteveen raised the specter of a global recession unless measures are taken to correct the growing imbalance. U.S. officials regard the current trade deficit and the accompanying plight of the dollar as a consequence of America's willingness to support other national economies by buying foreign imports. But the time has come, they add, for West Germany and Japan to carry a greater share of the deficit burden.

Uneven Growth Among Trading Partners

The most important factor in the weakening of the dollar is the disparity between the high growth rate of the U.S. economy and the lower growth rates of America's trading partners. The fact that American imports have outpaced exports reflects a slower growth in U.S. markets abroad than at home. That difference translates into a declining exchange value for the dollar, which has fallen about 20 per cent against the West German mark and Japanese yen in the last two years.

IMF strategy is to coordinate the growth of the biggest industrial countries — Japan, West Germany and the United States — to relieve the strain on the dollar and put the economies of developing nations on firmer ground. To this end, the Fund has called upon Germany and Japan to expand their domestic economies by opening their markets to more imported goods. Japan has announced that it will cooperate to a degree by lowering certain trade restrictions against U.S. agricultural imports. Germany, though, has been reluctant to stimulate its economy. "We will not be pushed [into expansion]," said

---

[3] Sidney Lens, "The Sinking Dollar and the Gathering Storm," *The Progressive*, May 1978, p. 22.
[4] See *U.S. Treasury Department Bulletin*, April 1978.

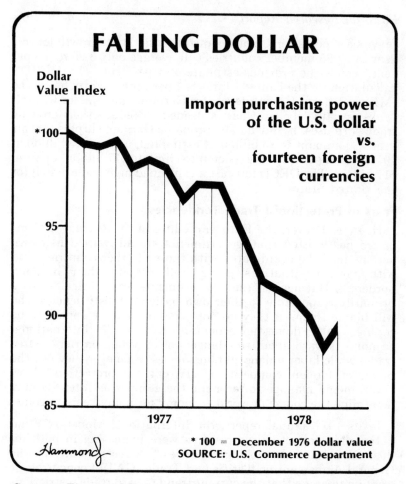

FALLING DOLLAR

Dollar Value Index

Import purchasing power of the U.S. dollar vs. fourteen foreign currencies

*100

95

90

85

1977   1978

* 100 = December 1976 dollar value
SOURCE: U.S. Commerce Department

Hammond

German Finance Minister Hans Matthoefer. "Germany wants growth," but not the sort that could cause high inflation, he added.[5]

In April, the IMF asked the United States to reduce its economic growth rate from an anticipated 4.5 per cent this year to 4 per cent in 1979; it asked Japan to accelerate from an expected 5.7 per cent this year to 7.5 per cent, and West Germany to increase from 3.1 to 4.5 per cent.[6]

Reaching these levels would have a positive influence on the balance of trade, the IMF predicted. However, new estimates released by the Organization for Economic Cooperation and Development[7] cast some doubt on whether growth rates will meet

---

[5] Quoted in *The Washington Post,* May 1, 1978.

[6] See *IMF Survey,* newsletter published by the International Monetary Fund, May 8, 1978.

[7] The OECD is made up of 25 industrial nations: Australia, Austria, Belgium, Canada, Denmark, Finland, France, Germany, Greece, Iceland, Ireland, Italy, Japan, Luxembourg, Netherlands, New Zealand, Norway, Portugal, Spain, Sweden, Switzerland, Turkey, United Kingdom, United States and Yugoslavia (a special status country).

previous expectations. The organization said that growth for this year in its 25 member countries will average only 3.25 to 3.5 per cent, below the previous estimate of 4 per cent. The OECD's calculation for the United States is 4 per cent, slightly below the IMF prediction. Growth levels for Germany and Japan will fall "substantially" below what is needed to reduce their growing trade surpluses, it added. The probable German surplus for this year will amount to $5 billion, it estimated, up from $3 billion in 1977; Japan's surplus is expected to climb to $17 billion, up from $11 billion. The OECD forecast a continued high trade deficit for the United States.

Fears of Protectionist Trade Tendencies

II. Peter Dreyer, the European editor of the *Journal of Commerce,* has written that "governments are all aware...their own actions must be coordinated with those of other countries, and with market situations going well beyond their national borders.... But against that, governments are political entities primarily responsible to their own national constituencies who will blame them...if they do not cope, or at least appear to be coping, with domestic economic troubles."[8] International economists warn about the dangers of imposing barriers to free trade, while labor unions and businesses, whenever they feel the pinch of foreign competition, cry out for protection.[9] How governments manage to reconcile these opposing interests may determine the course of world economy for many years to come.

In its 1977 annual report, the International Monetary Fund noted that protectionist pressures were increasing in both industrialized and developing countries.[10] A recent study by the General Agreement on Tariffs and Trade (GATT) concurred. It went on to argue that the current trend toward trade restrictions points up a refusal by some governments to adjust to changing patterns of supply and demand, and is as much a cause as it is a consequence of the difficulties being experienced by advanced economies.[11]

The present round of GATT negotiations being held in Geneva is seeking ways to minimize protectionism. A July deadline has been set for reaching agreement among the nearly 100 nations represented at the talks. U.S. officials have emphasized, however, that Congress probably will not ratify any agreement that does not contain provisions to guard against the use of

[8] H. Peter Dreyer, "International Economic Paradoxes," *European Community* (publication of the European Economic Community), November-December 1977, p. 3.
[9] See "Job Protection and Free Trade," *E.R.R.*, 1978 Vol. II, pp. 953-972.
[10] International Monetary Fund, "28th Annual Report on Exchange Restrictions," 1977.
[11] Richard Blackhurst, Nicolas Marian and Jan Tumlir, "Trade Liberalization, Protectionism and Interdependence," GATT Studies in International Trade, No. 5, 1977. GATT was established in 1947 by 23 nations, including the United States, to promote the reduction of tariffs and other trade barriers by multinational negotiations.

production subsidies and duties to protect domestic markets. Treasury Under Secretary Anthony M. Solomon said "increased discipline on subsidies should be accompanied by new guidelines on the use...of duties," specifying that they should be applied only when an import "threatens or causes injury to a domestic industry."[12] One proposal now under debate would cut existing tariffs among GATT nations by 40 per cent. An issue still being argued is whether certain allowable tariff practices can be applied selectively by country or must be applied equally to all "favored nation" trading partners, as GATT now requires.

Particularly affected by more liberal trade practices would be countries like Japan and Brazil where protective barriers permit only a minimal import trade. Largely because of its tariffs, Japan last year built up an $11 billion trade surplus. About half of that amount was accounted for by goods sold in the United States, which is effectively frozen out of most Japanese markets by strict quotas and other trade restrictions.

Recent Measures to Stabilize the Dollar

Virtually all economists agree that the dollar's problems abroad have many causes, ranging from trade setbacks to inflation. But there is no consensus among experts on what might be done to solve the dollar's problem. Recently, the U.S. Treasury auctioned off 300,000 ounces of gold at an average price of $180.38 per ounce. The announced aim of the sale was to reduce the balance-of-trade deficit. By selling gold, Treasury officials said they hoped to drive the price down and thus strengthen the dollar. Although the gold sold for about $3 below the prevailing world price, some observers believed the amount was too small to help the dollar significantly. The International Monetary Fund has been selling 500,000 ounces of gold monthly for the last two years, and these sales seem to have done little to hold down the world price of gold or prop up the dollar.

Concern about the condition of the dollar was heightened by bad economic news in the first quarter of 1978. The Labor Department reported that inflation in the United States climbed at an annual rate of 9.3 per cent during January, February and March, a much higher figure than the 6 per cent predicted by the Carter administration for the year. An 0.8 per cent rise in the April Consumer Price Index (CPI) puts the average yearly inflation rate at 9.6 per cent. Economists are divided on how much the federal budget deficit contributes to inflation. But many think that policies to restrict the growth of the money supply will reduce the domestic demand for goods and bring the inflation rate down.

---

[12] Quoted in *The Wall Street Journal*, May 12, 1978.

In an effort to limit the circulation of money and thus help to stabilize prices, the Federal Reserve Board in May raised the basic interest rate on loans to commercial banks to 7.5 per cent, from 7. Additionally, higher interest rates are expected to raise the dollar's exchange value by attracting foreign investment in Treasury bonds and other government securities.

In terms of international trade, a lower rate of inflation anticipated as a result of the Fed's action should improve the position of American exports. According to Paul McCracken, chairman of the Council of Economic Advisers under President Nixon, the persistent undervaluation of other currencies relative to the dollar has put the United States at a "chronic" trading disadvantage by tying the dollar to an "abnormally low exchange rate."[13]

Events Leading to Current Crisis

THE WORLD monetary system at the turn of the century was based on the gold standard. By law, national currencies represented and were exchangeable for a fixed quantity of gold. In 1914, monetary units were standardized as follows:

In Britain, 77 shillings, 10.5 pence equaled one ounce of gold.

In the United States, $20.67 equaled one ounce of gold.

In France, 3,447.74 francs equaled one kilogram of gold.

In Germany, 2,790 marks equaled one kilogram of gold.

International agreements stipulated that when gold left a country for any reason, an appropriate amount of currency had to be withdrawn from circulation. Conversely, when gold flowed into a country, more money had to be printed and added to the economy.

In theory, the gold standard was a self-correcting system. During periods of inflation — classically too much money chasing after too few goods — a nation would pay for imports with currency redeemable in gold. This reduced the purchasing country's money supply and thus helped end its inflation. Under "the rules of the game," countries were expected to solve their own economic problems. A country with a trade surplus, for example, was expected to expand its domestic economy, while a country with a trade deficit was expected to practice austerity.

This neatly arranged system was changed by the events of

---

[13] Paul McCracken, writing in *The Wall Street Journal*, June 2, 1978.

World War I. Warring nations suspended the gold standard at the outbreak of hostilities and removed the automatic limitations on the supply of paper money. Governments borrowed to pay for their wartime needs, and so did private suppliers of military needs. Banks were no longer restricted in the amount of credit they could extend since they did not have to pay out gold on demand. As a result, public debt and rising prices became acute.

Inflation ran rampant after the war, but European leaders were reluctant to impose austerity measures. Some countries printed more money than they had gold and were forced to devalue their currencies. In Germany, Poland, Hungary and Russia, paper money became virtually worthless by 1924. Just as European governments were unwilling to reform their economies, the United States was unwilling to take steps that would have caused inflation. Europeans imported American goods and paid for them in gold. However, the United States did not print as much money as its rising gold supply allowed.

When the European nations reestablished their export trade, gold began to flow out of the United States. The American money supply, though, did not shrink as it would have if the old agreements governing the ratio of gold to currency had been followed in the years immediately after the war. Despite an agricultural depression in this country, a period of easy credit fostered a stock market boom during the mid-Twenties. But later when credit conditions tightened, speculators could not borrow to cover their market debts and were forced to sell their stock holdings at any price. The outcome was the famous Wall Street "crash" of 1929.[14]

Dropping the Gold Standard; Trade Wars

Some economic historians regard the international money situation during the 1920s as the main cause of the stock market collapse and the worldwide recession that followed. Before World War I, gold owned by central banks was the foundation of the world's economy. Part of what went wrong in the decade after the war was that central banks held large parts of their official reserves in the form of bank deposits of securities rather than in gold. Historian Carroll Quigley wrote:

> In the United States credit was diverted from production to speculation, and increasing amounts of funds were being drained from the economic system into the stock market, where they circulated around and around building up the prices of securities. In other countries funds tended to flow to the United States where they could expect to roll up extraordinary earnings in capital gains in a relatively short time.... The stock market crash reduced the

---

[14] See "Wall Street: 40 Years After the Crash," *E.R.R.*, 1969 Vol. II, pp. 753-772.

volume of foreign lending from the United States to Europe. These events tore away the facade which until then had concealed the fundamental maladjustments between production and consumption, between debts and ability to pay....[15]

Britain's heavy investing abroad caused gold reserves to fall to record low levels. In September 1931, after a series of failing attempts to prop up the pound, British authorities cut it loose from the gold standard. Thirty-five countries followed suit, pegging their currencies to the depreciated pound. Britain's abandoning the gold standard, and at the same time adding to the amount of money in circulation, drastically altered the world's financial picture. For several years afterward, nations were divided into two main economic camps. One group organized around the British pound. The other was made up of countries still on the gold standard — the United States, France, Belgium, the Netherlands and Switzerland. But more important, over the long-run, the British action convinced many governments that the new way to deal with economic depression was by increasing, not reducing, the supply of paper money.

Almost immediately, the gold bloc nations adopted higher tariffs to prevent Britain from using its depreciated pound to gain a trade advantage. But as confidence in the pound began to grow, faith in the dollar declined. Finally, the United States dropped the gold standard on March 16, 1933, when President Roosevelt, who had taken office 12 days earlier in the midst of a bank crisis, proclaimed an embargo on the export of gold.

However, protective tariffs enacted during the Hoover administration continued in effect. The Hawley-Smoot Act of 1930[16] raised tariffs to the highest level in U.S. history. Although some economic theorists warned that these barriers would do more harm than good, many voters and politicians thought otherwise. Most Americans paid little heed to predictions of doom. They "did not seem to realize," wrote historian Thomas A. Bailey, "that a creditor nation like the United States could not expect repayment of [war] debts unless it was willing to let other nations earn the necessary dollars by exporting to it."[17] Prevented from selling their goods in America, many foreign countries retaliated by setting high tariffs of their own.

The World Monetary and Economic Conference, held in London in July 1933, proposed a number of emergency measures to remedy the foreign exchange situation; foremost among the recommendations was a general lowering of trade restrictions.

[15] Carroll Quigley, *Tragedy and Hope: The History of the World in Our Time* (1975), pp. 343-344.

[16] The measure was co-sponsored by Sen. Reed Smoot (R Utah) and Rep. Willis C. Hawley (R Ore.). For background, see "Job Protection and Free Trade," *E.R.R.*, 1977 Vol. II, pp. 960-962.

[17] Thomas A. Bailey, *A Diplomatic History of the American People* (1969), p. 656.

But at the time, the United States, which was enjoying a slight economic upswing, refused to join England and France in agreeing to abandon tariffs. A year later, though, Congress at the urging of Secretary of State Cordell Hull passed the Reciprocal Trade Agreements Act, liberalizing American trade policy. The 1934 law gave the President authority to reduce tariffs on a bilateral (two-party) basis. By incorporating "most favored nation" clauses in these agreements, tariff reductions negotiated with one country would be extended to others. Despite some improvement in foreign trade, the U.S. economy remained in a slump until the onset of World War II in Europe. In the end it was neither monetary nor trade policy but fiscal policy — in this case defense spending — that brought on prosperity.

Dollar and IMF Roles in Postwar System

With military victory at last in prospect, finance ministers from 44 allied nations met in June 1944 at Bretton Woods, a New Hampshire resort, to draw up plans for stabilizing the world's monetary system after the war. Their chief aim was to find a way to prevent a recurrence of the financial disasters of the previous two decades.

The basic principle settled on at Bretton Woods was that foreign currencies could be exchanged for U.S. dollars at essentially fixed rates. In effect, the dollar was chosen to fulfill the same function gold had served prior to World War I. The International Monetary Fund (IMF) was established in 1946 to regulate the flow of payments between member countries. Under rules agreed to by the 26 countries that signed the Bretton Woods accord, changes in parity between the dollar and other monetary units had to be sanctioned by the IMF.

Because demands on a nation's currency may vary from time to time, a government needs monetary reserves to support the value of its money in a system of fixed exchange rates. Reserves are held both in gold and in certain foreign currencies, usually in British pounds and U.S. dollars. All countries, except the United States, are required to meet their IMF obligations by buying and selling other currencies — mostly dollars. Until Aug. 15, 1971, when President Nixon declared dollars no longer redeemable for gold (see p. 183), the United States met its basic commitment under IMF rules by freely buying and selling gold to foreign monetary authorities at $35 an ounce.

The 134-member IMF plays the part of "economic tutor" to member nations. But since the United States released the dollar from a fixed rate of exchange in 1971, the organization has lost a good deal of its influence over the course of the world's monetary affairs. The oil crisis of 1973 (see p. 184) further eroded the

Fund's authority. As oil-producing countries have accumulated huge surpluses, some oil-consuming countries have been forced to endure trade deficits. And the IMF, many economists believe, has been all but powerless to correct the imbalance.

Most member nations have been reluctant to cooperate with the Fund's attempts to manage their finances. Poorer countries often have resisted pressure to repair their deficit economies, while certain major industrial nations — most notably Japan and West Germany — have been unwilling to reduce their trade surpluses. The IMF was designed to exercise "firm surveillance" over its members to make sure they do not "manipulate" their exchange rates to obtain "unfair [competitive] advantage." However, that duty is often hampered by ambiguities in the IMF charter. It does not define "manipulation" or "unfair advantage."

One of the original purposes of the Fund, outlined at Bretton Woods, was to..."facilitate the expansion and balanced growth of international trade, and to contribute thereby to the promotion and maintenance of high levels of employment and real income and to the development of the productive resources of all members...." But it has been charged that the IMF often has neglected this goal — that the Fund's emphasis on public spending reductions, devaluation and free trade has undermined governments and created unemployment and political repression in many areas of the world.

While there is growing debate over the best role for the IMF, many observers say that, in the present era of trade deficits and slow economic growth, it must reassert its regulatory authority. In international lending, former Federal Reserve Board Chairman Arthur F. Burns has said, the Fund should enforce "stricter terms" on its loans to borrower nations to assure that debts are paid and a banking crisis avoided.[18]

Devaluation and 'Floating' Dollar in 1970s

At the end of the 1960s, most industrial nations experienced recurrent periods in which wages rose faster than productivity and price trends would warrant. In an effort to control the resulting tide of inflation, the United States undertook a series of economic restraints.[19] But attempts to maintain the parity of the dollar in the face of years of deteriorating competitiveness led to massive U.S. balance-of-payments deficits, an increase in the foreign demand for gold, and ultimately the breakdown of the Bretton Woods agreement.

High inflation and the declining status of the dollar abroad "came about as Presidents pursued covert policies with con-

[18] Quoted in *The New York Times,* May 7, 1978.
[19] See "Economic Controls," *E.R.R.*, 1969 Vol. II, pp. 595-614.

GNP Growth in Major Industrial Countries

Country	Average 1963-64 to 1973-74	1975	From previous year 1976	1977
United States	4.0%	−1.8%	6.1%	4.75%
Japan	9.4	2.4	6.3	6.0
West Germany	4.4	−3.2	5.6	2.75
France	5.4	0.1	5.2	3.0
United Kingdom	2.7	1.8	1.4	0.25
Italy	4.7	−3.5	5.6	2.0
Canada	5.4	1.1	4.9	2.25

Source: OECD

cealed priorities," said Princeton political scientist Edward R. Tufte.[20] Political decisions by Presidents Johnson and Nixon, he argued, inflicted heavy strains on the world economic system. From 1965 to 1968, Johnson did not finance the Vietnam War adequately through taxes. Tufte contended that Johnson hid the true cost of the war effort from Congress, fearing lawmakers might take funds away from Great Society programs to cover military expenses. As a result of this "guns and butter" approach to spending, military and civilian outlays rose by $22 billion between mid-1965 and mid-1966.

The Federal Reserve Board initially resisted administration pressure to add to the amount of dollars in circulation. However, in 1966 the board authorized the first of many increases in the money supply,[21] an action that began an era of high inflation that has not yet ended. Early in 1967, Johnson did ask Congress to enact a 10 per cent tax surcharge to help defray war costs. The special tax took effect in 1968, but it did not offset the easing of money restrictions. The inflation cycle continued.

The inflationary trend persisted under the stimulative monetary policies of President Nixon. Despite temporary wage-price controls put in effect in 1971, the Federal Reserve Board during the Nixon administration pumped greater and greater amounts of money into the economy. The dollar's problems both at home and abroad led to two devaluations during the Nixon presidency. In 1971, it was devalued 8.57 per cent by executive proclamation. In 1973, central bankers meeting in Washington agreed to raise the price of gold from $38 per ounce to $42.22, which had the effect of an 11.1 per cent devaluation of the dollar on the world market.[22]

[20] Quoted in *Business Week*, May 22, 1978.
[21] See "Money Supply in Inflation," *E.R.R.*, 1969 Vol. I, pp. 143-162.
[22] Although the U.S. declared it would no longer redeem its dollar debts in gold after 1971, countries continued to use the dollar to buy gold from one another.

By far the biggest jolt to the international economic system and the condition of the U.S. dollar at home and abroad was registered in 1973-74 when the Organization of Oil Exporting Countries (OPEC)[23] quadrupled the price of oil. This ushered in a new round of inflation and made more apparent the existing faults in the world's monetary structure. In an effort to slow down the inflationary spiral, the United States and other countries hard-pressed by price increases adopted restrictive trade practices. The result was a worldwide recession. By 1974, total world production declined for the first time since the 1930s. Only massive borrowing saved many of the less developed nations from bankruptcy; even some countries in Western Europe ran up large account deficits because of the oil price rise.[24]

Outlook for Economic Reform

THE NEW ROUND of troubles for the dollar, many observers believe, is directly related to the current imbalance in U.S. trade. Oil imports are the most significant contributing factor to the trade deficit. According to the American Enterprise Institute, from 1976 to 1977 oil imports from OPEC to the United States increased from $27 billion to slightly over $40 billion, while U.S. exports to OPEC nations during the same period rose from $12.6 billion to $14 billion.[25]

In 1973, the United States was importing 6 million barrels of oil a day. In 1977, the daily average had risen to nearly 8.5 million. That steady increase in demand, some economists say, has been responsible for the continued rise in oil prices from just below $3 per barrel in 1973 to well above $13 this year. Lester R. Brown, author of a number of books on resource economics, wrote that "the steep rises in petroleum prices reflected the decision by members of OPEC to 'administer' prices, but the strength to make their resolution stick derived from the ability of principal suppliers such as Saudi Arabia and Kuwait to restrict production and from the lack of suitable substitutes for oil." By raising its prices, Brown suggested, OPEC has done "what market forces would do more gradually as oil reserves dwindle."[26]

[23] Current members are Algeria, Ecuador, Gabon, Iran, Iraq, Indonesia, Kuwait, Libya, Nigeria, Qatar, Saudi Arabia, United Arab Emirates and Venezuela.
[24] See "Arab Oil Money," *E.R.R.*, 1974 Vol. I, pp. 363-382, and "World's Slow Economic Recovery," *E.R.R.*, 1977 Vol. II, pp. 745-764.
[25] See *The Economist,* a monthly newsletter published by The American Enterprise Institute for Public Policy Research, April 1978, pp. 2-3.
[26] Lester R. Brown, "The Global Economic Prospect: New Sources of Economic Stress," Worldwatch Paper 20, May 1978, p. 23.

The oil price increase has shifted $80 billion a year in income and investments from the oil-consuming countries to the oil-producing countries, causing the rate of inflation to climb to record peacetime levels in many parts of the world. Carter administration officials contend that a stringent U.S. energy conservation program is the only way to bring OPEC prices down. However, Carter energy legislation, which would strictly limit fuel usage, has been stalled in Congress for more than a year. One adminstration proposal is a tax on domestic crude oil that would raise the fixed U.S. price to the level of OPEC prices and, officials predict, discourage consumption.

Sanford Rose of *Fortune* magazine has argued that the oil deficit by itself does not represent a serious threat to the dollar abroad, since most dollars paid out for petroleum "are never converted into other currencies and thus do not cross the foreign exchanges to help depress the value of the dollar."[27] However, the billions of dollars in revenues that OPEC has amassed is having a negative impact on the world economy. To the extent that this surplus is used to acquire property and other existing assets in the West, the effect is to take spending power out of the world's economic system without putting anything back in its place.

In a report to Congress in April, the Energy Information Administration forecast that U.S. oil imports will climb to 11 million barrels daily by 1985 and to 14.1 million barrels by 1990.[28] It also noted that left unchecked the consumption of energy would rise three-fourths as rapidly as the gross national product (GNP), the total amount of goods and services produced in this country. While the report pointed out that the U.S. economy between 1977 and 1985 would determine the terms on which financing would be available for energy projects, it concluded that such financing could be hampered by a shortage of credit and rising interest rates — conditions brought about by efforts to manage inflation.

President Carter's Effort to Curb Inflation

The dollar's ability to recover its lost value in international trading is being hampered by the current surge of inflation in the United States. Although inflation varies from country to country, the overall average for the 24 OECD nations of Western Europe, Japan and North America during the second half of 1977 was 7.25, just below the 8 per cent average for the last four years. "Once inflation gets going it tends to keep going," Geoffrey H. Moore of the Morgan Guaranty Bank Trust Co. observed.[29]

---

[27] Sanford Rose, "The Dollar Already on the Mend," *Fortune*, April 24, 1978, p. 35.

[28] See *Energy Information Administration Annual Report to Congress, Vol. II, 1977*, April 1978.

[29] Writing in the New York bank's monthly newsletter, *Morgan Guaranty Survey*, August 1977.

Growth of Consumer Prices

	1974	1975	1976	1977
Total OECD	10.5%	8%	8%	7%
United States	8	5.25	5.75	5.75
Japan	11	8.25	7.25	6
West Germany	6	4.5	3.75	4
Total OECD Europe	12.5	10	10	8.75

Source: Organization for Economic Cooperation and Development

Moore and other financial experts point to rising prices for oil, steel and manufactured products as evidence that the momentum of the present inflationary trend will continue.

Within countries, there is a natural motion to inflation as wages and prices race to catch up with each other. On the level of international trading, borrowing costs and the rate of return on investments are significantly affected by the relative rate of inflation among countries. If one country, such as the United States at present, has a comparatively high rate of inflation, its exports will cost more abroad and become less competitive; and it will pay more for its imports.

With the U.S. unemployment rate at 6 per cent for April, down from a 1975 peak of 9 per cent, the Carter administration has shifted its emphasis on expanding the economy to restraining it. This is best shown by a reduction in the administration's recently proposed tax cuts from $25 billion to $19 billion for fiscal year 1979[30] and by the creation of a voluntary anti-inflation program.

In April, President Carter announced that curbing inflation was his No. 1 domestic priority. He asked Congress to impose a 5 per cent ceiling on federal pay raises and called for labor and business to cooperate by holding down wages and prices. The President stopped short of requesting authority to impose wage-price controls.

Although they tend to approve the motive behind the President's effort, many international economic observers concur in the belief that the administration's action falls short of what is needed to manage inflation in the United States and bolster the dollar in foreign trading. Arvum Gruenwald, West German government spokesman for economic affairs, characterized Carter's anti-inflation program as "something of a disappointment" overseas. If the U.S. fails to conduct a more vigorous

---

[30] See "Tax Shelters and Reform." *E.R.R.*, 1978 Vol. I, pp. 241-260.

campaign against inflation, he said, the world could be led into a grave monetary crisis.[31]

The same opinion was voiced by Prime Minister Takeo Fukuda of Japan on a recent visit to Washington. Fukuda warned that world economy is being jeopardized by the inability of the United States to halt the climbing cost of its goods and services.[32] By the end of May, even the White House was pessimistic about its fledgling anti-inflation drive. The success of the voluntary program was "in doubt," a spokesman said, because few business and labor leaders had shown any willingness to make the necessary sacrifices.

Replacing the Dollar as Reserve Currency

Despite its ups and downs, the dollar remains the foundation of the world's monetary system. It is the currency most widely held in reserve by foreign countries and most often accepted in payment for international debts. But the dollar's decline against the West German mark and the Japanese yen has sparked renewed demands in many quarters for worldwide monetary reform.

A growing number of economists question the wisdom of relying on the money of any single country to serve as an international currency. The present monetary system is based on what many see as an illogical arrangement. As expressed by a British journalist: "The only way the world can enjoy an increase in its main source of international money is if the U.S. runs a deficit. But if the U.S. runs a deficit, that calls into question the strength of the dollars."[33]

The economy of the United States traditionally has been regarded as "the engine" that powers world trade. Yet recent fluctuations of confidence in the dollar and the effects they have had on the American economic system have led some theorists both here and abroad to suggest that the dollar be replaced by a new unit of exchange.

One proposal is that the hegemony of the dollar be divided into zones of economic influence, each clustered around the world's four strong currencies: the West German mark, the Japanese yen, the Swiss franc and the U.S. dollar. According to this plan, the strong currency countries would be required to maintain stable exchange rates among themselves and observe flexible, or floating, rates within their separate zones. The European Economic Community's consideration of a monetary union, link-

---

[31] Speaking at the National Economics Club, Washington, D.C., May 4, 1978.

[32] Speaking at a press conference in Washington, D.C., May 9, 1978.

[33] Frances Cairncross, writing in *The Manchester Guardian,* May 14, 1978.

Current Account Balances*
(in billions of U.S. dollars)

	1974	1975	1976	1977
Total OECD	−33	− 6.5	−26.5	−32
United States	− 2.3	11.6	− 1.4	−17.5
Japan	− 4.7	− 0.7	3.7	10
West Germany	9.7	3.8	3.4	2.25
Netherlands	2.1	1.7	2.4	.5
Switzerland	0.2	2.6	3.5	3.25
OPEC	62	31	42	40
Non-oil developing countries	−24.5	−40	−26	−22.5

* On goods, services and private transfers

Source: Organization for Economic Cooperation and Development

ing the principal European currencies to the mark, would be the initial step in this direction.

Monetary experts believe that the series of coming meetings of Common Market countries will result in establishing the mark as the dominant reserve currency in Europe. At present, five of the smaller member countries — Belgium, Luxembourg, the Netherlands, Denmark and Norway — use the mark to settle accounts among themselves. The dollar remains their reserve currency in trading with other countries.

There is now the prospect that Britain, France and Italy will follow the pattern of their five smaller neighbors. Observers are freely predicting that France will join in this arrangement. The British are reported to be willing to do so if West Germany takes steps to increase its low rate of growth — currently a source of British and Americn discontent. The gathering momentum for independence from the dollar is further underlined by a broadened reliance by Common Market Countries on the European Monetary Unit, an accounting device much like the IMF's Special Drawing Rights (SDRs). The unit is used frequently in transactions between European central banks.

Another suggestion, while not new, keeps returning the forekront — most recently at the International Monetary Fund meeting in Mexico City. It is that the IMF issue a new series of Special Drawing Rights (SDRs) to supplant the dollar as a form of reserve currency. The first SDRs were created by the fund in 1967. Intended to take the place of gold, they are in essence a bookkeeping device, certificates of account with the IMF that member nations use to settle international debts. Currently, one SDR is worth $1.22.

In the past, similar plans have enjoyed wide backing when the dollar has been weak in trading but lost support when it regained strength. For this reason, some economists are philosophically opposed to replacing the dollar. Any other unit of account, they say, would face the same periodic problems. Its stability, like that of the dollar, "would require [of countries] exactly those parallel price and balance-of-payment trends...that are today so conspicuously missing...."[34]

The dollar has served as an international medium of exchange for over three decades. How much longer it will fulfill that function depends largely on the ability of politicians and economists to shore up a world economic system that is threatening to fragment into regional and national entities. "Logic points inexorably to the formation of a genuine international political compact," economist Sidney Lens has written, "one that encompasses international planning to husband dwindling world resources and divide income and wealth equitably among nations."[35] Such a compact has long been the goal of economic planners, but it has remained elusive.

---

[34] Otmar Emminger, "On the Way to a New International Monetary Order," *Foreign Affairs Studies*, the American Enterprise Institute for Public Policy Research, 1976, p. 12. Emminger is vice president of the Deutsche Bundesbank and deputy of its central council.

[35] Sidney Lens, *op. cit.*, p. 24.

Selected Bibliography

Books

Hayek, Friedrich A., *Road to Serfdom,* University of Chicago, 1944.
Hirsch, Fred, *Money International,* Allen Lane, 1967.
—*Alternatives to Monetary Disorder,* McGraw, 1977.
—*Social Limits to Growth,* Harvard University Press, 1977.
Johnson, Harry G., *Trade Strategy,* George Allen and Unwin, 1971.
Odell, Peter R., *Oil and World Power,* Penguin, 1975.
Owen, Henry and Charles L. Schultze, *Setting National Priorities,* The
    Brookings Institution, 1977.
Quigley, Carroll, *Tragedy and Hope: The History of the World in Our
    Time,* Angriff Press, 1975.
Simon, William E., *A Time for Truth,* Reader's Digest Press, 1978.
Tufte, Edward, *Political Control of the Economy,* Yale, 1978.

Articles

Deaknews (foreign money newsletter), selected issues.
"How European Nations Control Inflation," *Business Week,* May 22,
    1978.
International Financial Statistics (publication of the International
    Monetary Fund), selected issues.
IMF Survey (publication of the International Monetary Fund), selected
    issues.
Lens, Sidney, "The Sinking Dollar and the Gathering Storm," *The
    Progressive,* May 1978.
Orbis (journal of world affairs), selected issues.
"Rich Countries Getting Poorer," *Economist,* Sept. 10, 1977.
Rose, Sanford, "The Dollar Is Already on the Mend," *Fortune,* April 24,
    1978.
"The Great Government Inflation Machine," *Business Week,* May 22,
    1978.
The *OECD Observer* (publication of the Organization for Economic
    Cooperation and Development), selected issues.

Reports and Studies

Brown, Lester R., "The Global Economic Prospect," Worldwatch In-
    stitute, 1978.
Editorial Research Reports, "World's Slow Economic Recovery," 1977
    Vol. II, p. 745; "Job Protection and Free Trade," 1977 Vol. II, p.
    955; "International Trade Negotiations," 1976 Vol. I, p. 343;
    "Economic Internationalism," 1973 Vol. II, p. 676.
"Government and the Nation's Resources," Report of the National
    Commission on Supplies and Shortages, December 1976.
Haberler, Gottfried, "Incomes Policy and Inflation: An Analysis of Basic
    Principles," American Enterprise Institute, 1977.

NUCLEAR PROLIFERATION

by

Sandra Stencel

**Mar. 17
1978**

Editor's Note: The Carter administration, on March 22, 1979, issued a report on the steps taken by the U.S. government in the preceding year to prevent nuclear proliferation. The four-volume report, required under the Nuclear Non-Proliferation Act of 1978, said that considerable progress had been made in increasing international appreciation of the importance of minimizing risks of proliferation inherent in future fuel cycle developments.

It pointed out that, through the International Nuclear Fuel Cycle Evaluation, the United States had stimulated a general re-examination of long-held technical assumptions concerning fuel cycle activities and awareness of the need to consider proliferation concerns. Progress was also reported in obtaining wider adherence to the 1968 Nuclear Non-Proliferation Treaty, in strengthening safeguards to ensure that governments do not divert nuclear materials from civilian uses to weapons programs, and in continued consultations among nuclear suppliers.

The report noted that a number of problems had been encountered, particularly in the perception by other countries that the United States is attempting to impose its own standards unilaterally on peaceful nuclear cooperation and that those standards are unnecessarily strict or impracticable. It also said that doubts persist about the reliability of the United States as a nuclear supplier.

NUCLEAR PROLIFERATION

A FTER a rocky beginning, President Carter's campaign to limit the further proliferation of nuclear weapons appears to be gaining support at home and abroad. Since taking office Carter has been trying to persuade other nations to follow America's lead by stopping — or at least reducing — the export of nuclear power technology that can be used for military purposes. What concerns the President is not the sale of nuclear reactors themselves. The danger lies in the ability of more countries to enrich uranium and reprocess used reactor fuel. It is in these stages of the nuclear fuel cycle *(see p. 195)* that weapons-grade nuclear material — plutonium or highly enriched uranium — is produced.

"The benefits of nuclear power are . . . very real and practical," Carter said in a policy statement issued on April 7, 1977. "But a serious risk accompanies worldwide use of nuclear power — the risk that components of the nuclear power process will be turned to providing atomic weapons." Carter said that the United States would "defer indefinitely the commercial reprocessing and recycling of plutonium" and would instead accelerate research "into alternative fuel cycles which do not involve direct access to materials usable in nuclear weapons."

Deferral of plutonium reprocessing and recycling also was recommended last year by the Nuclear Energy Policy Study Group — a 21-member committee set up by the Ford Foundation and the Mitre Corporation of McLean, Va. In its final report, the committee said that a decision by the United States to proceed with these technologies "would probably ensure worldwide movement to incorporate plutonium in the fuel cycle."[1] In the committee's view, the proliferation of nuclear weapons capability "is the most serious risk associated with nuclear power."

Representatives of 39 foreign nations met in Washington last Oct. 19-21 at a Nuclear Fuel Cycle Evaluation Conference, which had been proposed by Carter in his April 7 statement. The 39 nations agreed to join the United States in a two-year study of the relative economic and non-proliferation merits of

---

[1] Nuclear Energy Policy Study Group, *Nuclear Power Issues and Choices* (1977), p. 24. The Mitre Corporation describes itself as "a nonprofit systems engineering firm working solely for the public interest."

various nuclear fuel cycles. However, most of the representatives made it clear that in the meantime their countries intend to go ahead with domestic nuclear-energy programs. These programs include some aspects that the Carter administration considers dangerous, such as the development of "fast-breeder" reactors which produce more plutonium than they consume.

Congress voted last month to stiffen existing restrictions on American nuclear exports and give other countries incentives to adopt U.S. non-proliferation goals. The administration-supported Nuclear Non-Proliferation Act of 1978 passed by wide margins in both the House and the Senate despite strong opposition from the U.S. nuclear industry,[2] and it was signed into law by the President on March 10.

In September 1977, 15 nations that sell nuclear technology — materials and knowledge — agreed to guidelines governing future sales. They were the United States, the Soviet Union, Britain, France, West Germany, Japan, Canada, Poland, East Germany, Belgium, Czechoslovakia, the Netherlands, Italy, Sweden and Switzerland. The supplier nations agreed, among other things, to require strict safety controls from their customers before exporting additional nuclear technology and to exercise restraint in the sale of "sensitive" nuclear equipment that could be used for weapons production.

The Carter administration's efforts to reduce the spread of potentially dangerous nuclear technology were not always successful. Despite U.S. pressures, West Germany refused to cancel a 1975 agreement to sell reprocessing and enrichment facilities to Brazil and France decided to go ahead with its plan to sell a reprocessing plant to Pakistan.

International Agreement on Atomic Sales

The administration's emphasis on restricting nuclear exports continues a U.S. policy shift that started earlier in this decade. Particularly before 1974, the United States focused its non-proliferation efforts on reinforcing the international system of controls or safeguards. These were designed to prevent the secret diversion of nuclear material from peaceful uses into weapons.[3] But in recent years many experts have come to believe that safeguards are not always sufficient to insure that nuclear supplies are used only for peaceful purposes. This thinking has been prompted by several events:

1. The 1973-74 oil crisis, focusing world attention on the need to develop alternative energy sources.

---

[2] The Senate version of the bill passed Feb. 7, 1978, by a vote of 88 to 3. The House accepted the Senate version two days later by voice vote. A slightly different House version had been passed Sept. 28, 1977, by a vote of 411 to 0.

[3] See "Nuclear Safeguards," *E.R.R.*, 1974 Vol. II, pp. 865-884.

LIGHT-WATER REACTOR FUEL CYCLE

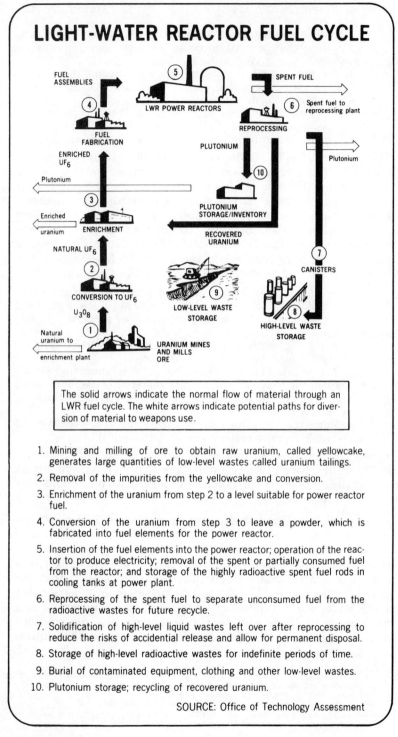

The solid arrows indicate the normal flow of material through an LWR fuel cycle. The white arrows indicate potential paths for diversion of material to weapons use.

1. Mining and milling of ore to obtain raw uranium, called yellowcake, generates large quantities of low-level wastes called uranium tailings.

2. Removal of the impurities from the yellowcake and conversion.

3. Enrichment of the uranium from step 2 to a level suitable for power reactor fuel.

4. Conversion of the uranium from step 3 to leave a powder, which is fabricated into fuel elements for the power reactor.

5. Insertion of the fuel elements into the power reactor; operation of the reactor to produce electricity; removal of the spent or partially consumed fuel from the reactor; and storage of the highly radioactive spent fuel rods in cooling tanks at power plant.

6. Reprocessing of the spent fuel to separate unconsumed fuel from the radioactive wastes for future recycle.

7. Solidification of high-level liquid wastes left over after reprocessing to reduce the risks of accidental release and allow for permanent disposal.

8. Storage of high-level radioactive wastes for indefinite periods of time.

9. Burial of contaminated equipment, clothing and other low-level wastes.

10. Plutonium storage; recycling of recovered uranium.

SOURCE: Office of Technology Assessment

195

2. India's detonation of a nuclear bomb in May 1974, demonstrating that a nation could secretly develop nuclear weaponry.[4]

3. An upsurge in international terrorism, raising the possibility of extremists acquiring and using radioactive materials or even nuclear weapons themselves.[5]

4. A commercial agreement between West Germany and Brazil, announced in June 1975, marking the first time reprocessing and enrichment facilities were sold to a Third World country.

These events led to a series of meetings in London, starting in mid-1975, of the seven major nuclear supplier nations — the United States, the Soviet Union, France, Britain, Japan, West Germany and Canada. Eventually membership was expanded to include eight other lesser suppliers — Poland, East Germany, Czechoslovakia, Belgium, the Netherlands, Italy, Sweden and Switzerland. It was at the Sept. 21, 1977, meeting that agreement was reached on the new guidelines. Under the agreement, nuclear exporters will require their customers to:

1. Provide "formal governmental assurances" that the material or facilities will not be used to produce any nuclear explosive device, whether a weapon or a supposedly "peaceful" nuclear explosion.

2. Place the material or facilities under "effective physical protection" to prevent theft or sabotage.

3. Accept international inspection by the International Atomic Energy Agency *(see p. 201)* of the material or facilities being imported and any similar items produced locally using the same type of design.

4. Agree that the same rules will apply to any re-export or sale of imported nuclear materials to a third country.

In the case of suspected or obvious violation, the guidelines call for "prompt" consultation among the supplier nations about the possibility of sanctions, including termination of all nuclear exports to that country.

The guidelines have been criticized for not insisting that future transactions include "full-scope" safeguards, under which a recipient nation would be required to permit international inspection of all of its nuclear facilities — no matter how or when acquired. State Department officials said that if the United States had pushed for full-scope safeguards, agreement would have been impossible. "A long-term solution to the proliferation problem requires political consensus, not confrontation," said Joseph S. Nye Jr. "Perfectionism on these questions is counterproductive."[6]

---

[4] India obtained the plutonium for its explosive device by processing nuclear waste from a small research reactor supplied by Canada in 1956.

[5] See "International Terrorism," *E.R.R.*, 1977 Vol. II, pp. 909-932.

[6] Quoted in *The New York Times*, Jan. 16, 1978. Nye is Deputy Under Secretary of State for Security Assistance, Science and Technology.

The same concerns that led the London suppliers group to adopt guidelines on nuclear exports prompted Congress to pass the Nuclear Non-Proliferation Act. It was the result of more than two years of congressional action. Sen. John Glenn (D Ohio), a principal sponsor, called it "the most comprehensive piece of nuclear legislation since the Atomic Energy Act of 1954."[7] It hews to recommendations Carter made to Congress in a message on April 27, less than three weeks after issuing his policy statement. As he sought, the act not only strengthens controls over U.S. nuclear exports but also attempts to assure foreign nations that the United States will continue to be a reliable supplier of nuclear fuel and technology. The act:

1. Sets criteria to be followed by the Nuclear Regulatory Commission *(see p. 198)* in granting export licenses for nuclear materials.

2. Mandates a cutoff of nuclear exports to any nation found, at any time after the act took effect, to have developed or tested atomic bombs, aided other countries in developing atomic weapons or violated international safeguards.

3. Directs the President to begin negotiations with other countries to establish an international nuclear fuel stockpile *(see p. 208)*.

4. Requires the President to undertake and to study the desirability of and options for foreign participation in any new U.S. enrichment facilities.

5. Directs the President to try to renegotiate existing nuclear cooperation agreements with other governments in order to incorporate the new non-proliferation standards in the act.

The Non-Proliferation Act is more stringent than the export guidelines adopted by the London suppliers group. It requires countries accepting nuclear material and technology from the United States to agree to "full-scope" safeguards on all their peaceful nuclear activities. This provision, to become effective in 1979, was denounced by Carl Walske, president of the Atomic Industrial Forum, an industry trade group. "Acceptance of such a requirement by any nation would be tantamount to its pledging not to build nuclear weapons," Walske declared in a speech delivered March 6 at the forum's 1978 fuel cycle conference in New York.

Other industry spokesmen said the legislation could divert business to countries with less restrictive export policies. The American Nuclear Energy Council, a lobbying group, forecast losses of up to $3 billion in foreign sales in the next few years. Carl Goldstein, assistant vice president of the Atomic Industrial Forum, said "there is no question that it complicates doing business overseas."

---

[7] *Congressional Record,* Feb. 2, 1978, p. S1064.

The American share of the nuclear export market has decreased substantially in recent years. Between 1972 and 1976, according to the Atomic Industrial Forum, the U.S. share of nuclear exports dropped from 85 to 42 per cent.[8] A survey done for the Westinghouse Electric Corporation[9] found that in 1972 the major U.S. nuclear manufacturers sold eight reactors overseas, while European manufacturers sold only one. In 1976, however, the Americans had only one export sale compared to nine for the Europeans. By the late 1980s the American share of the nuclear export market could drop to 25 or 30 per cent, according to a recent report by the congressional Office of Technology Assessment.[10]

Debate Over Role of Regulatory Agency

Much of the congressional debate over the Non-Proliferation Act centered on the role of the Nuclear Regulatory Commission (NRC). The commission is charged, under the Energy Reorganization Act of 1974, with primary responsibility for monitoring nuclear exports. Many persons in the nuclear industry, and their congressional supporters, wanted to remove the NRC's authority to regulate exports. They argued that this function was an extension of the President's conduct of foreign affairs and should therefore be carried out by the executive branch. NRC supporters argued that the nuclear industry's opposition to the commission was based on a belief that the State Department might be more accommodating in approving nuclear sales.

The NRC itself is divided on the question of its ability to assess the adequacy of nuclear safeguards in foreign nations — a primary requirement before nuclear exports can be approved. Commissioner Richard T. Kennedy said in a letter to Sen. Frank Church (D Idaho), dated Jan. 26, 1978: "Practically speaking . . . the commission is not equipped to independently examine the adequacy of foreign safeguards and must in practice accept the word of the executive branch as to their implementation and as to the foreign affairs implications of any export."

Since last September the NRC has licensed exports of nuclear materials without the approval of its own security and safeguards experts. Dr. Clifford V. Smith, head of the NRC's Office of Nuclear Material Safety and Safeguards, told the commissioners Jan. 11 that he based his decision to refrain from certifying the adequacy of overseas safeguards on a still-secret report prepared by the International Atomic Energy

---

[8] Atomic Industrial Forum, "U.S. Nuclear Export Policy," July 21, 1976.
[9] Dwight Porter, "Nuclear Exports and Non-proliferation Policy," undated.
[10] Office of Technology Assessment, "Nuclear Proliferation and Safeguards," June 1977, p. 256.

Agency. He said it found that the safeguard systems of certain unspecified countries were inadequate.

Despite this, NRC Commissioner Victor Gilinsky defended the agency's independent role. "In giving export licensing authority to an independent regulatory commission in 1974," Gilinsky wrote, "Congress was saying in effect that it wanted this country's nuclear trade to be handled consistently and to be subject to explicit protective standards rather than to the political exigencies of the moment. This still makes good sense."[11]

Congress apparently agreed with Gilinsky. The Non-Proliferation Act of 1978 preserved the basic independence and authority of the NRC in export decisions. Under the act, the commission retained the authority to (1) define adequate standards of physical security of nuclear facilities at foreign sites, and (2) determine what exports were relevant to nuclear proliferation and thus require approval under the bill's procedures. In certain cases, however, the President would be allowed to bypass NRC approval if the commission had not made up its mind within 120 days of receiving assurance from the executive branch that the proposed export license would not damage U.S. defense and security interests.

Changes in Control Strategy

THE UNITED STATES has gone through various phases in attempting to resolve the nuclear proliferation question — sometimes stressing control and other times stressing promotion of nuclear energy. "Nonproliferation policies have succeeded each other and can only be judged in the context of the days they were proposed and adopted," wrote Bertrand Goldschmidt, a French nuclear energy official. "They did not fail one after another; rather each of them added a stone to the building of a world in which the increase in the number of nuclear weapon states has been much slower than it was feared initially, but each of them had to be abandoned when it did not fulfill the exaggerated hopes put forward to convince all countries to adhere to it."[12]

The link between atomic energy and nuclear weapons

[11] Writing in *The Washington Post*, Jan. 26, 1978. NRC Commissioner Joseph Hendrie is said to side with Kennedy, while commissioner Peter A. Bradford is believed to side with Gilinsky. The commission's fifth seat is vacant.

[12] Bertrand Goldschmidt, "A Historical Survey of Nonproliferation Policies," *International Security*, summer 1977, p. 71. Goldschmidt is director of international relations for the French Atomic Energy Commission and the French representative to the International Atomic Energy Agency.

capability has been recognized since the dawn of the nuclear age. Within three months of the bombings of Hiroshima and Nagasaki, the United States, Britain and Canada jointly declared on Nov. 15, 1945: "The military exploitation of atomic energy depends, in large part, upon the same methods and processes as would be required for industrial uses." Therefore, the three countries concluded, information concerning "industrial application" of nuclear energy must not be shared among nations until effective safeguards were devised and implemented. Their declaration proposed that international controls be assumed by a United Nations commission.

American opposition to the spread of nuclear material and technology also was evident in the Atomic Energy Act of 1946, which created the Atomic Energy Commission.[13] The act imposed rigid restrictions on giving other countries information on nuclear technology. The restrictions were to apply "until Congress declared by joint resolution that effective and enforceable safeguards against the use of atomic energy for destructive purposes have been established."

The United States, realizing that such restrictions would not guard atomic secrets for long, drew up a plan to establish international controls over atomic energy. Bernard M. Baruch, chairman of the U.S. delegation to the U.N. Atomic Energy Commission, presented it at the commission's first meeting on June 14, 1946.[14] The Baruch plan called for creation of an International Atomic Development Authority to control "all phases of the development and use of atomic energy" and the subsequent destruction of existing nuclear weapons.

The Baruch plan has been described[15] as being "as revolutionary on the political level as fission was on the technical level." However, it incurred Soviet opposition and eventually was discarded. If the plan had been accepted when only the United States possessed atomic weapons, the U.S. Arms Control and Disarmament Agency said, "the nuclear threat would have been removed at the outset, and mankind would have entered the nuclear age in a joint and peaceful effort."[16]

---

[13] The Atomic Energy Commission was abolished by the Energy Reorganization Act of 1974 and its functions transferred to two agencies, the Energy Research and Development Administration and the Nuclear Regulatory Commission.

[14] The U.N. Atomic Energy Commission was established by the General Assembly in January 1946. The commission consisted of representatives of the 11 nations with seats on the Security Council and Canada. Canada was included because it had participated with the United States and Britain in the wartime development of the atomic bomb.

[15] By Bertrand Goldschmit, *op. cit.*, p. 71.

[16] U.S. Arms Control and Disarmament Agency, *Toward a World Without War: A Summary of United States Disarmament Efforts, Past and Present* (1962), p. 6. See also Joseph I. Lieberman, *The Scorpion and the Tarantula: The Struggle to Control Atomic Weapons, 1945-1949* (1970).

America's monopoly on nuclear technology was short-lived. Russia exploded its first atomic bomb in September 1949, much earlier than generally was expected. The first British atomic explosion took place in October 1952. At the same time there was growing interest throughout the world in the use of nuclear energy to generate electricity. International cooperation seemed essential both to spread the benefits of nuclear energy and to ensure that appropriate safeguards were applied to control the spread of nuclear-weapons technology.

Promotion of Atomic Energy in the 1950s

This was the basis for President Eisenhower's famous "atoms for peace" address, delivered on Dec. 8, 1953, before the U.N. General Assembly. Eisenhower proposed the creation of an International Atomic Energy Agency to which the nuclear powers would contribute fissionable materials from their stockpiles to "serve the peaceful pursuits of mankind." Such a step, he said, would stimulate development of the peaceful uses of atomic energy, "begin to diminish the potential destructive power of the world's atomic stockpiles," and demonstrate the peaceful intentions of the great powers.

The Eisenhower plan did not require prior agreement on a system of international inspection and control, a significant departure from the earlier stand taken by the United States in the Baruch plan. Despite this concession, the Soviet Union opposed the idea. The Russians argued that the diversion of a small part of the available fissionable materials to peaceful purposes would in no way lessen the danger of nuclear war and could, in fact, "serve to relax the vigilance of the peoples" with regard to the problem of nuclear weapons.

According to physicist Theodore B. Taylor and law professor Mason Willrich, the "atoms for peace" plan signaled a major shift in America's proliferation strategy. "Prior to 1953," they wrote, "international control came first and peaceful nuclear development second. Thereafter, development came first and international inspection and control second, if at all. Once taken, the decision to promote the peaceful uses of nuclear energy throughout the world soon became as irreversible as the presence of nuclear weapons."[17]

The U.N. approved the creation of the International Atomic Energy Agency (IAEA) in the fall of 1956 and it officially went into existence the following July 29. The Vienna-based organization, with 110 member nations today, operates autonomously under the aegis of the United Nations. Its primary role has become the administration of safeguards to ensure

---

[17] Mason Willrich and Theodore B. Taylor, *Nuclear Theft: Risks and Safeguards* (1974), p. 180.

Uranium Resources

A key question in the non-proliferation debate is whether enough uranium will be available to meet future nuclear power needs. There is an extremely wide range of opinion on how much recoverable uranium ore exists throughout the world. National Academy of Science geologists have concluded that there may be serious supply problems by the mid-1980s. But using the same basic facts, the Nuclear Energy Policy Study Group concluded that uranium supplies "will probably be adequate well into the next century."

The United States currently accounts for about 45 per cent of the world's production of uranium. Canada contributes about 25 per cent, South Africa less than 15 per cent, France less than 10 per cent, and Nigeria 6 per cent. Gabon, Spain, Portugal and Argentina make up the remainder. Australia, which possesses at least 20 per cent of the uranium reserves in the non-Communist world, exports only a minimal amount.

that governments do not divert nuclear materials from civilian uses to weapons programs.

The IAEA's safeguards system, as it has developed over the years, is one of strict statistical accounting involving four steps: (1) IAEA experts review the design of the nuclear plant to make sure effective controls are possible; (2) the nation is required to keep detailed records of plant operations and an inventory of nuclear material; (3) the government of the country concerned must supply periodic reports concerning those records; (4) the agency has the right to send inspectors for on-the-spot checks.[18] While "timely detection" is a basic objective of current international safeguards, they are not designed to prevent the theft of nuclear material or to recover it if it is stolen. This remains the responsibility of each nation. Critics of existing safeguards say that this is a major flaw in the system.

Aims of 1968 Treaty on Non-Proliferation

By the mid-1960s it was becoming clear that the spread of civilian nuclear power, encouraged by the "atoms for peace" plan, had increased the risk of nuclear war. Out of this concern evolved the Nuclear Non-Proliferation Treaty of 1968. Nations without nuclear weapons that signed the treaty made a formal commitment to remain weaponless. In exchange for this pledge, they were guaranteed access to peaceful nuclear technology.

Since 1968, 102 nations have ratified the treaty. But at least nine nations possessing advanced nuclear facilities have refused to join it. These are Israel, Spain, Argentina, Brazil, Pakistan, South Africa, and three of the six members of the "nuclear

---

[18] International Atomic Energy Agency, "IAEA: What It is; What It Does," 1972.

club" — France, China and India.[19] This lack of participation is not the only weakness in the treaty. Article X allows a party to withdraw from the treaty's obligations on three months' notice if it determines that "extraordinary events" have placed its "supreme interests" in jeopardy. "Despite these weaknesses," notes a recent report by the Office of Technology Assessment, "the NPT was a momentous achievement and remains a significant deterrent."[20]

Search for Safer Technologies

E UROPE AND JAPAN generally have supported President Carter's efforts to tighten controls on nuclear exports and to limit the spread of potentially dangerous nuclear technology. They are, however, more skeptical about his plan to "defer" the use of plutonium as a fuel. Many of America's allies believe that this policy is unfair and unrealistic. They say that while nuclear power might be viewed as an energy source of "last resort"[21] in the United States, it is an unavoidable necessity for other countries that do not have America's coal, oil, natural gas and uranium resources.

Some foreign leaders have said that Carter's anti-plutonium policy could be counterproductive. The longer the United States foregoes the use of plutonium as a fuel, they say, the faster it will use up the world's supply of uranium. This could encourage other countries to turn more quickly to the use of plutonium — a result totally inconsistent with Carter's nonproliferation objectives. Some Europeans have said that Carter's opposition to the breeder reactor is just an attempt to quash a technology in which Europe leads and America trails.

America's non-proliferation strategy also has evoked considerable opposition in the Third World. According to an Indian official,[22] it is seen "as a manifestation of neo-colonialism and technological hegemony." He went on to say: "The price of this strategy is to convert the nuclear issue into a confrontation between north and south and make the development of nuclear technology a symbol of assertion of autonomy from neo-colonialist dependence."

---

[19] The other three nations possessing nuclear weapons are the United States, the Soviet Union and Britain.

[20] Office of Technology Assessment, *op. cit.*, p. 224.

[21] Phrase used by Carter during the 1976 presidential campaign.

[22] K. Subrahmanyam, "The Nuclear Issue and International Security," *Bulletin of the Atomic Scientists,* February 1977, p. 19. Subrahmanyam, formerly the director of the Institute for Defense Studies and Analyses in New Delhi, is now Home Secretary to the Government of Tamil Nadu, Madras.

This country's non-proliferation initiatives often have been "misunderstood or misrepresented," according to Deputy Under Secretary of State Joseph S. Nye Jr. Nye told a nuclear energy conference in West Germany last October that Carter's policy is neither anti-nuclear nor anti-breeder reactor.[23] What Carter is opposed to, Nye said, is premature entry into a plutonium economy without investigating more proliferation-resistant fuel cycles.

> If we are to develop and coordinate effective policies to reach our mutual goal of nuclear power without nuclear proliferation [Nye said], we must avoid assuming that there are no alternatives to the technological path upon which we are now embarked. At the very least, we owe to future generations the assurance that we examined real alternatives and were not simply carried along by the momentum of the past.

This is the purpose of the Fuel Cycle Evaluation Program, which Carter first proposed last April. An international group working on the project held its first meeting in mid-December in Vienna.[24] Over the next two years several international "working groups" will seek to identify ways to minimize the proliferation danger without jeopardizing energy supplies or the development of nuclear energy for peaceful purposes.

Reprocessing and Breeder-Reactor Efforts

While the fuel cycle evaluation continues, most countries are pushing ahead with reprocessing and breeder-reactor programs. West Germany intends to build a large reprocessing and storage center in lower Saxony. After months of discussion, the United States and Japan on Sept. 12, 1977, signed an agreement allowing Japan to open its newly built Tokai Mura reprocessing plant north of Tokyo. Because the United States provides the enriched uranium that is used in Japanese nuclear power plants, it has the right to rule on the use of the spent fuel and so had a virtual veto over the reprocessing plant. The agreement permits the Japanese to open the plant on a controlled experimental basis for two years while conducting research into alternative recycling methods.

France, which has the only commercially viable reprocessing plant in the West,[25] has contracted with 10 Japanese utilities to handle 1,600 tons of spent fuel over a 10-year period beginning in 1983. It is holding talks with West Germany, Switzerland, Sweden and Austria on similar contracts. France's Japanese

---

[23] Friedrich Ebert Conference on Problems of Nuclear Energy Supply, Oct. 3, 1977. Remarks reprinted in *Department of State Bulletin,* Nov. 14, 1977, pp. 666-671.

[24] China is the only nuclear power not taking part in the project.

[25] Three commercial reprocessing facilities have been built in the United States: the Nuclear Fuel Services plant in West Valley, N.Y.; General Electric's Midwest Fuel Recovery Plant at Morris, Ill.; and the Allied-General plant in Barnwell, S.C. All three have been plagued by technical and financial difficulties, and none is operating.

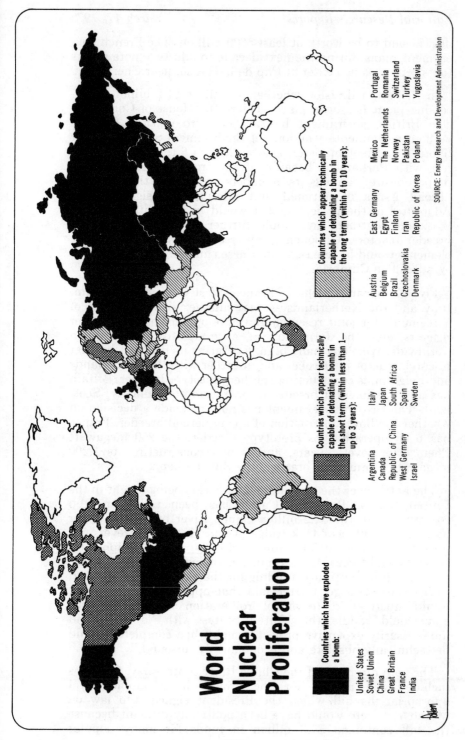

World Nuclear Proliferation

Countries which have exploded a bomb:

United States
Soviet Union
China
Great Britain
France
India

Countries which appear technically capable of detonating a bomb in the short term (within less than 1— up to 3 years):

Argentina   Italy
Canada   Japan
Republic of China South Africa
West Germany   Spain
Israel   Sweden

Countries which appear technically capable of detonating a bomb in the long term (within 4 to 10 years):

Austria   East Germany   Mexico   Portugal
Belgium   Egypt   The Netherlands Romania
Brazil   Finland   Norway   Switzerland
Czechoslovakia   Iran   Pakistan   Turkey
Denmark   Republic of Korea Poland   Yugoslavia

SOURCE: Energy Research and Development Administration

deal is said to be worth at least $600 million. The French government plans during the next decade to add two more plants to its reprocessing center at Cap de la Hague, near Cherbourg.

In Britain, a decision whether to build a $1.2 billion reprocessing plant has been placed before the House of Commons. The British government has authority to make a decision without parliamentary action but Environment Secretary Peter Shore, a Cabinet minister, said on March 6 the matter would rest with Parliament because of a "strong, widespread and proper desire" among its members to debate the project's "broad issues of national and international significance." Advocates of the project said it would be a profitable source of export contracts and would further development of fast-breeder reactors. Opponents expressed fears that radioactive elements would be released into the sea and air from the site, at Windscale in Cumbria.

Five European nations — France, West Germany, Belgium, Italy and the Netherlands — last summer signed a series of agreements for joint research and development of fast-breeder reactors and the formation of a group to market them worldwide. West Germany began operating its first fast-breeder research reactor in October and, together with the Netherlands and Belgium, is constructing another prototype breeder. Britain has an experimental breeder in operation at Dounreay, Scotland. The British government has not yet made a decision on whether to allow construction of a commercial breeder. France has been operating its prototype breeder, the 250 megawatt Phenix, for several years, and is now constructing its 1,200 megawatt commercial breeder, the Super Phenix.

The battle over the breeder reactor also is being fought in the United States. President Carter has been trying to stop construction of the $2.2 billion Clinch River breeder, a major prototype plant near Oak Ridge, Tenn. He has, however, run into strong opposition from industry, trade union and congressional forces. In November he vetoed a bill authorizing $80 million in continued funding for the experimental reactor. In his veto message, Carter said that approval of the project would imperil efforts to control proliferation of nuclear weapons and would saddle the United States with "a large and unnecessarily expensive project, which when completed would be technically obsolete and economically unsound."

The veto did not end the Clinch River controversy. Congress included $80 million for the project in a supplemental appropriations bill which the President signed into law on March 7. A veto would have been politically difficult because the bill contained $7.3 billion in funds for many popular projects. The future of the Clinch River project still is in doubt. In signing the bill, Carter said he would spend the Clinch River money on that project, as required by law.[26] But he said it would be spent to "complete the system design . . . and to terminate" the project. However, U.S. Comptroller General Elmer B. Staats has said[27] that the executive branch cannot shut down Clinch River without legislative approval.

Carter's opposition to the Clinch River project was reflected in the budget for fiscal year 1979 which he sent to Congress in January. He asked for only $13 million for the project, an amount Department of Energy officials said would cover the cost of ending the project. His budget proposed $445 million for the overall breeder program in 1979, about $165.6 million less than it is receiving in 1978. Much of the new funds would be spent "to accelerate investigations of alternative breeder concepts especially those that do not involve fuels that can be readily used to produce nuclear weapons."

Alternative Plutonium Recycling Systems

Among the alternative plutonium recycling systems that will be studied is one that was unveiled Feb. 27 at an energy technology conference in Washington by Dr. Walter Marshall, deputy chairman of the British Atomic Energy Authority, and Dr. Chauncey Starr of the U.S. Electric Power Research Institute.[28] Unlike the existing Purex reprocessing system, the new process — called Civex — does not at any stage produce pure, weapons-grade plutonium. This is accomplished by leaving the unfissioned uranium, plutonium and some radioactive waste products mixed together. This mixture is so radioactive, Marshall and Starr said, that it would kill anyone trying to steal it. Because of the presence of waste products in the recycled fuel, the Civex process is better suited for use with fast-breeder reactors than with conventional light-water reactors. The Civex can, however, reprocess spent or used fuel from either light-water or fast-breeder reactors.

The Carter administration already has expressed an interest in Civex. "It's an example of the kind of fruitful suggestions we want to see studied," said Joseph S. Nye.[29] The administration's optimism is not universally shared. Carl Walske of the Atomic Industrial Forum said that the risk of theft from conventional reprocessing plants is too small to justify the expense of a conversion to Civex.[30] Dr. Starr estimates that a

---

[26] Under the 1974 Impoundment Control Act a President cannot simply refuse to spend appropriated funds.

[27] In a letter to Rep. Olin E. Teague (D Texas), dated Dec. 5, 1977.

[28] The Electric Power Research Institute is the research arm of the U.S. electric utility industry.

[29] Quoted in *Newsweek*, March 13, 1977, p. 60.

[30] Address to the forum's 1978 fuel cycle conference, March 6, 1978, in New York.

pilot plant to test the economics of the Civex system would cost $100 million to build and at least $30 million a year to operate during a decade of testing.

Foregoing or deferring plutonium recycling and the commercial use of breeder reactors presupposes that an adequate supply of enriched uranium fuel will be available. To assure doubters, President Carter has proposed the creation of an international nuclear fuel bank. The United States and other major supplier nations would donate enriched uranium to the fuel bank. The fuel would be drawn out by nuclear importers in the event that a supplier nation was unable or unwilling to fulfill the terms of a nuclear contract. The idea of an international fuel bank is not new. It was first proposed by President Eisenhower in his "atoms for peace" address.

In a related development, Carter proposed on Oct. 18 that the United States buy and store radioactive wastes from foreign reactors that use American fuel. His hope is that reducing nuclear waste storage problems in other countries will reduce their interest in reprocessing.[31] The proposal has sparked heated debate in Congress since no method for disposing of nuclear wastes is yet acceptable to all parties.

Conflicting U.S. Foreign Policy Objectives

The Nuclear Fuel Cycle Evaluation Program has been criticized for its emphasis on technical solutions of the proliferation problem. Experts point out that the decision to acquire nuclear weapons is only partly based on the availability of requisite technology. "If capability itself were the driving force," wrote Richard K. Betts, a research associate at the Brookings Institution, "Germany, Japan, Italy, the Netherlands, Belgium and Sweden would have acquired weapons long ago. . . . Proliferation . . . is a political problem as much as a technical one."[32]

The motives for countries to acquire nuclear weapons fall into two principal categories: (1) military security and (2) the desire for international or regional influence and status. According to a list published by the Ford Foundation-Mitre Corporation study, the first category includes "insecure states" such as Israel, South Africa, South Korea, Taiwan and Yugoslavia. The list of status-seeking states that might "go nuclear" includes Brazil, India, Iran and Spain. The study group also listed as potential nuclear powers four traditional rivals of the insecure or status-seeking states — Argentina (as a rival of Brazil), Egypt (of Israel), Pakistan (of India), and North Korea (of South Korea).[33]

---

[31] See "Nuclear Waste Disposal," *E.R.R.*, 1976 Vol. II, pp. 884-906.

[32] Richard K. Betts, "Paranoids, Pygmies, Pariahs and Non-proliferation," *Foreign Policy*, spring 1977, p. 163.

[33] Nuclear Energy Policy Study Group, *op. cit.*, p. 284.

The study suggested that the United States give strong security guarantees to states like South Korea, Israel and Taiwan, while strengthening its links with the status seekers and their rivals to dissuade them from making weapons. One reason for the administration's emphasis on the technical side of the proliferation problem may be that many of the proposed political solutions conflict with other foreign policy goals. For example, in order to prevent some repressive or corrupt regimes from obtaining the bomb, the United States might have to reaffirm or strengthen alliances with them. And some have been attacked by the administration for violating human rights. Countries in this category include South Korea, South Africa and Brazil.

However, the administration has demonstrated a willingness to compromise for the sake of its non-proliferation objectives. Last fall the administration approved the export of 54 tons of low-enriched uranium to Brazil despite Carter's criticism of Brazil's human rights record and his opposition to Brazil's purchase of reprocessing and enrichment technology from West Germany. U.N. Ambassador Andrew Young, in a television interview Oct. 30, ruled out an American ban on the shipment of nuclear fuels to South Africa because such a prohibition might encourage its government to step up development of South Africa's capacity to produce atomic weapons.[34]

Young said that while he might personally favor an embargo on nuclear exports to South Africa as further pressure on the government to alter its apartheid policies, "things have gone too far for that to be a realistic possibility." He said the only way the United States could monitor South Africa's nuclear development "is to keep some kind of relationship." The administration's main concern has been over South Africa's decision in 1973 to build its own uranium enrichment plant and its refusal to put that plant under international control. This has raised the possibility that South Africa could produce its own weapons-grade nuclear material. South Africa already possesses about 20 per cent of the world's raw uranium reserves.

A decision by the United States to cut off nuclear supplies to South Africa could also undermine the President's attempt to convince other nations that the United States is and intends to remain a reliable source of low-enriched uranium fuel and that they therefore need not reprocess or recycle plutonium. Decisions such as those involving South Africa are difficult to make. But then no one in the Carter administration believed that curbing the spread of nuclear weapons would be easy.

---

[34] Young was interviewed on ABC's "Issues and Answers."

Selected Bibliography

Books

Bader, William B., *The United States and the Spread of Nuclear Weapons*, Pegasus, 1968.

Nuclear Energy Policy Study Group, *Nuclear Power Issues and Choices*, Ballinger, 1977.

Willrich, Mason and Theodore B. Taylor, *Nuclear Theft: Risks and Safeguards*, Ballinger, 1974.

Articles

Alexander, Tom, "Why the Breeder Reactor Is Inevitable," *Fortune*, September 1977.

Annals of the American Academy of Political and Social Science, March 1977 issue.

Betts, Richard K., "Paranoids, Pygmies, Pariahs and Non-Proliferation," *Foreign Policy*, spring 1977.

Far Eastern Economic Review, Jan. 6, 1978 issue.

Gall, Norman, "Atoms For Brazil, Dangers For All," *Foreign Policy*, summer 1976.

Goldschmidt, Bertrand, "A Historical Survey of Non-Proliferation Policies," *International Security*, summer 1977.

Gwynne, Peter, "Plutonium: 'Free' Fuel or Invitation to a Catastrophe?" *Smithsonian*, July 1976.

Mandelbaum, Michael, "A Nuclear Exporters Cartel," *Bulletin of the Atomic Scientists*, February 1977.

Nye, Joseph S. Jr., "Nuclear Power Without Nuclear Proliferation," *Department of State Bulletin*, Nov. 14, 1977.

Ribicoff, Abraham A., "A Market Sharing Approach to the World Nuclear Sales Problem," *Foreign Affairs*, July 1976.

Walske, Carl, "Nuclear Electric Power and the Proliferation of Nuclear Weapon States," *International Security*, winter 1977.

Wohlstetter, Albert, "Spreading the Bomb Without Quite Breaking the Rules," *Foreign Policy*, winter 1976-77.

Reports and Studies

Atomic Industrial Forum, "United States Nuclear Export Policy," July 21, 1976.

Committee for Economic Development, "Nuclear Energy and National Security," September 1976.

Congressional Research Service, "Nuclear Proliferation Factbook," Sept. 23, 1977.

Editorial Research Reports, "Nuclear Safeguards," 1974 Vol. II, p. 865; "Nuclear Waste Disposal," 1976 Vol. II, p. 883; "International Terrorism," 1977 Vol. II, p. 909.

Guhin, Michael A., "Nuclear Paradox: Security Risks of the Peaceful Atom," American Enterprise Institute, 1976.

Office of Technology Assessment, U.S. Congress, "Nuclear Proliferation and Safeguards," June 1977.

INDEX

A

X, Y, Z